Toward Sustainable Communities

A Resource Book for Municipal and Local Governments

Mark Roseland

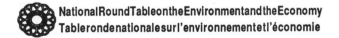

NationalRoundTableontheEnvironmentandtheEconomy
Tablerondenationalesurl'environnementetl'économie

Canadian Catalogue Information in Publication Data
Roseland, Mark

Toward sustainable communities: a resource book for municipal and local governments

(National Round Table series on Sustainable Development)
ISBN 1-895643-09-0
1. City planning - Canada.
2. City planning - environmental aspects - Canada
3. City planning. 4. City Planning - Environmental aspects.
I. National Round Table on the Environment and the Economy
II. Title. III. Series
HT169.C3R67 1992   307.1'2'0971   C92-094941-X

Book Design, Typesetting and Graphic Consultants for Series:
sla Graphicus *Specialists in environmental graphic design*
Sims Latham Group, 190K Memorial Avenue, Suite 201,
Orillia, Ontario, L3V 5X6 Tel: (705) 327-2191

Cover
Zebra Photo Design Studio with sla Graphicus

This book has been set in New Century Schoolbook, Helvetica and printed on Environmental Choice paper containing over 50% recycled content, including 5% post-consumer fibre, using vegetable inks. The cover board also has recycled content and is finished with a water based, wax free varnish.
Printed and bound in Canada by The Alger Press.

National Round Table on the Environment and the Economy
Table ronde nationale sur l'environnement et l'économie
1 Nicholas Street, Suite 1500, Ottawa, Ontario, K1N 7B7

Series General Editor: Daniel Donovan
Tel: (613) 992-7189 Fax: (613) 992-7385

NATIONAL ROUND TABLE SERIES
ON SUSTAINABLE DEVELOPMENT

Aussi disponible en français

Canadä

A Resource Book for Local Government

NRTEE MEMBERS

Dr George Connell, Chair
National Round Table on the Environment and the Economy
R.C. (Reg) Basken *President, Energy and Chemical Workers Union*
The Honourable Carole Carson *Minister of Environment,*
Government of Saskatchewan
The Honourable Jean Charest *Minister of Environment,*
Government of Canada
The Honourable J. Glen Cummings *Minister of the Environment,*
Government of Manitoba
Pat Delbridge *President, Pat Delbridge Associates Inc.*
The Honourable Jake Epp *Minister of Energy, Mines and*
Resources, Government of Canada
Josefina Gonzalez *Research Scientist, Forintek Canada Corp.*
Diane Griffin *Executive Director, Island Nature Trust*
Dr Leslie Harris *Memorial University, Newfoundland*
Tony Hodge *School of Planning, McGill University*
Susan Holtz *Senior Researcher, Ecology Action Centre*
John E. Houghton *Chairman and C.E.O., Quebec and Ontario*
Paper Company Ltd.
David L Johnston *Principal and Vice-Chancellor, McGill University*
Pierre Marc Johnson *Directeur de Recherche, Centre de médecine,*
d'éthique et de droit de l'Université McGill
Geraldine A. Kenney-Wallace *President and Vice-Chancellor,*
McMaster University
Margaret G. Kerr *Vice President, Environment, Health and Safety,*
Northern Telecom
Lester Lafond *President, Lafond Enterprises Ltd.*
Jack M. MacLeod *President and C.E.O., Shell Canada Ltd.*
Jim MacNeill *Senior Fellow, Sustainable Development Program,*
Institute for Research on Public Policy
The Honourable Donald Mazankowski *Minister of Finance,*
Government of Canada
David Morton *Chair and Chief Executive Officer, Alcan Aluminium*
Dr Bob Page *Faculty of Environmental Design, University of*
Calgary
Leone Pippard *President and Executive Director, Canadian Ecology*
Advocates
Barry D. Stuart *Judge of the Territorial Court*
The Honourable Michael Wilson *Minister of Industry, Science and*
Technology, Government of Canada

Executive Director: Ron Doering

The National Round Table on the Environment and the Economy is pleased to present this book as a further contribution to the greater understanding of the concepts of Sustainable Development and Sustainable Communities.

The views expressed in its pages are those of its author and do not necessarily represent those of the NRTEE or its Members.

Foreword

For generations, environmentalists in North America have fought to protect "nature," but have been ambivalent in the struggle to create healthy, equitable, and economically sustainable communities for the human family. *Toward Sustainable Communities* confronts this major contradiction and shortcoming of the North American environmentalist tradition with practical, hopeful guidance.

The intellectual roots of the North American environmental movement in Anglo-Romantic traditions of the 19th century has inspired many battles to protect a pure and wild nature, but they have failed to guide humankind on a course that is sustainable. While we have tended to nature's ecosystems, we have permitted our cities and towns to become engines of resource extraction and exploitation, waste generation and release, so much so that even the chemistry of the Earth's atmosphere is no longer spared from their effects.

During the period that environmentalism became a force in North American public life, our cities and communities have sprawled without consideration for resource efficiency. Infrastructure has been constructed – housing, roadways and sewage systems, for instance – which encourages disregardful resource consumption. Water sources have been taxed or polluted. Built environments have been designed which alter micro-climates and promote photochemical smog formation. Environmental services, such as public transit systems, have been left without public support. Our settlements have not only become less and less habitable for humans and most other species. They now stand as the geographic point sources of most regional and global environmental problems, and threaten even the most distant wild areas saved by environmental advocates.

Over the most recent decades, a new humanistic tradition in the environmental movement has developed, which focuses attention directly upon the state, form, and management of human communities. It includes the Habitat movement, the Healthy Cities movement, and the more recent "sustainable communities" and eco-cities movements. These movements share the perspective that the most direct and effective means to protect the environment is to redevelop, retrofit, and redesign our own communities – in other words, to make them sustainable communities.

Toward Sustainable Communities chronicles many of the practical outcomes of this new movement. Built upon a sound theoretical basis – the application of the concept of sustainable development through an ecosystem approach to human settlements management – the book explores the subcomponents of human community life and its impact on the environment. *Toward Sustainable Communities* is a rare compendium of tested, practical suggestions, helpful contacts, and essential references to use in setting community planning and development on a sustainable course.

Jeb Brugmann
Secretary General
The International Commission for Local Environmental Initiatives

ACKNOWLEDGEMENTS

The author gratefully acknowledges financial support for this project from The Forum for Planning Action, The University of British Columbia Centre for Human Settlements, The University of British Columbia Task Force on Healthy and Sustainable Communities, and Friends of the Earth.

This publication was initiated by the Forum for Planning Action to continue the momentum generated by its conference on sustainable communities held in Vancouver in 1989. The conference was funded by Environment Canada and the British Columbia Ministry of Municipal Affairs, and was organized with financial assistance from The Koerner Foundation, BC Hydro, Cominco, Alcan, and Inco.

I am particularly obliged to Brahm Wiesman and William Rees of the University of British Columbia's School of Community and Regional Planning, Councilmember Nancy Skinner of the Berkeley, California City Council, Michael Replogle of the Institute for Transportation and Development Policy in Washington, D.C., Peter Burch of the City of Vancouver, David Loukidelis of Lidstone, Young, Anderson in Vancouver, Jeb Brugmann of the International Commission for Local Environmental Initiatives, and several anonymous reviewers for reviewing all or parts of the manuscript prior to publication.

Thanks also to Kevin Lee for providing additional research assistance on bicycle transportation initiatives; to the staff of the National Round Table on the Environment and the Economy for their enthusiasm; and to Renée Roseland for graciously tolerating the many weeks I seemed married only to this project.

Toward Sustainable Communities

CONTENTS

Toward Sustainable Communities

INTRODUCTION

This book is intended to enable local government officials and citizens who want to apply the concept of "sustainable development" in their communities. The rationale for writing it is that many of our most critical global environmental issues (e.g., atmospheric and potential climate change) are rooted in local, day-to-day problems (e.g., traffic congestion and inefficient land use patterns). It follows that enlightened local decisions about these issues will be of global as well as local benefit.

The people who prompted me to write this book were the people for whom I wrote it – elected officials, municipal staff, and concerned citizens. In the last few years I have spoken widely on the topics described in these chapters. Invariably, people ask me during or after my lectures where they can find out more. The answer, until now, has been "in my files."

That isn't good enough any longer. While global environmental change is accelerating, there is a wealth of important and exciting information that really can help us make the 1990s the "Turnaround Decade" that sets the planet on a sustainable course. Unfortunately, most of this information is not available through the mainstream media. I have endeavoured to make these ideas, tools and resources accessible.

The book is designed to be both stimulating and useful. Each chapter begins with an introductory overview explaining the topic and its relevance to sustainable communities and/or municipal and local government, followed by a set of Tools, Initiatives, and Resources. Each chapter's Resources section includes the bibliographic references for that chapter.

The book is not intended to be comprehensive; rather, it attempts to identify and document the current range of municipal and local government initiatives toward sustainable communities. Dozens of tools, initiatives and resources are presented in these pages, accompanied by hundreds of references to aid interested readers in their own research. Certain tools and initiatives may be missing because I didn"t know about them, but many others were omitted because of space and budget limitations. I have presented those which seemed most readily transferable to other communities.

The mixed use of Canadian and American spellings throughout the book (e.g., centre vs. center, neighbour vs. neighbor) is because I have kept the original spellings intact in all excerpts from the literature of not only Canada and the US but also from several other countries.

This volume is part of a larger, ongoing research project. If you are aware of sustainable community initiatives and resources other than those described here, or are involved in developing your own sustainable community initiatives, please send your information and/or documentation to me in care of the publisher.

I dedicate the book to the municipal and local government politicians, staff and citizen activists around the world who have developed the wide array of initiatives that make it possible. Your efforts to create a sustainable future have sustained me as well.

2

PART ONE

From Sustainable Development to Sustainable Communities

Toward Sustainable Communities

1

The Meaning of Sustainable Development

> *"Each generation is entitled to the interest on the natural capital, but the principal should be handed on unimpaired."*
> Canadian Conservation Commission, 1915

The environment has changed. Equally important, so has our perception. We are beginning to realize that we too have to change.

In 1970 our major environmental problems were perceived to be local: smog, DDT, oil spills, jet exhausts, and mercury. By 1990 the list and scale of environmental problems had grown to global proportions, including desertification, rising sea-levels, temperate and tropical rainforest depletion, forest die-back, acid rain, toxic contamination of food and water supplies, soil erosion, species extinction, freshwater scarcity, water table depletion, marine pollution, fisheries collapse, ozone depletion, greenhouse gas buildup, climatic change, and urban growth.

Awareness of environmental deterioration has itself been growing, in part due to a cascade of warnings (e.g., *The Limits to Growth, Global 2000, The World Conservation Strategy*) that what we have until now called "development" is in fact jeopardizing our future.

In December 1983, in response to a United Nations General Assembly resolution, the UN Secretary-General appointed Gro Harlem Brundtland of Norway as Chairman of an independent World Commission on Environment and Development. The mandate of the Brundtland

Commission, as it became known, was threefold (WCED 1987):

"• to re-examine the critical issues of environment and development and to formulate innovative, concrete, and realistic action proposals to deal with them;

• to strengthen international co-operation on environment and development and to assess and propose new forms of co-operation that can break out of existing patterns and influence policies and events in the direction of needed change; and

• to raise the level of understanding and commitment to action on the part of individuals, voluntary organizations, businesses, institutes and governments."

For the next few years the Commission studied the issues and listened to people at public hearings on five continents, gathering over 10,000 pages of transcripts and written submissions from hundreds of organizations and individuals. In April 1987 the Commission released its report *Our Common Future*. At the core of the report is the principle of "sustainable development." The Commission's embrace of sustainable development as an underlying principle gave political credibility to a concept many others had worked on over the previous decade. The Commission defined sustainable development as meeting "the needs of the present without compromising the ability of future generations to meet their own needs." This simple, vague definition has been criticized by some and hailed by others (see Starke 1990).

Unfortunately, many people mistakenly use the term "sustainable development" to mean either environmental protection or else sustained economic growth (presumably to pay for, among other things, environmental protection). Even the Brundtland Commission accepted the need for a five- to ten-fold increase in world industrial output as essential for sustainable development.

> ### *Sustainable Confusion*
> "The term [sustainable development] has been criticized as ambiguous and open to a wide range of interpretations, many of which are contradictory. The confusion has been caused because 'sustainable development,' 'sustainable growth' and 'sustainable use' have been used interchangeably, as if their meanings were the same. They are not. 'Sustainable growth' is a contradiction in terms: nothing physical can grow indefinitely. 'Sustainable use' is applicable only to renewable resources: it means using them at rates within their capacity for renewal."
>
> (IUCN 1991)

Environmental protection is like foam padding – it offers some protection from a fall. We congratulate ourselves if we double our spending to double the thickness of the foam, because we assume thicker foam means more protection. However, *we only get more protection if we fall the same distance.* Meanwhile, *unsustainable* development constantly increases the distance we're likely to fall. Sustainable development must therefore be more than merely "protecting" the environment: it requires economic and social change to *reduce the need for environmental protection.*

Like other political objectives of its kind (e.g., democracy), we all agree with the need for sustainable development and disagree over what it entails. Nevertheless, sustainable development has a core meaning which remains however it is interpreted. There are three elements to this (see Jacobs 1991):

- *Environmental considerations must be entrenched in economic policy-making.* Environmental and economic objectives must be placed within a common framework in which a variety of parallel objectives can be

7

Natural Capital

The term "natural capital," coined by ecological economists, can help us understand the meaning of sustainability. Like financial capital, natural capital consists of assets. There are three kinds of "ecological assets":

- non-renewable resources, such as minerals and fossil fuels;
- the finite capacity of natural systems to produce "renewable resources" such as food crops, forestry products and water supplies – which are renewable only if the natural systems from which they are drawn are not overexploited; and
- the capacity of natural systems to absorb the emissions and pollutants which arise from human actions without side effects which imply heavy costs passed onto future generations (such as activities that release chemicals which deplete the atmosphere's ozone layer and greenhouse gases which may cause serious climatic imbalances).

"No one can doubt that the stock of non-renewable resources are finite. No one can doubt that ecosystems (individually and collectively within the biosphere) have limits in their capacity to absorb pollutants. There is agreement that some environmental assets are irreplaceable – for instance areas [...] of outstanding natural beauty. The debate centres on which environmental assets are irreplaceable and the extent to which current (and projected) future levels of resource use degrade the capital stock of environmental assets for future generations, the extent to which one resource can be substituted for another (for instance, a synthetic substance replacing a natural one) and the extent to which pollutants derived from human activities are damaging the biosphere."

(Mitlin and Satterthwaite 1991)

recognized. In particular, we must learn to live on the "interest" generated by remaining stocks of living "natural capital" (Rees 1991). Growth at the expense of sustainability actually makes us poorer rather than richer (Daly and Cobb 1989).

• *Sustainable development incorporates an inescapable commitment to social equity.* This requires not simply the creation of wealth and the conservation of resources, but their fair distribution both between and within countries, including at least some measure of redistribution between North and South. Sustainability also requires the fair distribution of environmental benefits and costs between generations.

• *"Development" does not simply mean "growth,"* as represented by faulty measures of economic performance such as increases in Gross National Product (GNP). Development implies qualitative as well as quantitative improvement.

In sum, sustainable development must be a *different kind of development.* It must be a *pro-active strategy to develop sustainability.*

This applies particularly in developed countries, where one quarter of the world's people consume three quarters of the world's resources. Given that North Americans are among the world's most inefficient and wasteful consumers of materials and energy (see WCED 1987), it is incumbent upon us to find ways of living more lightly on the planet. For North Americans to contribute to global sustainability will require major shifts in the lifestyles of the affluent. A wide variety of approaches are called for, including appropriate technologies, recycling, and waste reduction. The most important adaptation, however, is a reduction of our *present* levels of materials and energy consumption. This will require a more globally conscious kind of local development than we are accustomed to.

Social Equity and Sustainable Development
Today the poorest fifth of the world's population has less than two percent of the world's economic product while the richest fifth has 75 percent; the 26 percent of the world's population living in the developed countries consumes 80-86 percent of nonrenewable resources and 34 to 53 percent of food products. Bringing the Third World up to North American living standards would require a five- to ten-fold increase in world industrial output (see WCED 1987), yet the contingent combination of depleted resource stocks (e.g., fossil fuels, fisheries, forests) with degraded life-support systems (e.g., ozone depletion, global warming, acid rain) demonstrates the impossibility of the entire world consuming and polluting at the rate of North Americans. Social equity demands that we balance the needs of the biosphere with the needs of the vast majority of the human population, the world's poor. Within the developed nations, this in turn means that we must balance the needs of the biosphere with the needs of our own poor. But in doing so we can no longer rely on our 200-year tradition of material growth as the primary instrument of social policy.

"The opposite of wealth is not poverty but sufficiency. This is critical. Sufficiency is not a matter of sacrifice and deprivation. It is a means of working out different ways of achieving satisfaction in our own lives."

Porritt 1989

Toward Global Equality
"To try to solve the economic problems of the high-consumption welfare states or the poor countries by stimulating further growth in the former, as the Brundtland Commission and many others propose, will exacerbate problems for both rich and poor countries. Even the stimulation of growth in the poor countries will be counterproductive unless the growth is oriented toward solar energy and is based on ecologically sound renewable resource production. To attempt to deal with international disparities by trickling aid from growth-stimulated rich countries to poor countries will at best be insufficient to reduce those countries' poverty; at worst, such an approach increases their dependency on technology and oil, deepens their debt, and leads to more ecological destruction. If we in the rich countries are to help those in the poor, we must reduce our own consumption[...]Whether or not such a path is sufficient to move toward global equality, it is necessary."   (Boothroyd 1991)

INITIATIVES

United Nations Conference on Environment and Development (UNCED)
The first-ever "Earth Summit" was held in Rio de Janeiro, Brazil, in June 1992. Ironically, because of political sensitivity the official agenda generally avoided direct discussion of what many analysts perceive to be the two key global sustainability issues: consumption in the North and population growth in the South. Despite the possibility of important international agreements on critical global issues arising from UNCED, many people now realize that the General Agreement on Tariffs and Trade (GATT) may

have a more profound impact on the future of the global environment than all the handshaking and speechmaking by heads of state at the Earth Summit. UNCED information is available in North America from:

National Secretariat UNCED '92
Environment Canada
10 Wellington Street, 4th Floor
Hull, Quebec K1A 0H3
Tel: 819/953-1420   Fax: 819/953-3557

UNCED New York Office
Room S-3060, United Nations
New York, NY 10017
Tel: 212/963-5959   Fax: 212/963-1010

National "Green Plans"

Canada is one of a handful of nations that has produced a "Green Plan" for a healthy environment. The Plan was prepared by the Government of Canada after cross-country consultations in 1990. It claims that its measures will reverse environmental damage, maintain future development, and secure a healthy environment and a prosperous economy. Time will tell if the plan lives up to its claims. Whatever its weaknesses, however, the simple fact of *having* a plan demonstrates environmental leadership relative to most other countries. Available from Environment Canada Communications Offices or from:

Canada's Green Plan
c/o Environment Canada
Ottawa, Canada K1A 0H3

Round Tables on the Environment and the Economy

Apparently unique to Canada, Round Tables are founded upon the conviction that the success of sustainable

12

development will be determined through the definition of a new consensus. Round Tables attempt to bring together a representative selection of people from all facets of society – governments, industry, ecology groups, unions, universities, native peoples – to create a forum for divergent points of view. The idea is that the consensus, alliances, and synergy essential for effective sustainable development policy may emerge through these new institutions. Provincial and many community Round Tables have also been established throughout Canada. More information is available from:

> National Round Table
> on the Environment and the Economy
> 1 Nicholas Street, Suite 520
> Ottawa, Ontario K1N 7B7
> Tel: 613/992-7189   Fax: 613/992-7385

RESOURCES

THE WORLD CONSERVATION UNION (IUCN), THE UNITED NATIONS ENVIRONMENT PROGRAMME (UNEP), AND THE WORLD WIDE FUND FOR NATURE (WWF),*Caring for the Earth: A Strategy for Sustainable Living* (Gland, Switzerland: IUCN/UNEP/WWF, 1991). Dozens of governments and international agencies contributed to this report, which sets out 132 measures that must be implemented over the next ten to twenty years if the Earth is to remain capable of supporting its population. The report estimates that ensuring the long-term survival of the planet will cost $1,288 billion over the next decade (equal to three times Canada's national debt), much of which could come from reducing military spending, selling "Earthcare Bonds," and other financial mechanisms. Additional recommendations include creating an international body to monitor the environment on a global scale, controlling population growth, minimizing the depletion of non-renewable resources, and sharing resources between rich and poor countries and with future generations. This report stands out as essential reading for two reasons. It is the first such document to propose a global action plan that will – sooner or later, in this format or another – *have* to be adopted. It is also the first such report to recognize that local governments are key units for environmental care. Available from:

United Nations Environment Programme
Room DC 2 - 0803
United Nations
New York, NY 10017
Tel: 212/963-8093

WORLD COMMISSION ON ENVIRONMENT AND DEVELOPMENT, *Our Common Future* (New York: Oxford University Press, 1987). This is the report of the Brundtland Commission discussed above. The Commission's main recommendations are to revive economic growth; change the quality of growth; conserve and enhance the resource base; ensure a sustainable level of population; re-orient technology and manage risks; integrate environment and economics in decision-making; reform international economic relations; and strengthen international co-operation. The Commission's call for a five- to ten-fold increase in world industrial output, without any analysis to show whether such expansion is ecologically possible, is highly questionable.

LINDA STARKE, *Signs of Hope: Working Towards Our Common Future* (NY: Oxford University Press, 1990). Starke's book records some of the progress made in the first few years after publication of *Our Common Future,* and points to initiatives underway around the world by governments, industry, scientists, non-governmental organizations, the media, and young people. While not intended to be comprehensive, it shows that those working toward a sustainable future no longer toil alone.

LESTER BROWN, ET AL, *State of the World: A Worldwatch Institute Report on Progress Toward a Sustainable Society* (NY: W.W. Norton & Co., annual). This annual volume includes consistently credible research relating to the challenge of sustainable development. Topics addressed in 1991 included energy, waste, forestry, urban transport, over-consumption, green taxes, and the environmental impacts of war. The Worldwatch Institute also publishes an excellent series of papers and a bimonthly magazine, *World Watch*. Available in bookstores or from:

Worldwatch Institute
1776 Massachusetts Ave., NW
Washington, DC 20036-1904
Tel: 202/452-1999
Fax: 202/296-7365

MICHAEL JACOBS, *The Green Economy: Environment, Sustainable Development and the Politics of the Future* (London: Pluto Press, 1991). This book is primarily about environmental economic policy in industrialized countries, which Jacobs argues are mainly responsible for the environmental crisis. Jacobs rejects both the traditional Green movement demand of "zero growth" and the new economic orthodoxy which seeks to give the environment a monetary value. He argues that sustainability provides an objective both morally defensible and capable of being translated into policy. He then describes a range of instruments by which economic activity can be constrained within environmental limits, and shows how environmental policies need not hurt the poor. His discussion includes regulation versus financial incentives, the role of government expenditure, and integrating equity with social policy. The last section of the book addresses questions of measurement in the context of environmental decision-making.

Jacobs' final chapter addresses the impact of a Green economy on our lives. Jacobs makes a cogent distinction between "standard of living," as equated simply with disposable income, and "quality of life," the sum of all things which people purchase collectively, whether through public expenditure (e.g., public education) or not purchased at all (e.g., air quality).

Will people be willing to forgo constant expansion of material possessions in favour of a more sustainable lifestyle? The important point, he notes, is not how *likely* such a change in culture might be – whether or not the change occurs is for us to decide. Cultures and tastes are influenced by a whole range of social and political factors which themselves can be changed and developed by political parties, pressure groups, voluntary organizations, individual behaviour and cultural activity. In this sense achieving a sustainable economy in industrialized societies is not ultimately a question of economics but rather a question of manifesting the desire and will to change.

HERMAN E. DALY AND JOHN B. COBB, JR., *For the Common Good: Redirecting the Economy Toward Community, the Environment, and a Sustainable Future* (Boston: Beacon Press, 1989). Daly, a World Bank economist and Cobb, a theologian, teamed up to critique "mainstream" economic thinking and offer a new paradigm for economics, public policy, and social ethics. Their work is based on a concern with building community, achieving equity and social justice, and maintaining high levels of economic well-being while conserving and enhancing environmental resources.

Daly and Cobb argue that the "welfare approach to social justice" must be replaced by a more comprehensive approach in which municipalities expand their authority and responsibility in order to work with local citizens on projects designed to enhance community capacity environmentally, socially and economically. They believe that the promotion of greater levels of self-reliance within the geographic boundaries of the municipality should provide one basis for this new approach. For example, they suggest that using wastes as raw materials and emphasizing the local production of goods and services for local use, using locally-based resources, is likely to have a far greater positive impact on social welfare than is the further expansion of human services.

Perhaps Daly and Cobb's greatest contribution is their index of sustainable economic welfare (ISEW). As an alternative accounting system to the GNP, the ISEW attempts to factor in the social and environmental costs of growth in measures of:

• income distribution, as a measure of equity;
• net capital growth, in order to assess whether capital formation is proceeding "in step" with population growth, as a measure of the sustainability of current economic activity;
• sources of capital (i.e., internal or external), as a measure of self-reliance;
• natural resource depletion, as a measure of how much future generations will need to be compensated for the loss of services from exhausted nonrenewable resources;
• environmental damage, as a measure of the costs of noise, air and water pollution;
• value of unpaid household labour, in order to ensure that the index does not discriminate against non-waged contributions to general welfare.

Whereas GNP for the US has risen annually for the last few decades, the ISEW shows a similar pattern of

17

improvements in the 1960s, little growth in the 1970s, and *decline* in the 1980s. The exercise underscores the authors' argument that growth at the expense of sustainability makes us poorer rather than richer. The important question, they conclude, is whether we continue to focus our efforts on increasing total output or whether we redirect our focus toward sustainability.

References

BOOTHROYD, P., "Distribution Principles for Compassionate Sustainable Development," in A.H.J. Dorcey, ed., *Perspectives on Sustainable Development in Water Management: Towards Agreement in the Fraser Basin* (Vancouver: Westwater Research Centre, 1991).

BROWN, L., ET AL, *State of the World: A Worldwatch Institute Report on Progress Toward a Sustainable Society* (NY: W.W. Norton & Co., annual).

CANADIAN CONSERVATION COMMISSION, 1915; cited in Metropolitan Toronto Planning Department, *Towards a Liveable Metropolis* (Toronto: Metropolitan Plan Review Report No. 13, May 1991).

DALY, H.E. AND J.B. COBB, JR., *For the Common Good: Redirecting the Economy Toward Community, the Environment, and a Sustainable Future* (Boston: Beacon Press, 1989).

JACOBS, M., *The Green Economy: Environment, Sustainable Development and the Politics of the Future* (London: Pluto Press, 1991).

INTERNATIONAL UNION FOR CONSERVATION OF NATURE (IUCN), THE UNITED NATIONS ENVIRONMENT PROGRAMME (UNEP), and THE WORLD WIDE FUND FOR NATURE (WWF), *Caring for the Earth: A Strategy for Sustainable Living* (Gland, Switzerland: IUCN/UNEP/WWF, 1991).

MITLIN, D. AND D. SATTERTHWAITE, "Sustainable Development and Cities," prepared for How Common Is Our Future? A Global NGO Forum. Mexico City: Habitat International Coalition, March 4-7, 1991.

PORRIT, J., "Seeing Green: How We Can Create A More Satisfying Society," *Utne Reader* No. 36, Nov/Dec 1989, pp. 70-77.

REES, W.E., "Understanding Sustainable Development" (Vancouver: UBC School of Community and Regional Planning, 1991).

STARKE, L., *Signs of Hope: Working Towards Our Common Future* (NY: Oxford University Press, 1990).

WORLD COMMISSION ON ENVIRONMENT AND DEVELOPMENT (WCED), *Our Common Future* (New York: Oxford University Press, 1987).

2

Toward Sustainable Communities

> *"It is becoming apparent that almost every issue of sustainable development which emerges at the local level will be replicated, in one form or another, at the provincial, national and international levels."*
>
> George E. Connell, Chair,
> National Round Table on the Environment and the
> Economy, letter to the Prime Minister, 1991.

> ### *Importing Sustainability*
> "Our preliminary data for industrial cities suggest that the land 'consumed' by urban regions is typically at least an order of magnitude greater than that contained within the usual political boundaries or the associated built-up area. If we take the lower Fraser Valley (Vancouver to Hope) as an example, our regional population uses 18 times as much land as it actually occupies. The missing land is, in effect, 'imported' from distant elsewheres which may not be ecologically secure or politically stable [...] However, brilliant its economic star, every city is an ecological black hole drawing on the material resources and productivity of a vast and scattered hinterland many times the size of the city itself."
>
> **(Rees 1992)**

Nearly half of the world's people will live in urban areas by the turn of the century (see WCED 1987). The way these urban areas are developed will largely determine our success or failure in overcoming environmental challenges

21

and achieving sustainable development. Cities provide enormous, untapped opportunities to solve environmental challenges, and local governments must and can pioneer new approaches to sustainable development and urban management. They must also assume the responsibility and marshall the resources to address the environmental problems facing their communities (see Toronto Declaration 1991).

Although common environmental themes unite the world's communities, the communities of the developing (Southern) world face distinctly different challenges than those faced by the communities of the developed (Northern) world. From the perspective of sustainable development, the basic problem with Northern cities is that they are unsustainable, whereas the basic problem with Southern cities is that they are underdeveloped. Most Northern city dwellers are adequately housed and fed, but they meet their needs by consuming at rates the planet cannot afford and polluting at rates the planet cannot tolerate. Most Southern city dwellers cannot meet their basic needs for food, clean water, clean air, fuel, transport and an environment free of disease-causing agents. While this dichotomy is not entirely clear cut – i.e., there is poverty in many Northern cities, and many Southern cities live beyond their means in terms of consumption of natural resources such as firewood and water – it helps illuminate the essential challenge of urban sustainability both North and South: meeting basic needs without depleting or degrading environmental capital (see Holmberg, Bass, and Timberlake 1991).

The role of the cities of the industrial world deserves much more scrutiny in the context of human settlements and the environmental crisis, precisely because their impact on the world's changing ecosystems is so enormous. Although some of our cities may appear to be sustainable,

> *"The reality with which we must come to terms is that the world is not bountiful enough to support this kind of behaviour by the world's present human population of 5 billion, let alone the 10 billion we might have before the population levels off [...] The challenge for human settlements policy is not to replicate the rich country patterns in today's poor countries. The challenge is to design and manage human settlements in such a way that all the world's people may live at a decent standard based on sustainable principles."*
>
> White and Whitney 1990

analysis of the "ecological footprint" of industrial cities shows that they "appropriate" carrying capacity (see Wackernagel 1991) not only from their own rural and resource regions but also from "distant elsewheres" (Rees 1992) – in other words, they "import" sustainability. Furthermore, the cities of the industrial world, with their inadequate urban policies and technology, set the standard to which city managers in low-income countries aspire — low density single family dwellings, cars, expressways, waste creation, air conditioning and profligate water use (see White and Whitney 1990).

The focus of this book is on the postwar pattern of Western urban development, as typified by many North American (i.e., Canadian and US) cities and towns. Many ideas mentioned briefly in this chapter are elaborated in succeeding chapters.

Most North American cities were built using technologies which assumed that abundant and cheap energy and land would be available forever. Communities therefore grew inefficiently, and became dependent on lengthy distribution systems. Cheap energy influenced the construction of our spacious homes and buildings, fostered our addiction to the automobile, and increased the separation of our workplaces from our homes (see Environment Council of Alberta 1988).

Urban sprawl is one legacy of abundant fossil fuel and our perceived right to unrestricted use of the private car whatever the social costs and externalities. Per capita gasoline consumption in US and many Canadian cities is now more than four times that of European cities, and over 10 times greater than such Asian cities as Hong Kong, Tokyo, and Singapore. The biggest factor accounting for these differences in energy use appears to be not the size of cars or the price of gasoline, but the efficiency and compactness of land use patterns (see Newman and Kenworthy 1989). One conclusion of a study prepared for the US Government was that "sprawl is the most expensive form of residential development in terms of economic costs, environmental costs, natural resource consumption, and many types of personal costs [...] This cost difference is particularly significant for that proportion of total costs which is likely to be borne by local governments" (Real Estate Research Corporation 1974).

Other local and regional consequences of sprawl, such as congestion, air pollution, jobs-housing location "imbalance," and longer commuting times are now commonly recognized. Yet, until recently, few researchers acknowledged that the land use pattern of North American cities also has serious *global* ecological ramifications. For example, residents of most Canadian cities annually produce about 20 tons of carbon dioxide per capita, placing Canada among the top three or four nations in terms of per capita contribution to potential climate change. In contrast, citizens of Amsterdam produce only 10 tons of carbon dioxide per capita per year. Sprawl, exclusionary zoning and low density account for much of this difference. According to recent research at the International Institute for Applied Systems Analysis, if North American cities modelled future development on cities like Amsterdam, future carbon dioxide emissions here would only be half as much as

24

"Sprawlsville is flawed because it over-emphasizes the private, individualized world at the expense of our commons. It provides for private splendour in our houses and backyards and in our cars, but public squalor in our air and water, at the urban fringe as it falls under the subdivision's bulldozer, in the global environment due to the greenhouse effect, in the feeble attempts at community which characterize our suburbs, and in our public transport, which is allowed to run down and become vandalized."

Newman 1991

"The current round of suburban growth is generating a crisis of many dimensions: mounting traffic congestion, increasingly unaffordable housing, receding open space, and stressful social patterns. The truth is, we are using planning strategies that are forty years old and no longer relevant to today's culture. Our household make-up has changed dramatically, the work place and work force have been transformed, real wealth has shrunk, and serious environmental concerns have surfaced. But we are still building World War II suburbs as if families were large and had only one breadwinner, as if jobs were all downtown, as if land and energy were endless, and as if another lane on the freeway would end congestion."

Calthorpe 1989

current gloomy projections now indicate (see Alcamo 1990).

The postwar pattern of Western urban development is not only ecologically unconscionable but economically inefficient and socially inequitable. In contrast, sustainable development implies that the use of energy and materials be consistent with production by such "natural capital" processes as photosynthesis and waste assimilation (see Rees 1990a,b). To some authors this implies increasing community and regional self-reliance to reduce dependency on imports (see RAIN 1981, California Office of Appropriate Technology 1981, Morris 1982). The benefits would be reduced energy budgets, reduced material consumption, and a smaller, more compact urban pattern interspersed with productive areas to collect energy, grow crops, and recycle wastes (see Van der Ryn and Calthorpe 1986).

Cities with low "automobile dependence" are more centralized; have more intense land use (more people and jobs per unit area); are more oriented to non-auto modes (more public transit, foot traffic, and bicycle usage); place more restraints on high-speed traffic; and offer better public transit (see Newman and Kenworthy 1989). This suggests a new approach to transportation and land use planning in North America. In the absence of comprehensive planning, transportation has, almost by default, guided land use. Instead, land use planning should guide transportation, and transportation should be designed to accommodate and support planned growth, inducing the needed changes in urban form (see Cervero 1991; Replogle 1990).

The ideal urban form for a particular locale will depend to some extent on the nature of the energy supply options: for example, higher densities make most efficient use of district heating and public transport networks, while lower densities may make solar energy more viable. The location, gross density and form of new development should therefore be determined in conjunction with programs for energy supply and conservation technologies (see Owens 1990). This principle is illustrated by a recent San Jose, California study which compared development pressures with or without a "greenbelt" to constrain development. Without it, 13,000 exurban homes would be developed which, compared to an equivalent number of units downtown and along the transit corridor, would require at least an additional 200,000 miles of auto commuting plus an additional three million gallons of water *every day,* as well as 40 percent more energy for

The City as Ecosystem

"In this century, the city has been imagined by sociologists, planners, and engineers as a bazaar, a seat of political chaos, an infernal machine, a circuit, and, more hopefully, as a community, the human creation 'par excellence.' These different ways of thinking about cities, their social forces, their market behaviours, their reliance on materials and processes from the natural world, both shape and constrain the programmes and policies that local governments put forward to serve the needs of urban people.

The city can also be imagined as an ecosystem. Such a concept provides a tool to understand the complex relations between human activities and the environment, and how communities can organise their activities to both meet human needs and benefit the environment [...]

Like a natural system such as a pond or forest, an urban ecosystem transforms energy (human labour, capital, fossil fuels) and materials (timber, iron, sand & gravel, information, etc.) into products that are consumed or exported, and into by-products. In natural systems by-products are recycled. We have designed and managed our cities so that these by-products often go unused as wastes. The impact of human activity on the environment can be highlighted by charting the dynamics of the system – the movement of materials and people, the flows of energy and capital, the locations where energy is stored or expended, the rates at which wastes are generated and recycled. By looking at the city as a whole, by analyzing the pathways along which energy and pollution move, we can begin to see how human activities create and direct pollution into local, regional, and global ecosystems. We can also see how these activities can be reorganised and reintegrated with natural processes to increase the efficiency of resource use, the recycling of 'wastes' as valuable materials, and the conservation of energy."

(Brugmann and Hersh 1991)

> "A [typical North American] city of 100,000 people imports
> 200 tons of food a day, 1000 tons of fuel a day, and 62,000 tons
> of water a day [...] it dumps 100,000 tons of garbage a year
> and 40,000 tons of human waste a year."
>
> Morris 1990

heating and cooling (see Yesney 1990).

Another study, by Montgomery County, Maryland, found that continued growth in an automobile-dependent pattern would produce traffic congestion levels high enough to choke off economic development. However, an anticipated doubling of population and employment could be accommodated without excessive traffic problems if most new growth were clustered in pedestrian- and bicycle-friendly centres focused on an expanded rail transit and busway system. Through such strategies, the share of County work trips made by non-auto alternatives could double to 50%, resulting in only half the level of energy use and air pollution compared to the sprawled, automobile strategy (see Replogle 1990).

Such studies demonstrate that *the pattern of growth is more important than the amount of growth* in determining the level and efficiency of resource use and traffic congestion.

Australian researcher Peter Newman notes (1990) that "the most unsustainable form of settlement yet developed – the low density suburb – has been a relatively recent phenomenon, motivated by a strong anti-urban Anglo-Saxon sentiment and facilitated by the automobile. Social organisation for ecological sustainability will need to reverse this settlement pattern." His analysis of settlement patterns and sustainability suggests that sustainable settlements require making cities more urban and making the countryside more rural.

Making cities more urban can be accomplished by "re-

Local Governments for a Sustainable Future
"Local governments have been timid to act in the face of overwhelming evidence of global environmental decline. While resources at the local government level have been scarce, they have been even more inhibited by a narrow and ineffectual conception of the domain of local government concern. The result has been a lack of mobilization to address global problems that are largely rooted in local, day-to-day activity. Indeed, it is the world's industrial cities that produce most of the world's solid and liquid wastes, consume most of the world's fossil fuels, emit the majority of ozone depleting compounds and toxic gases, and give economic incentive to the clearing of the world's forests [...]

Fortunately, in the face of global challenges, many local governments have started taking singlehanded initiatives to address the root causes of environmental decline. From recycling systems and traffic reduction programs to local bans of CFCs and city-to-city Third World development partnerships, local governments are serving as laboratories for policy invention in the environmental arena [...]

While broad policy parameters are being formulated at the international level, local governments are developing the thousands of concrete changes in economic, political and social behaviour required to forestall an environmental crisis. The concrete innovations that they are testing are providing models for national level policies and programs."

(from "Call to a World Congress of Local Governments for a Sustainable Future," United Nations Environment Program, September 5-8, 1990)

urbanising" city centres and sub-centres; re-orienting transport infrastructure away from the automobile; removing subsidies on the automobile; and providing a

The Failure of the Conventional Urban Model
"By the 1960s, the traditional main street, which had been set in and was the center of a particular neighbourhood, built on a human scale and haphazardly accommodating shopping, businesses and homes, came to be regarded as passé. The wave of the future was to be a city where the various activities of human life were to be compartmentalized, physically separated from one another; a city designed with the car in mind. In place of the main street was to be the suburban shopping mall, set in the middle of the asphalt square that serves as a temporary resting spot for the automobiles the customers had no choice but to use. Many urban residential neighbourhoods, with what was seen as a disorderly mix of architectural styles and streetscapes that did not fit the planners' logic, were to be demolished wholesale, to make way for the erection of uniform towers, cut off from the street by walls, berms and open space masquerading as landscaping.

It is now generally conceded that the quality of urban life can suffer seriously in cities built entirely upon this model because of dependence on the automobile, the loss of diversity and public places built on a human scale, and the consequent multiplication of areas where pedestrians fear to tread. These cities aren't very efficient, either, because commuters spend a tremendous amount of time and energy, and cause enormous pollution, by constantly having to drive on congested streets."

*(**Globe and Mail** Editorial 1991)*

more public-oriented urban culture, assisted by attractive urban design (townscapes, streetscapes, malls and squares) and by "traffic calming" measures to facilitate bicycle and pedestrian use of residential areas and major roads. Making the countryside more rural can be accomplished by means such as protecting and encouraging sustainable agriculture in rural areas and moving towards bioregionalism (e.g., air- and watershed management) as the basis of local government boundaries and responsibilities.

Figure 1a: Creative Development

Site A Before Development

Reprinted with permission from the Center for Rural Massachusetts/University of Massachusetts at Anmherst, from the Center's Design Manual, by R.D. Yaro, et al, *Dealing With Change in the Connecticut River Valley: A Design Manual for Conservation and Development.*

Figure 1b: Creative Development

Site A After Conventional Development

Reprinted with permission from the Center for Rural Massachusetts/University of Massachusetts at Anmherst, from the Center's Design Manual, by R.D. Yaro, et al, *Dealing With Change in the Connecticut River Valley: A Design Manual for Conservation and Development.*

Figure 1c: Creative Development

Site A After "Creative Development"

Reprinted with permission from the Center for Rural Massachusetts/University of Massachusetts at Anmherst, from the Center's Design Manual, by R.D. Yaro, et al, *Dealing With Change in the Connecticut River Valley: A Design Manual for Conservation and Development*.

Yaro *et al* (1988) have developed practical planning standards which rural New England towns can adopt to protect their distinctive character and accommodate economic growth. Their drawings of actual sites in western Massachusetts show each site before development, after conventional development and after "creative development" (Figure 1). In both schemes, the same number of units have been added. The most critical difference is that the conventional approach dramatically alters the land use pattern (e.g., agricultural lands lost to suburban sprawl), while the creative approach absorbs growth without destroying future options (e.g., agricultural "capital" remains intact).

Norwood (1990) illustrates a similar concept within the setting of a typical suburban block (Figure 2). An existing single-family neighbourhood, with under-utilized back yards, garages, attics, basements and bedrooms, has been transformed into an "urban cooperative block." Variations on this theme are increasingly popular in new private market developments. This concept could be: organized around one or more small or home businesses; designed to "recycle" obsolete corporate/industrial parks, shopping centres, and office complexes; or, as shown here, the centre of a "village cluster" typical of Danish cohousing communities, with a community house, common back yards, parking, and resources. Many forms of ownership are possible: a condominium corporation, a non-profit corporation with resident control, a limited equity cooperative, a community land trust or a mutual housing association. Economic advantages include lowering housing costs through creating additional infill units and/ or bedrooms, renting rooms and units, and allowing cottage industries or home businesses. By improving affordability, this model has the potential of serving a diversified and intergenerational cross-section of the population.

Figure 2 An Urban Cooperative Block

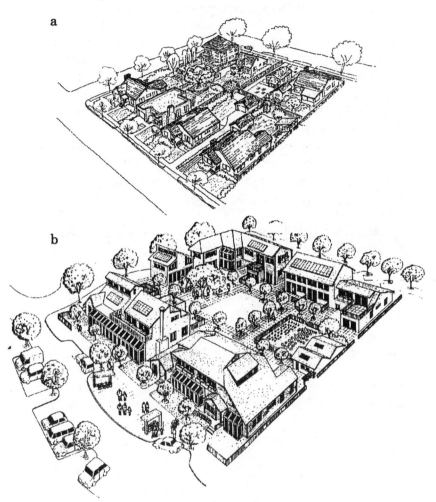

a

b

A traditional development (a) compared to an urban "village cluster" (b) which could include a community house, common back yards, common parking, and common resources.

Reprinted with permission from the Shared Living Resource Center, a non-profit organization dedicated to creating supportive shared living communities that integrate housing with cooperative living, ecological design and affordability. Shared Living Resource Center, 2375 Shattuck Ave., Berkeley, CA 94704, 415/548-6608.

Figure 3 A Sustainable City Vision

This emphasizes mixed-use zoning, pedestrian-, bicycle-
and transit-friendly streets, renewable energy sources,
and urban greenery.

From a drawing by Diane Schatz, reprinted with permission from *Rain* Magazine, PO Box 30097, Eugene, OR 97403, 503/683-1504.

Rethinking Urban Transport

"What would the future look like if cities were not dominated by cars? The very heart of a city would be reserved for people on foot and passengers arriving by metro or trolley. Proceeding outward from the center, streets would become the shared domain of pedestrians, cyclists, trolleys, and buses. Slow automobile traffic would be allowed beyond the city's densest core, but convenient bus and rail services – running between stops placed within walking or cycling distance of most points – would offer a faster way to get around. Express public transport routes would link outlying areas to each other and to the downtown. Car parking would be progressively less restricted as you moved away from the city center.

People would make most short trips by foot or on a bicycle, and longer ones by walking or biking to transport stops, then continuing by bus, metro, or trolley. Many long drives between cities would be replaced by train trips. Cars would be used mainly for trips for which these other modes are inconvenient, such as the transport of loads of things or groups of people, travel at odd hours when public transport is running infrequently, and some recreational outings.

The challenge of creating an alternative transport future is ultimately a political one. As elected officials in most societies are well aware, many people continue to support the policies that have nurtured overreliance on cars – from driving subsidies, to tax benefits, to expansion of parking lots and roads. Even more resistance to change lies in the colossal power of the automobile and road lobby.

But as the enormous problems caused by excessive dependence on the automobile continue to plague cities, a political transformation may occur. Indeed, people around the world are beginning to see that the costs of depending on cars are already outweighing the benefits. If cities are to achieve the dream of clean, efficient, reliable transportation once promised by the automobile, they will have to steer toward sustainable alternatives."

(Lowe 1991)

Figure 3 illustrates a similar concept, but this time the setting is in a downtown core. Many ideas for urban sustainability are illustrated in this drawing, such as mixed-use zoning; streets devoted to walking, cycling, and public transport; heavy reliance on renewable energy sources; rooftop gardens and greenery; and separate "waste" containers for compost and trash. Note the integration of work and home, which reduces the need for travel. As described earlier, a recent San Jose, California study compared the impacts of 13,000 units of this kind of development downtown and along the transit corridor to an equivalent number of exurban homes. It found that the kind of development pictured here saved at least 200,000 miles of auto commuting plus an additional three million gallons of water *every day*, and required 40 percent less energy for heating and cooling (see Yesney 1990).

Calthorpe's "Pedestrian Pocket" is another variation on this theme, at the level of a compact neighbourhood. The "Pedestrian Pocket" is defined as a balanced, mixed-use area within a quarter-mile or a five-minute walking radius of a transit station. The functions within this 50 to 100-acre zone include housing, offices, retail, day care, recreation, and parks. Up to two thousand units of housing and one million square feet of office space can be located within three blocks of the transit station using typical residential densities and four-story office configurations (see Kelbaugh 1989).

Figure 4 brings the discussion to the level of the urban region, using the city of Berkeley, California as an example. Although these maps may at first appear to show the *history* of Berkeley, they actually demonstrate a sustainable *future* development pattern for this urban region. The first map in this set shows Berkeley and its town and neighbourhood "centers." These centres were selected as a compromise between the "ideal" centres – according to the

---

A Sustainable City Vision
"[A] sustainable city [...] thinks of itself whole, moves with change, and plans for permanence. Above all, this implies an acceptance of responsibility and nurturing of solutions at the local level: conserving indigenous resources and managing them for sustained yield; fostering local production to meet more of local needs; designing political systems to support decision-making at the lowest possible level; and, everywhere, encouraging low-cost, community self-help strategies that empower people to help themselves. The vision is still a distant one. It may require nothing less than a reorientation of our values. But doing such things, a city will survive and endure.

Pieces of such a vision have already begun to appear: neighbourhoods that have experimented with integral food, energy and waste systems; cities that have built energy conservation into their street design, zoning and building codes; urban regions that are assessing the levels of growth and development that can be supported by their air- and watersheds; whole states that are being studied to determine their ability to become self-reliant in food production. Make no mistake about it, the transition has begun.

But, as yet, no major community has come forward with a new image of itself that integrates all these ideas and uses that image to build its future."

(RAIN 1981)

---

natural features of the landscape such as ridgelines and steep slopes – and the existing centres. Over time, urban development is concentrated near these centers while surrounded by non-urban lands. Once again, the key feature is the *pattern* of urban growth.

These drawings demonstrate a "nodal" rather than a "centralized" vision – a network of smaller, compact communities surrounded by *non-urban* land. As the city grows, and its "centers" become increasingly compact, the surrounding land can be reclaimed – as open space, forests, agricultural land, and wildlife habitat – to simultaneously benefit people and the environment.

Figure 4a (Reprinted with permission from *Ecocity Berkeley*)

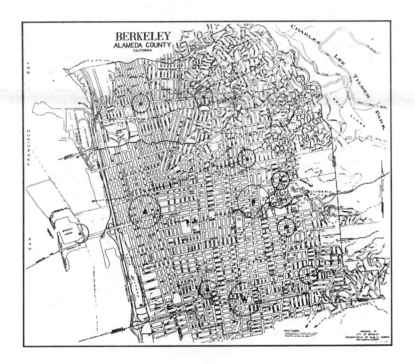

Berkeley and its Centres

"The underlying concept behind drawing these circles is simply that distance requires energy and time to traverse. The greater the distance people have to travel, the higher the use of resources and the greater the production of pollution and waste of time. ...

Figure 4b (Reprinted with permission from *Ecocity Berkeley*)

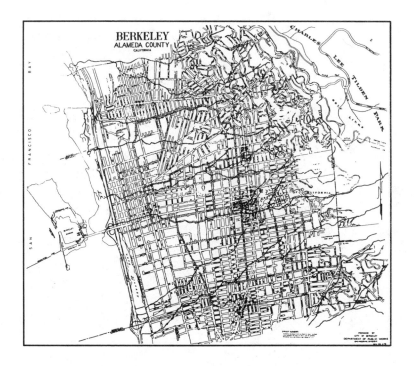

Berkeley, 15 to 50 Years Hence

... Therefore, we should build relatively compact centers. These areas will then work well with any public transit connecting them to other relatively high-use areas. ...

Figure 4c (Reprinted with permission from *Ecocity Berkeley*)

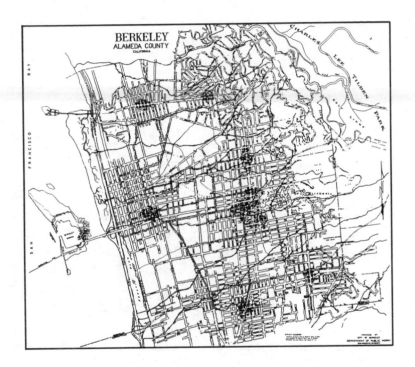

Berkeley, 25 to 90 Years Hence

... Within and between the spots of higher activity people can find it easy and pleasant to walk and bicycle. This pattern of 'spots' of development is based on the size of the human body and the speed of walking. ...

Figure 4d (Reprinted with permission from *Ecocity Berkeley*)

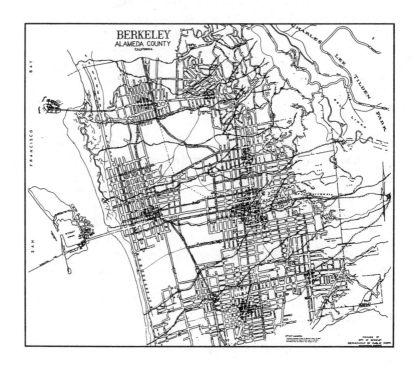

Berkeley, 40 to 125 Years Hence

> ... It contrasts sharply with 'strip' (one-dimensional or linear development) and 'sprawl' (two-dimensional or flat development) created by and for things that weigh 10 to 40 times as much and travel up to 50 times as fast: automobiles." **(Register, 1987)**

Local Governments for Sustainable Communities
"Despite being centres of industry and commerce, many cities display extreme poverty and environmental degradation. In high-income countries, as older industrial towns decline and inner city districts decay, the less educated, the poor and the elderly find themselves trapped and sometimes homeless in places where services are disappearing and crime rates are high. Ethnic minorities, immigrants, and the disabled suffer disproportionately, the victims of a growing equity gap [...]

Cities can provide high-quality living for all their inhabitants at sustainable levels of consumption. The poverty suffered by the minority of urban dwellers in richer nations and the majority in poorer nations can be drastically reduced without a large expansion in consumption. In both instances, more effective and representative local governments, and more far-sighted national governments are required."

(IUCN 1991)

INITIATIVES

World Congress of Local Governments for a Sustainable Future

The world's local governments are represented through the International Union of Local Authorities (IULA), which consists of 56 national associations of local government in 34 nations, as well as hundreds of individual local governments and local government institutes. In September 1989, the U.S.-based Center for Innovative Diplomacy (CID) – which was leading an international campaign to have cities ban and phase-out chemical compounds that are depleting the ozone layer – initiated discussions with IULA about creating an international environmental agency to serve local governments. At the same time, CID interviewed more than 100 local government officials from 20 countries to get their input on the idea. A few months later, the United Nations Environment Programme, Regional Office for North America, joined the discussions. These three institutions jointly resolved to establish the International Council for Local Environmental Initiatives (ICLEI) at a World Congress of Local Governments for a Sustainable Future.

On September 5-8, 1990, more than 400 local government leaders from 41 nations gathered for an unprecedented and historical meeting at the United Nations. The delegates represented the range of world communities from mega-cities like Mexico City and Los Angeles to small communities of indigenous people in the Amazon Basin. Most delegates represented cities of medium size, with populations from 200,000 to 2 million people – the places where most of the world's human population live their daily lives.

The World Congress delegates discussed the need to integrate environmental factors into all aspects of municipal management (including procurement, investment, budgeting, and environmental impact assessment) and to see waste as a resource of the future. They recognized their ability to mobilize participation and collaboration for environmental protection (for example, by transforming school systems into centers for environmental ethics). As well, they recognized the value both of local partnerships (for example, with private industry to reduce CFC emissions) and global partnerships (such as North-South municipal partnerships between Calgary, Canada and Daqing, China, and between Palo Alto, USA and Oaxaca, Mexico).

The Congress also discussed the need to understand and

manage urban environments as ecological systems; take charge of the structure of our municipalities, rather than letting them grow and sprawl in uncontrolled fashion; to look for indigenous solutions to local environmental problems; decentralize energy production and distribution; and reintegrate native species into the urban environment.

In the numerous strategy sessions, the Congress asked that the International Council for Local Environmental Initiatives serve as a clearinghouse for innovative policies, strategies and techniques for local environmental protection; facilitate international partnerships among municipalities; provide technical assistance; provide financial assistance for specific pilot projects; and represent local government interests and concerns in the process of the 1992 UN Conference on Environment and Development.

Sustainable Cities Project

The cities of *San Jose* and *San Francisco*, California, and the city of *Portland*, Oregon, together with representatives from the State of Washington and Lawrence Berkeley National Laboratory, teamed up to develop a far-sighted strategy to increase the overall efficiency and sustainability of their communities. The project, begun in 1988, was supported by the US Departments of Energy and of Housing and Urban Development. The primary objectives of the project were to conserve the natural environment while "reshaping" the built environment. Specific attention for the natural environment focused on energy conservation in buildings and transportation, conservation of water and urban forest resources, and the improved management of toxic materials, solid wastes, sewage and urban runoff. Efforts for the built environment addressed a wide range of life extension procedures complemented by rehabilitation and reuse initiatives. Reshaping efforts included innovative management procedures and incentives to limit the spread of urban sprawl, encourage center city activity, and reduce vehicle commuting.

The project's efforts were initiated in the self-interest of each participating city, rather than addressing national or international concerns with environmental quality. Rather than isolate the "environment" from overall community goals, the project integrated environmental concerns into objectives for a community's economic and cultural vitality. Significantly, the project was not designed to require substantial capital investment, but rather to emphasize the improvement of local management techniques, regulatory provisions and land development incentives to reshape traditional patterns of consumption, development and employment into more efficient and sustainable patterns. (see Zelinski and Broun 1989)

RESOURCES

THE INTERNATIONAL COUNCIL FOR LOCAL ENVIRONMENTAL INITIATIVES (ICLEI) was established at the World Congress of Local Governments for a Sustainable Future at the United Nations in September 1990. ICLEI's North American headquarters opened in Toronto in September 1991:

> The International Council for Local
> Environmental Initiatives
> New City Hall, East Tower, 8th floor
> Toronto, Ontario M5H 2N2
> Tel: 416/392-1462   Fax: 416/392-1478

THE UNITED NATIONS CENTRE FOR HUMAN SETTLEMENTS SUSTAINABLE CITIES PROGRAMME was launched in 1990 to address the environmental implications of rapid urbanization. Six megacities in Asia, Africa, Latin America, and Eastern Europe will initially participate in this programme, which aims to strengthen local capacity to plan, coordinate, and manage environment-development interactions in the framework of broad-based participatory systems. It also promotes integrated development plans and sector investment strategies. For more information, contact:

Mr. M. Hildebrand, Chief
Technical Co-operation Division
UNCHS (Habitat)
PO Box 30030
Nairobi, Kenya

THE MEGA-CITIES PROJECT is a network of professionals and institutions in the world's largest cities, committed to promoting urban innovations for the 21st century. Its focus is reducing poverty and environmental degradation, and encouraging popular participation. Mega-cities are cities with over 10 million inhabitants – by 2000 there will be 23 of them. The North American mega-cities are New York, Los Angeles, and Mexico City. The project gives particular attention to urban innovations that empower women. For more information, see the special issue of *Cities* on "Urban Innovation for the 21st Century" (Volume 7, Number 1, February 1990) or contact:

Dr. Janice Perlman, Director
Mega-Cities Project
4 Washington Square North
New York University
New York, NY 10003
Tel: 212/998-7520   Fax: 212/995-3890

MARCIA D. LOWE, *Shaping Cities: The Environmental and Human Dimensions* (Washington, D.C.: Worldwatch Institute, Paper 105, 1991). This paper provides an overview of urban environmental planning issues in cities around the world, with considerable attention to the challenges facing Third World cities. The future growth of cities "can either recognize the limits of the natural environment, or destroy the resources on which current and future societies depend; it can meet people's needs equitably, or enrich some while impoverishing or endangering others." It concludes with a framework for urban land use policy which emphasizes adequate information, regional cooperation, and strong support from national governments.

ORGANIZATION FOR ECONOMIC CO-OPERATION AND DEVELOPMENT (OECD), *Environmental Policies for Cities in the 1990s* (Paris, OECD, 1990). This report examines various existing urban environmental improvement policies, proposes ways and means to improve policy coordination with regard to urban environmental impacts, and describes policy instruments available to national, regional and local governments. It also assesses local initiatives in three areas of concern: urban rehabilitation, urban transport and urban energy management, and proposes policy guidelines for improvement in these areas. The report emphasizes the need to develop long-term strategies, adopt cross-sectoral approaches, facilitate cooperation and coordination, enable polluters to absorb environmental and social costs through fiscal and pricing mechanisms, set and enforce minimum environmental standards, increase the use of renewable resources, and encourage and build upon local initiatives. Several descriptions of urban environmental policies and programs in OECD countries are included.

RICHARD STREN, RODNEY WHITE, AND JOSEPH WHITNEY, editors, *Sustainable Cities: Urbanization and the Environment in International Perspective* (Boulder, CO: Westview Press, 1991). Based on a 1990 colloquium at the University of Toronto, this volume brings together comprehensive studies of the urban experience in the U.S., Canada, Western Europe, Eastern Europe, Japan, Southeast Asia, China and Hong Kong, Africa, and Latin

America. The chapters examine the meaning of sustainable development in a specific region, the growth and structure of urban systems, the effects of possible climatic changes on urban areas, and the political environment within which cities operate. Chapters conclude with policy proposals for increasing sustainability.

URBAN ECOLOGY, *Report of the First International Ecocity Conference* (Berkeley, CA: Urban Ecology, 1990). At the First International Ecocity Conference in 1990, over 700 attendees from around the world gathered in Berkeley, California to discuss urban problems and submit proposals toward the goal of shaping cities upon ecological principles. Over 80 sessions addressed the broad spectrum of ecocity concerns. The Second International Ecocity Conference is in Adelaide, South Australia in 1992. Available from:

Urban Ecology
P.O. Box 10144
Berkeley, CA 94709
Tel: 415/549-1724

SIM VAN DER RYN AND PETER CALTHORPE, editors, *Sustainable Communities: A New Design Synthesis for Cities, Suburbs and Towns* (San Francisco: Sierra Club, 1986). Architects Sim Van der Ryn and Peter Calthorpe's seminal volume grew out of an intensive week-long workshop with thirty leading innovators in ecology and community design. It includes contributions from biological designer John Todd, economist David Morris, planner Clare Cooper-Marcus, businessman Paul Hawken, bioregionalist Peter Berg and agriculturalists David Katz and Fred Reid.

Hawken postulates that the shift to a post-industrial economy requires a design shift from consumption toward efficiency, i.e., doing more with less. Katz argues that the post-industrial suburb will be more site-specific and rely more on local people and local intelligence rather than standard formulations from afar. Reid argues for diversity in transportation options, noting that lighter, more efficient autos are only an interim step towards diversity in land use planning, with more emphasis on clustering, density, and mixed-uses.

Cooper-Marcus notes our existing land use patterns are built on outdated notions of the nuclear family with one wage earner (as much as on outdated notions of cheap oil, land and water), and that the shift toward a service economy should mean more work opportunities in or close to residential neighbourhoods and greater accessibility to public transport. Morris argues that cities and neighbourhoods will gain greater economic and political independence as local self-reliance provides cheaper and more stable services than can be provided by large centralized industries or government (e.g., utilities). Todd argues that the sustainable settlement can reintegrate today's "producer" and "consumer" roles at home and elsewhere, with the household, through its design, producing some of its own food, energy, and even employment on site, rather than being merely a place of consumption.

Despite a wide range of expertise and opinion, the common perspective of these authors is characterized by an emphasis on energy efficiency, stressing passive solar heating and cooling; encouraging local food production and reliance on local resources; and fostering creation of on-site jobs and neighbourhood stores to revitalize communities and eliminate wasteful commuting. These physical layouts, in turn, encourage social interaction by clustering dwellings and creating common-use areas and shared facilities, while increasing security and stressing appropriate scale.

References

ALCAMO, J.M., "Compact City Design as a Strategy to Cut Dangerous Air Pollution," presented to the First International Ecocity Conference. Berkeley, CA: Urban Ecology, March 29-April 1, 1990.

BRUGMANN, J. AND R. HERSH, *Cities as Ecosystems: Opportunities for Local Government* (Toronto: ICLEI, 1991), draft.

CALIFORNIA OFFICE OF APPROPRIATE TECHNOLOGY (CALOAT),*Working Together: Community Self-Reliance in California* (Sacramento: California Office of Appropriate Technology, 1981).

CALTHORPE, P., "Introduction: A Reverse Definition," in D. Kelbaugh, ed., *The Pedestrian Pocket Book: A New Suburban Design Strategy* (New York: Princeton Architectural Press, 1989).

CERVERO, R. 1991. "Congestion Relief: The Land Use Alternative," *Journal of Planning Education and Research* 10(2): 119-129.

CONNELL, G.E., Chair, National Round Table on the Environment and the Economy (NRTEE), letter to the Prime Minister, in *A Report to Canadians* (Ottawa: NRTEE, 1991).

ENVIRONMENT COUNCIL OF ALBERTA. *Environment By Design: The Urban Place in Alberta*, ECA88-PA/CS-S3 (Edmonton: Environment Council of Alberta, 1988).

Globe and Mail, "The Fight for Humane Cities" (Editorial), November 4, 1991, p. A22.

HOLMBERG, J., S. BASS, AND L. TIMBERLAKE, *Defending the Future: A Guide to Sustainable Development* (London: International Institute for Environment and Development/ Earthscan 1991).

INTERNATIONAL COUNCIL FOR LOCAL ENVIRONMENTAL INITIATIVES, *Congress Report: World Congress of Local Governments for a Sustainable Future* (Cambridge, MA: ICLEI, 1990).

INTERNATIONAL UNION FOR CONSERVATION OF NATURE (IUCN), THE UNITED NATIONS ENVIRONMENT PROGRAMME (UNEP), and THE WORLD WIDE FUND FOR NATURE (WWF), *Caring for the Earth: A Strategy for Sustainable Living* (Gland, Switzerland: IUCN/UNEP/WWF, 1991).

KELBAUGH, D., ed., *The Pedestrian Pocket Book: A New Suburban Design Strategy* (New York: Princeton

Architectural Press, 1989).

LOWE, M.D., "Rethinking Urban Transport," in Brown, L. R., et al, *State of the World 1991: A Worldwatch Institute Report on Progress Toward a Sustainable Society* (NY/London: W.W. Norton & Co., 1991), pp. 56-73.

LOWE, M.D., *Shaping Cities: The Environmental and Human Dimensions* (Washington, D.C.: Worldwatch Institute, Paper 105, 1991a).

MORRIS, D., *Self-Reliant Cities: Energy and the Transformation of Urban America* (San Francisco: Sierra Club Books, 1982).

MORRIS, D., "The Ecological City as a Self-Reliant City," in D. Gordon, ed., *Green Cities: Ecologically Sound Approaches to Urban Space* (Montreal: Black Rose Books, 1990), pp. 21-35.

NEWMAN, P., "Social Organization for Ecological Sustainability: Toward a More Sustainable Settlement Pattern," in P. Cook, ed., *Social Structures for Sustainability,* Fundamental Questions Paper No. 11 (Canberra: Centre for Resource and Environmental Studies, Australian National University, 1990).

NEWMAN, P., "Sustainable Settlements: Restoring the Commons," *Habitat Australia,* August 1991, pp. 18-21.

NEWMAN, P.W.G. AND J.R. KENWORTHY. *Cities and Automobile Dependence* (Brookfield, VT: Gower Technical, 1989).

NORWOOD, K., "The Urban Cooperative Block," *The Permaculture Activist* VI (4), November 1990.

ORGANIZATION FOR ECONOMIC CO-OPERATION AND DEVELOPMENT (OECD), *Environmental Policies for Cities in the 1990s* (Paris, OECD, 1990).

OWENS, S.E., "Land Use Planning for Energy Efficiency," in Cullingworth, J.B. ed., *Energy, Land, and Public Policy* (New Brunswick, NJ: Transaction Publishers, 1990), pp. 53-98.

THE EDITORS OF RAIN, *Knowing Home: Studies for a Possible Portland* (Portland: RAIN, 1981).

REAL ESTATE RESEARCH CORPORATION. *The Costs of Sprawl,* Volume I: Detailed Cost Analysis (Washington, DC: US Government Printing Office, 1974).

REES, W.E., "Sustainable Development and the Biosphere: Concepts and Principles," *Teilhard Studies* No. 22 (Chambersburg, PA: Anima Books for the American Teilhard

Association, 1990a).

REES, W.E., "The Ecology of Sustainable Development," *The Ecologist* 20(1):18-23, 1990b.

REES, W.E., "Ecological Footprints and Appropriated Carrying Capacity: What Urban Economics Leaves Out," presented to Globe '92, Vancouver, British Columbia, March 18, 1992.

REGISTER, R., *Ecocity Berkeley: Building Cities for a Healthy Future* (Berkeley, CA: North Atlantic Books, 1987).

REPLOGLE, M., "Sustainable Transportation Strategies for World Development," presented to the World Congress of Local Governments for a Sustainable Future, United Nations, New York, September 7, 1990.

STREN, R., R. WHITE, AND J. WHITNEY, eds., *Sustainable Cities: Urbanization and the Environment in International Perspective* (Boulder, CO: Westview Press, 1991).

Toronto Declaration on World Cities and Their Environment (Toronto: World Cities and Their Environment Congress of Municipal Leaders, August 28, 1991).

UNITED NATIONS ENVIRONMENT PROGRAM, "Call to a World Congress of Local Governments for a Sustainable Future," United Nations, New York, September 5-8, 1990.

URBAN ECOLOGY, *Report of the First International Ecocity Conference* (Berkeley, CA: Urban Ecology, 1990).

VAN DER RYN, S. AND P. CALTHORPE, *Sustainable Communities: A New Design Synthesis for Cities, Suburbs, and Towns* (San Francisco: Sierra Club Books, 1986).

WACKERNAGEL, M., "Assessing Ecological Sustainability: A Background Paper On Indicating the Health and Sustainability of a Community By Measuring Its Appropriated Carrying Capacity," unpublished paper (Vancouver: UBC Task Force on Planning Healthy and Sustainable Communities, 1991).

WHITE, R. AND J. WHITNEY, "Human Settlements and Sustainable Development: An Overview," (Toronto: University of Toronto Centre for Urban And Community Studies; draft prepared for the Colloquium on Human Settlements and Sustainable Development, June 21-23, 1990).

WORLD COMMISSION ON ENVIRONMENT AND DEVELOPMENT (WCED), *Our Common Future* (New York: Oxford University Press, 1987).

PART TWO
Sustainable Community Tools

Part I explored the meaning of sustainable development and its implications for communities. Parts II and III are a "toolbox"—these chapters include planning tools, practical initiatives, and associated resources which have helped municipal and local governments move toward sustainable communities. While not every tool will "fit" every community, many of them will fit quite well.

If local governments think and act creatively, they can make tremendous progress toward sustainable communities. The "tools" which follow emphasize the role of local initiative and innovation in the movement toward sustainable communities.

Events such as the World Congress of Local Governments for a Sustainable Future, held at the United Nations in 1990, demonstrate how much is offered by these tools and how far we have come in such a short time. From recycling systems and traffic reduction programs to local bans of CFCs and city-to-city Third World development partnerships, local governments are serving as laboratories for policy invention in the environmental arena. The concrete innovations that they are testing are providing models for national level policies and programs.

Since the powers of municipal and local governments vary considerably, proponents of sustainable community initiatives must research their issues and fashion an approach which works within the specific legal framework of their jurisdiction. For example, a creative municipal solid waste management bylaw will have to fit the specific municipal situation as well as the legislative framework of the province or state.

3

Atmospheric Change and Air Quality

> *"Given the uncertainty associated with the effects of atmospheric change, should decision-makers act now or wait for more information? Global warming and the destruction of the ozone layer are essentially irreversible processes. If we wait to see the proof of these phenomena, the costs of dealing with changes in agriculture, forestry, and weather patterns will be much greater than if we act now to start reducing the likelihood of these events occurring."*
>
> City of Vancouver 1990

There are three key areas of atmospheric change that concern local governments: local air quality, ozone layer depletion, and potential climate change (e.g., global warming). Local air quality obviously varies according to local conditions, but shares causes and solutions with broader atmospheric change issues. Ozone layer depletion and climate change are discussed below.

Many scientists believe that the context for thinking about sustainable development for the next several decades will be global atmospheric change. Put simply, we are changing the composition of the earth's atmosphere. If the change continues at current rates, the world's weather may be significantly altered by the middle of the next century.

Climate Change
Global warming is one possible consequence of atmospheric change. In essence, we might be giving the planet a fever by increasing the Earth's natural "greenhouse effect." We

know from personal experience that a fever allowed to rise unchecked poses serious health risks to the brain, the immune system, and many other key bodily functions. Likewise, an unchecked *global* fever poses serious health risks to food production systems (irrigation, growing seasons, crop failures, etc.) and many other key social and ecological functions that human civilization depends upon.

Although atmospheric change is a complex technical issue, most local decision-makers require only a few basic concepts in order to comprehend its implications at the community level and to design community strategies to reduce the threat of atmospheric change.

The greenhouse effect refers to heat retention in the earth's atmosphere. There has always been a natural greenhouse effect; without it the earth would be too cold for life. The problem now is what scientists call the enhanced greenhouse effect; in the last several decades we have dumped additional quantities of "greenhouse gases" into the atmosphere which greatly increase its heat retention.

For the majority of North American local governments, the most significant greenhouse gases to address are chlorofluorocarbons (CFCs), carbon dioxide, and methane.

Ozone Layer Depletion

Scientists now believe that CFCs and other ozone-depleting compounds are largely responsible for the deterioration of the ozone layer that shields the Earth from the sun's harmful ultraviolet rays. These gases also contribute to the greenhouse effect, lingering 60-100 years in the atmosphere and, molecule for molecule, trapping 20,000 times more heat than carbon dioxide. Because it takes so long for ozone depleting chemicals to reach the atmosphere, the ozone depletions now being observed are actually the result of releases prior to the 1980s. Most CFCs and related chemicals are still on their way up.

Ozone Layer Depletion
In the upper layer of the Earth's atmosphere, the stratosphere, is a thin shield of ozone that limits the amount of ultraviolet radiation that can reach the Earth's surface. Depletion of the ozone layer causes an increase in ultraviolet radiation, which is expected to result in higher incidences of skin cancer, cataracts, immune system disorders, damage to crops and plant life, and destruction of marine phytoplankton. Ozone layer destruction is caused primarily by the release of a group of human-made chemicals known as halocarbons. Chlorofluorocarbons (CFCs), halons, and chlorocarbons including methyl chloroform and carbon tetrachloride drift up to the stratosphere where they destroy ozone molecules for up to 100 years. They also contribute to the greenhouse effect. Ozone depleting chemicals are used as coolant materials in refrigerators, and in building and automobile air conditioners. They are also used as the blowing agent for foam products such as seat cushions, insulation, and foam containers and they are used as cleaning solvents in the computer, aerospace, and metal products industries. Halon fire extinguishers and hospital sterilants also use ozone depleting chemicals.
(see Local Government Commission 1990)

In 1987, 32 nations signed an international agreement to limit the production of CFCs. This agreement, known as the Montreal Protocol on Substances that Deplete the Ozone Layer, was an important first step, but unfortunately even eliminating CFC production and use by 2000, as agreed to in London in the 1990 revision of the Protocol, is not sufficient to halt further destruction of the ozone layer. Recent reports suggest that damage to the ozone layer is accelerating and that ozone levels are dropping by some 8 percent per decade over North America (see Stolarski *et al* 1991).

For this reason, many local governments are calling for stricter actions. Making fast progress toward eliminating the release of ozone depleting chemicals is important since their ozone depleting capacity lasts for so long.

Carbon Dioxide

Carbon dioxide lingers for 100 years in the atmosphere and accounts for about half of the greenhouse effect. Carbon dioxide is fully integrated into our daily activities since it is released largely from fossil fuel combustion and from burning forests and plants. While deforestation may have contributed as much as 40% to the increase of carbon dioxide earlier in the century, 80% of today's carbon dioxide emissions are from fossil fuels – coal, oil, and natural gas – and these will continue to be the most significant source (see Bolin 1986; Rees 1989).

On a per capita basis, Canada and the U.S. are among the world's largest consumers of fossil fuels and producers of carbon dioxide. For example, despite its relatively small population (0.5% of the world's population), Canada is responsible for fully 2% of global greenhouse emissions. Other industrialized countries such as Japan and the U.K., with comparable standards of living, produce only half as much carbon dioxide per capita as do the U.S. and Canada (see Flavin 1990). If North Americans are to help in reversing climate change, we must reduce our carbon dioxide emissions and contribute to the development of cleaner and more energy-efficient technologies.

Reducing atmospheric carbon dioxide emissions may require major long-term commitments and social reorganization. Later chapters on transportation, land use, energy, and urban ecology are all directly concerned with the challenge of reducing our carbon dioxide emissions.

> **Methane**
> Methane is released from rotting organic matter such as bogs, wetlands, and landfills. Local governments can construct methane gas collection systems for their landfills. When collected, methane can also be used as an energy source for the landfill or sewage plant, or sold to other users.

The US Environmental Protection Agency has estimated that merely to stabilize atmospheric concentrations of CO_2 at the current level, carbon emissions must be cut by 50-80 percent by the middle of the next century. A recent global action plan calls for the governments of all high- and medium-energy consuming countries to reduce their carbon dioxide emissions by 70% by 2030. Scientists and policymakers meeting in Toronto in June 1988 offered a short-term goal: cutting them by 20 percent by 2005 (see Flavin 1990; IUCN 1991; Toronto Conference Statement 1988). Yet while international bodies and national governments struggle to formulate policies to achieve this goal, it is at the community level where most of these policies will be implemented.

In the face of such challenges, many local governments have started developing initiatives to address the root causes of environmental deterioration and to contribute solutions toward a sustainable future. They recognize that net fiscal, economic, and ecological benefits will accrue to those who get their environmental house in order.

Global Warming as a Municipal Issue

"In 1990 the United Nations Intergovernmental Panel on Climate Change, a panel of world-renowned scientists, concluded it was certain that 'emissions resulting from human activities are substantially increasing the atmospheric concentrations of the greenhouse gases [...] resulting on average in an additional warming of the Earth's surface.' Although the timing and impacts of the warming trend are not fully understood, sufficient evidence is now available, the Panel reported, to indicate that the warming trend could have very significant consequences. These include:

• regional shifts in food production;
• loss of forests and natural terrestrial ecosystems;
• rising sea levels;
• large regional changes in water resource availability;
• increased risks to coastal cities and lowland communities from storm surges.

Even a nominal rise in temperatures may be magnified in cities, where asphalt, concrete, and black roofing tar absorb solar radiation, producing heat, and air conditioning blows out hot air. This 'heat island effect' facilitates the formation of ground level ozone, degrades local air quality, harms human health, and creates stresses on urban forests. Urban water supplies may also be at risk, as reservoirs dry up during more frequent periods of drought, and salt water from rising seas intrudes into the groundwater supplies of coastal cities.

The major 'greenhouse gas' forcing the rise in global temperatures is carbon dioxide (CO_2), produced largely through the burning of fossil fuels for energy use. The concentration of CO_2 in the atmosphere has risen about 25 percent since pre-industrial times and is continuing to rise at the rate of 0.5 percent annually due to human activities.

Scientific concern about global warming culminated at the Second World Climate Conference in October 1990 in agreement about its causes and potential effects, and possible measures to slow down the rate and reduce the ecological risks of warming. Conference participants agreed that:

• without action to reduce emissions of greenhouse gases from human activities, global warming may reach 2 to 5 C°, and sea levels may rise 30 to 100 centimetres over the next century;

• a continuous world-wide reduction of net CO_2 emissions of 1-to-2 percent per year would stabilize atmospheric concentrations of CO_2 by the middle of the next century;

• many studies conclude that technical and cost-effective opportunities exist to reduce CO_2 emissions by at least 20 percent by 2005 in industrialized nations;

• these nations must implement reductions even greater than those required, on average, for the globe as a whole, to allow for increased emissions from developing countries.

[...] Cities, among the most energy-intensive ecosystems on the planet, are major producers of CO_2. As over half the world's population will live in urban areas by 2000, the reduction of fossil fuel use in cities will be vital to the implementation of an international climate change convention. Furthermore, many of the actions necessary to reduce CO_2 emissions – licensing, building codes, land use planning, zoning, transit, and transportation plans – fall under the jurisdiction of municipal or regional governments."

(ICLEI 1991)

Public Transportation and Greenhouse Gases
"It is now a political necessity to draw up strategies for reducing greenhouse gases by 20% or 30% some time over the next 10-15 years. Substantial cuts are possible [...] yet in nearly all reports transport in cities is seen as the really difficult area in which to make reductions.

[Data from a study of 32 major world cities show that] those [...] with the highest public transport utilization (and these are virtually all rail-based systems) have the lowest greenhouse gas emissions. This is important as it is sometimes claimed that if we are going to use more public transport then it is not much better than the automobile when it comes to emissions per capita. However, this is because simplistic assumptions are being made about changing from one mode to the other. It is not just a matter of one trip by car being replaced by one trip on public transport. Once a mode is provided that can adequately compete with the automobile, then a range of other changes also occur. Only by considering these kinds of changes is it possible to do justice to the full benefit of rebuilding our cities around non-automobile modes.

[The study data show that] the cities with highest CO_2 emissions have the greatest provision for the automobile in terms of roads and car parking.

The data also show that the cities with the lowest CO_2 emissions have the slowest moving traffic; this goes against the often stated theory that free-flowing traffic saves fuel and reduces emissions due to greater vehicle efficiency. A more realistic explanation is that congestion does indeed reduce vehicle efficiency but it also facilitates other modes, and most of all it keeps a city from sprawling and hence building in extra travel distances. The conclusion has been applied in the US, where the Environmental Protection Agency has now requested all new highway applications to consider the effect of increased vehicle miles of travel (VMT) on emissions from new highways, not just the effect of improved vehicle efficiency. This is an important step in recognizing the need for cleaner cities and not just cleaner cars.

In short, electric rail-based cities are clearly the way we should be heading in a greenhouse future."

(Newman 1991)

TOOLS

Total Emissions Model for Integrated Systems (TEMIS)
The Total Emissions Model for Integrated Systems (TEMIS Model) is a tool for assessing local CO_2 sources and likely impacts of CO_2 reduction options. The TEMIS model estimates emissions of relevant gases based upon energy use. It is an "integrated systems" model in that total energy impacts of an action are assessed. For example, in considering the energy impact of recycling aluminium versus reusing glass bottles, the TEMIS model would estimate energy use – and resultant emissions – from extraction of raw materials to transporting cans or bottles to smelters or processing plants for recycling. The TEMIS Model is presently being further developed by the U.S. Department of Energy for use in national energy policy development in the United States. The Öko-Institut in Darmstadt, Germany – author of the model – has agreed to provide access to the model for simulations of proposed CO_2 reduction strategies throughout Phase I of the Urban CO_2 Project (see Resources below and ICLEI 1990)

INITIATIVES

Bans on Ozone-Depleting Compounds
Newark, New Jersey and *Irvine,* California (see Resources) have passed comprehensive bans on the use, sale and manufacture of ozone-depleting compounds within their jurisdictions. Their by-laws:
- prohibit the use, sale, and manufacture of nearly all ozone-depleting compounds, except in the manufacture of drugs and medical devices and when military specifications call for them; and
- require all service stations and repair shops to capture and recycle CFCs.

CFC Recycling

Montréal collects CFCs found in discarded refrigerators and air conditioners. Municipal employees pick up the appliances and send them to a company that stores the CFCs in sealed tanks. The recycled CFCs are used in repairing old appliances that still use the product (see Ville de Montréal 1991).

Stratospheric Protection Accord

Twenty-four North American municipalities – including Los Angeles and Toronto – joined together in a Stratospheric Protection Accord. They have agreed to ban the local use of ozone-depleting substances by early 1992 unless no technically feasible alternatives exist by then, and to require the recovery and recycling of CFCs from products such as refrigerator-coolant units (see Starke 1990).

Carbon Reduction Targets

In 1990, *Toronto* made a commitment to reduce the city's *net* CO_2 emissions by 20 percent, relative to the 1988 level, by the year 2005. By "net" emission reduction, the city's Special Committee meant some combination of direct emissions reductions and creation of an offsetting "carbon sink" (e.g., financing reforestation in Southern Ontario or Central America). In 1991 the Toronto Special Committee revised its position, arguing that the city can reduce its gross carbon dioxide emissions by a full 20% *without* the need for an offsetting carbon sink. They outlined a set of strategies to achieve this target while still accommodating up to 20 percent growth in the number of people living and working in the city. The report includes strategies for measuring and allocating CO_2 emissions reductions, electricity use, natural gas use, district heating and cooling, building, transportation, urban forestry, energy efficiency, education and advocacy (see Resources).

Vancouver's Task Force on Atmospheric Change

recommended in June 1990 that Vancouver commit itself to achieving the following three targets:

1) A complete phase out of all uses of products containing ozone-depleting chemicals within the City by the year 1995;
2) Immediately reducing emissions levels of sulphur dioxide and methane; and
3) A 20% reduction in 1988 level carbon dioxide emissions by the year 2005; and bringing all related atmospheric pollutants within federally determined acceptable levels.

To achieve these targets, the Vancouver Task Force proposed a set of 35 far-reaching recommendations in the areas of transportation, land use, energy conservation and efficiency, and administrative organization (see City of Vancouver 1990). Vancouver City Council approved the report's recommendations in October 1990.

Ottawa, Ontario's Official Plan includes City Council's stated objective to reduce carbon dioxide emissions 50% by the year 2005 by increasing non-auto transportation, regulating polluting development, improving energy efficiency, planning land uses to reduce distances and vehicle trips, and improving the urban forest (see City of Ottawa 1991). While the Ottawa Plan is admirable in many respects, the goal of reducing carbon dioxide emissions 50% by 2005 may be over ambitious.

Airshed Quality Management

"In early 1989, an extensive three stage programme to substantially improve air quality was adopted for the metropolitan area of *Los Angeles,* California. The programme's first stage (1989-93) includes tightening restrictions (at a cost of $2.8 billion per year) on the use of private automobiles and on pollution-causing industrial and household activities. During its second stage (1993-

> *"Alfonso Cipres Villareal, head of the Mexican Ecologists Movement, said his organization plans to put up 10 booths on street corners around Mexico City to sell clean air. Thirty-second shots of oxygen will sell for about $2 Cdn."*
>
> Reuter 1991

98), all diesel buses, 70 per cent of freight vehicles, and 40 per cent of private automobiles will be required to convert to cleaner fuels, with an additional 50 per cent reduction of industrial and consumer-related emissions. The final stage of the programme anticipates the total prohibition of gasoline fuels in automobiles by the year 2007 – a prohibition that assumes the availability of new [perhaps] unknown, technologies emerging as viable commercial alternatives to gasoline fuelled vehicles. A key to the success of the plan is a 'redirection' of development patterns, employment and housing locations, and a substantial reduction in travel from homes to employment centres. This 'redirection' must be led co-operatively by communities within the Los Angeles metropolitan area.

For especially significant environmental problems, local governments have the ability and the will to take equally significant corrective actions. While a major incentive for local action may be provided through national standards, the actions themselves cannot be taken by the national government alone. The Los Angeles (South Coast Air Quality District) plan is the most drastic, comprehensive and expensive effort to improve air quality ever drawn up locally in the United States. While specific actions proposed were not mandated by the Federal government, court decisions in response to the region's non-compliance with Federal air quality standards were a major factor in the development of the local plan. Implementation of the plan will be a local responsibility." (OECD 1990; see also SCAG 1989; SCAQMD 1989)

RESOURCES

CITY OF TORONTO, *The Changing Atmosphere: Strategies for Reducing CO₂ Emissions, Volume One: Policy Overview, Volume Two: Technical Volume* (Toronto: City of Toronto, Special Advisory Committee on the Environment, Report Number Two, March 1991). Available from:

> Maria Mandarino, Committees Secretary
> City Clerks Department, City Hall
> 100 Queen Street West
> Toronto, Ontario M5H 2N2
> Tel: 416/392-6745

CITY OF VANCOUVER, *Clouds of Change: Final Report of the City of Vancouver Task Force on Atmospheric Change* (Vancouver: City of Vancouver, 1990, 2 Volumes). After public consultations based upon its research, Vancouver's Task Force on Atmospheric Change published its two-volume *Clouds of Change* report in June 1990. Volume One explains the causes of global and local atmospheric change, the known and probable effects of atmospheric change, and the role of the City in acting to protect public health by reducing the hazards posed by atmospheric change. The report sets forth a framework for action based on targets to eliminate or reduce emissions of ozone-depleting chemicals, carbon dioxide and related pollutants. Thirty-five major recommendations are presented regarding administrative organization, transportation planning and traffic management, land use planning, energy efficiency, public health, a regional carbon dioxide tax, urban reforestation, waste reduction and recycling, leadership by example (e.g., procurement policies), and public involvement and education. Volume Two is a set of model and example by-laws from other jurisdictions which are referenced in the report. Vancouver

City Council approved the report's recommendations in
October 1990. Available from:
Planning Department
City of Vancouver
453 West 12th Ave.
Vancouver, B.C. V5Y 1V4
Tel: 604/873-7344

THE INTERNATIONAL COMMISSION FOR LOCAL
ENVIRONMENTAL INITIATIVES (ICLEI), *The Urban CO₂
Project: Formulating Municipal Strategies to Reduce
the Emission of Greenhouse Gases* (Toronto: ICLEI,
1991). ICLEI established The Urban CO_2 Project to help
municipal governments develop effective strategies to
reduce emissions of greenhouse gases. The Project is
designed to tap into already existing resources and expertise
to:

- develop a municipal policy framework for CO_2
  reduction, including analytical and modelling tools for
  assessing its technical and economic feasibility;
- assess the cost, equity, employment, and institutional
  implications of reducing CO_2 emissions by 60 percent
  from present levels over the next 25 years, or 2 percent
  annually, in urban areas; and
- encourage wider municipal interest and action on
  global warming by facilitating the growth of a network
  of local governments concerned with the issue.

For more information, contact:
Phil Jessup, Director
The Urban CO_2 Project
The International Council for Local
    Environmental Initiatives
New City Hall, East Tower, 8th floor
Toronto, Ontario M5H 2N2
Tel: 416/392-1462   Fax: 416/392-1478

KAI MILLYARD, *A Preliminary Carbon Dioxide Inventory for the City of Ottawa* (Ottawa: FOE, 1992). This report attempts to inventory carbon dioxide emissions not only from city operations but from the entire municipality. Although the focus is on Ottawa, appendices describing the methods used to ascertain these figures may be useful in estimating carbon dioxide emissions in other jurisdictions. Available from:

Friends of the Earth
251 Laurier Ave. West
Ottawa, Ontario K1P 5J6
Tel: 613/230-3352

Irvine, California's 1989 ordinance "Governing the Manufacture, Distribution, Sale and Recycling of Products Which Utilize Ozone Depleting Compounds" went into effect July 1, 1990. Irvine is a major center of aerospace, computer, and hi-tech manufacturing, and the ordinance was estimated to affect between 400 and 500 businesses in the community. Knowing the ordinance was coming, Irvine's businesses began reducing their emissions even before the measure took effect. During 1988 and 1989, the large users of CFCs in Irvine reduced their emissions by approximately 46%, and city officials expected further reductions in 1990. For more information, contact:

Michael S. Brown
Manager of Environmental Affairs
City of Irvine, Box 19575
Irvine, CA 92713
Tel: 714/724-6000 ·

References

BOLIN, B "How Much Carbon Dioxide Will Remain in the Atmosphere?" in B. Bolin, B. Doos, J. Jaeger, and R. Warrick, eds., *The Greenhouse Effect, Climatic Change and Ecosystems* (SCOPE 29) (Chichester: John Wiley, 1986)

CITY OF OTTAWA, *Official Plan Volume I: The Primary Plan*

(Ottawa: City of Ottawa, Final Draft, February 1991).

CITY OF VANCOUVER,*Clouds of Change: Final Report of the City of Vancouver Task Force on Atmospheric Change* (Vancouver: City of Vancouver, 1990, 2 Volumes).

FLAVIN, C., "Slowing Global Warming," in Brown, L.R., *et al, State of the World 1990: A Worldwatch Institute Report on Progress Toward a Sustainable Society* (NY/London: W.W. Norton & Co., 1990), pp. 17-38.

INTERNATIONAL COMMISSION FOR LOCAL ENVIRONMENTAL INITIATIVES (ICLEI), "The Urban CO_2 Project," Project Proposal (Cambridge, MA: ICLEI, 1990).

INTERNATIONAL COMMISSION FOR LOCAL ENVIRONMENTAL INITIATIVES (ICLEI), *The Urban CO_2 Project* (Toronto: ICLEI, 1991).

INTERNATIONAL UNION FOR CONSERVATION OF NATURE (IUCN), THE UNITED NATIONS ENVIRONMENT PROGRAMME (UNEP), and THE WORLD WIDE FUND FOR NATURE (WWF), *Caring for the Earth: A Strategy for Sustainable Living* (Gland, Switzerland: IUCN/UNEP/WWF, 1991).

LOCAL GOVERNMENT COMMISSION, *Model Ordinances: Addressing Ozone Layer Destruction* (Sacramento, CA: Local Government Commission, 1990).

NEWMAN, P., "Greenhouse, Oil and Cities," Futures, May 1991, pp. 335-348.

ORGANIZATION FOR ECONOMIC COOPERATION AND DEVELOPMENT (OECD), *Environmental Policies for Cities in the 1990s* (Paris: OECD, 1990).

REES, W.E. "Atmospheric Change: Human Ecology in Disequilibrium" UBC Planning Papers Discussion Paper No.17 (Vancouver: UBC School of Community and Regional Planning, 1989).

REUTER, "Mexico City Street-Vending Machines to Sell Oxygen," *Vancouver Sun*, February 8, 1991, p. A8.

SOUTH COAST ASSOCIATION OF GOVERNMENTS (SCAG) and SOUTH COAST AIR QUALITY MANAGEMENT DISTRICT (SCAQMD), *Air Quality Management Plan: South Coast Air Basin* (Los Angeles: SCAG/SCAQMD, 1989).

SOUTH COAST AIR QUALITY MANAGEMENT DISTRICT (SCAQMD), *The Path to Clean Air: Attainment Strategies* (El Monte, CA: SCAQMD, 1989).

STARKE, L., *Signs of Hope: Working Towards Our Common*

Future (NY: Oxford University Press, 1990).

STOLARSKI, R.S., P. BLOOMFIELD, R.D. MCPETERS AND J.R. HERMAN, "Total Ozone Trends Deduced From Nimbus 7 TOMS Data," *Geophysical Research Letters* 18(6): 1015-1018, June 1991.

TORONTO CONFERENCE STATEMENT, "The Changing Atmosphere: Implications for Global Security" (Toronto: Environment Canada, June 27-30, 1988).

VILLE DE MONTRÉAL, *Montréal: The Sustainable Development Option* (Montréal: Ville de Montréal, 1991).

4

TransportationPlanningandTraffic Management

As discussed in the previous chapter, the burning of fossil fuels in motor vehicles and the associated release of carbon dioxide is one of the prime contributors to atmospheric change. Beyond this, governments at every level are in fiscal crisis and mostly unable to adequately maintain and expand transportation infrastructure to keep pace with traffic growth. If we continue our present trends for the next few decades, we can also expect to see increasing congestion, longer commuting times, increasing demands for shorter work hours to compensate for longer travelling hours, and higher prices due to reduced worker productivity.

Efforts to relieve traffic congestion alone do little to reduce polluting emissions or the amount of fuel consumed. Cities must now stress *reduction of single occupancy vehicle trips* as the only sound way to achieve improved air quality, reduce the energy consumption that is contributing to atmospheric change, and relieve traffic congestion.

Transportation planning and traffic management initiatives are critical for sustainable urban development. These initiatives are usually motivated by goals to reduce the number of automobile trips; increase opportunities for non-auto transportation including bicycles, walking, rail, buses, and alternative vehicles; and reduce the use of gasoline and diesel fuel in conventional buses, autos and trucks.

In general, local initiatives should aim to:
• encourage transit over personal automobile use by, for

75

"Differences in travel behavior arise largely from public policy differences, especially from differences in automobile taxation. In addition, variations in transit subsidies, land use controls, and housing programs significantly influence travel choice, although sometimes only indirectly. The success of public transportation depends more on supportive urban development and automobile taxation policies than on transit subsidies."

Pucher 1988

"Culture plays little or no role in travel mode choice. One could argue, for example, that extensive bicycle use is part of the Dutch culture. But in this context culture is the result, not the cause, of bicycle prominence."

Kilcoyne 1990

"If we really want to get people out of their cars, we need to pay attention to land-use planning and pricing. If you add together auto subsidies such as free parking and personal costs of owning and operating a car (insurance, fuel, depreciation, loans and purchase) using a car costs about 40 cents a mile. Between 80-90 percent of people in the Bay Area have free parking. But it really isn't free. Parking structures run about $10,000 to $20,000 per space. These numbers don't include [other] environmental costs, which run about 3 cents per mile in the San Francisco Bay Area and about 9 cents per mile in Los Angeles."

Deakin 1990

example, reducing the subsidies to private vehicles;
* identify means for managing transportation demands, especially of commuters; and
* emphasize bicycle and pedestrian networks as valid components of a regional transportation strategy.

Environmental Impacts of Transportation
"The environmental impact of transport can be separated into four main components:

Vehical manufacture   Impact on the environment of resource extraction, and the pollutants generated both at the time of manufacture and disposal...

Infrastructure effects   Congestion, visual intrusion, severance and consumption of resources, particularly land.

Vehicular effects   The contributions of differrent types of vehicles to air, water, noise or visual pollution; their contribution to global warming; general health risks; safety to the user and non-user; the efficiency with which they use resources.

Traffic volume effects   [Congestion may not only increase vehicular effects proportionately, but also increase the effects further as vehicle efficiency dimishes.] Providing new infrastructure to accommodate increased traffic is likely to generate further infrastructure effects. Sometimes the best solution may lie elsewhere."

(ACC 1990)

Transport Infrastructure Policies

A study of 32 major world cities, funded by the Australian Government, shows that there are very clear relationships between transport and urban form. Economic factors such as income and gasoline prices are less important than the direct policy instruments of transportation planners and urban planners, such as the relative provision of infrastructure for automobiles and rapid transit, or the density of population and jobs. The data suggest that city transport patterns would become more sustainable if the set of policies excerpted here were adopted. "Readers who wish to examine the data upon which these policies are based should consult the source document."

"•*A policy to restrict the amount of road supply within a city to something around 2 m to 3 m per capita.* This would essentially mean curtailing new road projects that pass through the city. It would also depend on urban form policies" [(see Land Use chapter). In particular, since roughly three quarters of city road mileage is comprised of minor and local streets, this would imply a move away from the single family house with a typical wide street frontage in favour of innovative family housing which shares road access more intensively and needs less roads because of its public transport, walking, and bicycling orientation.]

•*A policy to restrict central city parking to a level around 200 spaces or less per 1000 CBD workers.* This would require a concurrent policy that provides good public transport access and a series of central city policies on housing, cultural attractions, urban design, pedestrianization and commercial activity that allows a central city to compete strongly with suburban centres where easy parking is available.

•*A policy accepting that average speeds in a city of around 30 km/h are adequate.* This means rejecting the notion that fuel is saved by increasing average speeds.

•*A policy that provides a rapid transit option (most likely to be rail) which is substantially faster than the average traffic speed in the city and together with other improvements slowly builds up public transport in stages so that it provides something more like 20 to 30% of total passenger km.* This would be a considerable change for many cities where the present situation has public transport at less than 10% and in some cities less than 1% [...]

•*A policy that encourages pedestrianization, traffic-calming treatment of streets and bicycle facilities so that the proportion of work journeys by bicycling and walking rises to something more like 20% rather than its present 5%.* Like the others, this policy is not really contentious, but is unlikely to be successful unless wedded to [appropriate urban form policies (see Land Use chapter)]."

(Newman and Kenworthy 1991)

> ***The True Costs of Private Automobile Use and Abuse***
> The environmental and social costs associated with
> private automobile use and abuse span an enormous
> range – from government expenditure on highway
> construction and maintenance to crop and health
> damage from ground-level ozone to traffic- and
> insurance-related court activity. Attempting to
> estimate an overall social cost for the automobile,
> West German studies found annual total social and
> other costs in the mid-1980s to range between DM 50
> billion and DM 110 billion. Adjusting for population
> and inflation, this would amount to around $30 billion
> for Canada in the early 1990s. The social cost of the
> private automobile in West Berlin in 1985 was
> estimated at DM 0.64 per passenger-kilometre –
> equivalent to about 65¢ in Canada today. To recover
> this cost from gasoline taxes would require prices on
> the order of $5.00 per litre – about nine times the
> present price.
>
> **(see CUI 1991)**

TOOLS

Air Quality and Congestion Relief
"Transportation demand management (TDM) and
transportation system management (TSM) consist of a
wide range of measures aimed primarily at improving air
quality and relieving traffic congestion. In the process,
these strategies can result in energy savings as well.

All too often, transportation planning takes projected
demand as a given and attempts to satisfy it rather than
trying to reduce it. The goal of TDM strategies is to
influence people to shift to more-efficient modes of
transportation and to travel during off-peak hours. Some

> *"A re-orientation of transport priorities involves the following major elements:*
> * *Less high speed road services*
> * *More traffic management and 'traffic calming'*
> * *Better public transport infrastructure*
> * *Better bicycling facilities*
> * *Better pedestrian facilities*
> * *Less parking in the city centre"*
>
> Kenworthy and Newman 1990

strategies attempt to manage transportation demand with regulations and pricing schemes, such as parking management and time-of-day charges for roads; others manage demand by promoting alternative-mode choices, such as ridesharing and telecommuting. In complementary fashion, TSM strategies aim to affect the supply of transportation services. The most successful policies integrate supply and demand strategies to create a transportation network that promotes efficient, low-polluting choices." (Gordon 1991)

Specific TDM/TSM strategies include:
* parking measures (described elsewhere in this chapter)
* ridesharing
* high-occupancy vehicle (HOV) facilities
* variable-pricing schemes (e.g., congestion or time-of-day pricing)
* telecommuting
* alternative work schedules
* bicycle and pedestrian use
* innovative land-use planning
* innovative transportation technologies (e.g., traffic-signal synchronization)

> *"Approval for a new development can be made contingent upon participation in programs such as ridesharing, flextime, and employee public transport passes [...] If instituted systematically, along with even modest parking price increases, such measures could shift an estimated 10-15 percent of trips in many areas from one-occupant vehicles."*
>
> Lowe 1991b

Transportation Control Measures

Transportation Control Measures include employer-based transportation management; improved public transit; park-and-ride lots and fringe parking; parking management programs; rideshare (car- and van-pooling) incentives; road pricing (tolls); traffic flow improvements; trip-reduction by-laws; voluntary no-drive days; and work schedule changes. These measures "not only reduce emissions and congestion, but also save energy and money." The U.S. Department of Transportation reviewed 40 current transportation control programs and found that the most successful combined these elements:

• Site-specific planning, including a transportation coordinator, personalized in-house car-pool matching, priority car-pool parking, transit encouragements, bicycle facilities and promotions, and flex-time;

• Environmental incentives, including tight parking supply, moderate to high parking prices, low level of parking cost subsidy, little on- or off-street parking nearby, and well-enforced car-pool preferential parking; and

• Convenient transportation alternatives, including frequent transit service, ample transit capacity, and stable fares. (see US DOT 1989)

Road Pricing Strategies

There is growing interest in road pricing strategies to check the trend in increased automobile use and its adverse

---

Public Pressure on Transit Authorities

In return for agreeing not to sue to block the reconstruction of a Boston-area interstate highway, the Conservation Law Foundation has convinced transit authorities to adopt a long-term transportation policy that requires the city to construct high-speed trains to New York, begin 15 mass-transit expansion projects, add 20,000 parking spaces at commuter rail stations, install bus and carpool lanes on commuting routes, index mass transit fares so that they remain competitive with driving, and agree that there will never be further expansion of any highway into Boston.

(see RMI 1991)

---

environmental effects, especially in inner city areas. The Singapore "Area Licensing Scheme," a form of road pricing instituted in 1975, demonstrated that such schemes can be used successfully for reducing peak hour traffic volumes, reducing single-occupant vehicle traffic, and encouraging buses and car pools.

More recently, several politically feasible policy measures were analyzed for Stockholm. Of considerable interest was an Area Licensing Scheme combined with different public transport subsidy levels. "Four different policies were evaluated in this context:

1. A decrease in the public transport fare by 50 per cent;
2. An area licensing scheme around the inner city of Stockholm;
3. An area licensing scheme combined with a public transport fare reduction of 50 per cent;
4. An area licensing scheme combined with a public transport fare increase of 50 per cent.

The area licensing scheme would totally surround the

inner city of Stockholm, with approximately 30 checkpoints on the cordon line. Because of the geographical location of Stockholm County, the inner city and the road transport network, through traffic would be exempt from toll payment on certain routes. A toll fee of 25 SK (app. Canadian $4.65) per passenger car per round trip was adopted for analysis, the fee level being based on the achievement of environmental goals.

Each of the transport policy measures was evaluated according to the following criteria:

1. The achievement of the national environmental goal of reduction of NOx emissions by 30 per cent by 1995;
2. Forecasts of NOx and CO emissions from car traffic in Stockholm County and the inner city area and a partial estimate of the environmental costs of car emission based on NOx and CO emission;
3. Changes in the travel pattern by car and public transport in Stockholm County and the inner city;
4. Changes in the amount of vehicle kilometres travelled in Stockholm County and in the inner city;
5. Changes in the estimates of travel time by car and public transport and the average speed on the road network;
6. Estimation of public transport revenue and toll revenue.

The analysis of the policy options against the above criteria concluded that two policy measures satisfy the achievement of the national environmental goal. First, an area licensing scheme combined with a public transport fare reduction of 50 per cent adequately achieves the 30 per cent reduction; and second, an area licensing scheme with no change in the public transport fare almost meets this goal. An area licensing scheme combined with a public transport fare reduction of 50 per cent ranked highest in all the other criteria except for that of combined revenues generated from public transport and tolls but it generates enough revenue to finance the public transport network. An area licensing scheme with no change in the public transport fare produces substantially more revenue and if these revenues were allocated to finance the public transport network (as well as the road network), public transport ridership would further increase as the result of the increase in the level of service of public transport." (OECD 1990; see also Pendakur 1986)

New Approaches to Transportation Analysis
"Inefficient transportation and land use patterns brought about by excessive hidden subsidies and the failure of market price signals inevitably translate into reduced economic competitiveness. Governments at every level are in fiscal crisis and mostly unable to adequately maintain and expand transportation infrastructure to keep pace with traffic growth [...]

Conventional transportation analysis often disregards the potent effects of urban design changes on transportation demand and the impact of transportation investments and policy on land use patterns [...] Estimates of trip generation, distribution, and choice are often based on look-up engineering formulas that have been determined from the existing automobile-dependent environment [...]

Recent advances in geographic information systems (GIS) make possible new approaches to deal with small scale pattern and urban design factors that influence travel behavior, such as the quality of the pedestrian and cycling environment, the accessibility of jobs and housing to transit stops, TDM incentives, parking supply and cost, and the micro-scale pattern and mix of land uses." (Replogle 1991)

Light Rail

More than 300 cities around the world have joined the light rail revolution. The English-speaking world has been generally slow to take on light rail. A UK study concluded that professional fashion rather than economics was a major reason the UK had missed the light rail revolution; even there interest now appears to be increasing.

"Started in France and Germany, light rail combines the speed and comfort of a traditional train with the flexibility and pedestrian-friendliness of the traditional street car or tram. But it has all the hi-tech electronics and modern materials that can solve many of today's urban transport problems, including:

- ground-level access, making it easy for people of all ages, even for those in wheelchairs or with a pram;
- comfortable seats and spaces for hanging bikes and prams;
- easy movement through people-filled city squares and grassy-tracks out to suburbs; [...] and
- fast access along permanent way areas including heavy rail lines[...]" (Newman 1991a; see also1991b)

Bicycle Transportation: Beyond the "Integration-Segregation" Debate

"The city's [Vancouver] Comprehensive Bicycle Plan has encouraged cycling by recommending improved street design, educating cyclists, and enforcing cycling regulations.

There is one main drawback to the Bicycle Plan. It caters largely to those who already cycle. It proposes that bicycles and cars should travel on the same arterial roads, rather than try to stay apart on separate rights-of-way. As a result, it has not led directly to a significant increase in cycling in the city, nor do we believe it is likely to.

The rationale for the Comprehensive Bicycle Plan

approach came mainly from a controversial California bicycle enthusiast and engineer named John Forester. Unlike most international cycling specialists, Forester has argued it is safest to 'integrate' bikes with cars on main streets. He believes 'segregated' routes for cyclists cause accidents when cyclists and cars meet at intersections. Although Forester has not changed his opinion, he recently acknowledged that his 'theory' is impossible to prove with existing quantitative data.

Even if one were to adopt Forester's view that main roads are safe for everyday cycling, most people still don't see it that way. Perceptions are powerful. To encourage more people to cycle regularly, a network of bicycle routes that are perceived as safe must be provided.

It would be a daunting challenge for the city to find the space or finances to build separate bicycle paths. But we do have a huge network of quiet residential side-streets running parallel to main arteries. They offer the potential for a compromise solution that will satisfy both the 'integrationists' and the 'segregationists.' We believe these residential streets can provide the basis for a network of bicycle routes that will be both safe and perceived as safe – leading to a significant jump in cycling." (Vancouver Bikeway Network Group 1991)

Bike to the Future
The Toronto City Cycling Committee argued that the City's 1991 Plan should strive for a well-balanced, diverse transportation system and that serious traffic reduction schemes can only be successful if the alternatives are made more attractive than driving. Here is a summary of their proposals.

"1. Set realistic targets and develop strategies for reducing automobile trips and increasing transit, bicycle and walking trips in the City [...]

2. Encourage the development of programs that expand the range of mode choice for commuters.

3. Encourage the development of road design and maintenance standards which reduce the risk of accidents and injuries to cyclists.

4. Establish a network of exclusive bicycle lanes and paths, available from within one kilometre from any point in the City, so that cyclists never have to travel more than one kilometre in mixed traffic to a bike lane or path.

5. Encourage the development of bike paths in and along the hydro and rail corridors, abandoned rail lines, and other linear right-of-ways.

6. Encourage the development of a bicycle ring-route encircling the city [...]

7. Establish a policy requiring an appropriate percentage of the City's annual roads budget to be set aside for energy-efficient or non-polluting modes of transportation, and that all new road construction or road widening proposals must include strategies to encourage energy-efficient and non-polluting modes of transportation.

8. Encourage increases in transit and bicycle ridership by providing secure, covered bike parking at all subway and [transit] stations, providing bike routes to and from stations, and actively promoting combined bike-transit trips.

9. Encourage strategies which improve cycling and surface transit together, while at the same time reducing the convenience of driving, such as by providing bus-bike lanes on major bus routes.

10. Encourage strategies that use the existing roads more efficiently by recycling automobile dominated space for transit and bike lanes, and wider sidewalks.

11. Replace on-street car parking spaces in retail strips

with bus or bike lanes, and/or wider sidewalks.

12. Encourage the development and evaluation of neighbourhood 'green streets,' on which pedestrians and cyclists have priority, and motor-vehicles are restricted to bicycle and pedestrian speeds.

13. Close certain arterial roads to cars on Sundays to provide safe opportunities for non-polluting recreation and travel in the City.

14. Provide secure, covered bike parking, and shower/change rooms for bike commuters in all new developments. Provide bike parking in all new sidewalk construction, at parks and recreation facilities, in City-owned parking lots, and at public buildings.

15. Provide wide curb lanes, by reducing the inside lanes to ten feet, whenever a road is resurfaced or the lane markings are repainted.

16. Require all development proposals to include strategies for minimizing automobile use and encouraging transit and bicycle use.

17. Introduce a permit system for motorists who want to drive in the Central Area, and apply the revenues generated by it towards transit, cycling, and pedestrian amenities."

(Toronto City Cycling Committee 1990)

Trip Reduction Bylaws
Trip reduction bylaws (TRBs) are designed to reduce single-occupant vehicle trips. This is a summary of a model TRB being developed in Vancouver, B.C.

"Applicable To: All employers of 25 or more employees, all employers in non-exempt designated commercial districts, commercial buildings of 25,000 gross square feet or

more, and any multi-tenant building or
group of buildings on one site with 100 or
more employees.

Objectives: To reduce peak hour trips and increase
the number of people to vehicles from 1.3
to 1.75.

Requirements: Employers and contractors are required
to implement a trip reduction program,
including appointment of a transportation
coordinator and any reasonable
combination of commute alternative
programs designed to achieve the
required target.
The City is required to monitor and report
annually on the success of the trip
reduction programs, by administration
and analysis of employee surveys. The
City is also required to support trip
reduction activities by gathering and
disseminating material and providing car
pool and van pool matching services.

Enforcement: Failure to comply would enable the City
to impose an effective trip reduction
program or fine. Fines are to be kept in
a Trip Reduction Fund for improvement
of public transit and for education
programs on commute alternatives."
                    (City of Vancouver 1990)

INITIATIVES

Trip Reduction Bylaws
Montgomery County, a suburb of Washington, D.C., has instituted both developer requirements and a Ride Share Ordinance. Developers must prepare a ten year trip reduction plan that includes elements such as personalized ridesharing assistance, shuttle van services, transit pass subsidies and other measures. The Ride Share Ordinance requires new employers to achieve a specified increase in transit use by their employees; penalties are exacted if goals are not met. This ordinance has achieved a 31.7% increase in the number of carpools and a 59.6% increase in transit commuters within just one year. Other communities that have adopted similar ordinances include *Bellevue,* Washington, and at least 37 cities and counties in California (see Local Government Commission 1990; Cal DOT 1990).

Regulation XV of the South Coast Air Quality Management District in **Southern California** requires all work sites with 100 or more employees to implement a ridesharing program and to increase the organization's "average vehicle ridership" to a specified target. After more than a year of experience, the first evaluation of the program's results show that there has been a small but significant increase in average vehicle ridership, and a corresponding decrease in commuting by single-occupant vehicle. Most of the initial change appears to be from increased carpooling, while the use of compressed work hours and walking and bicycling also increased. (see Giuliano *et al* 1991)

Automobile Restrictions
Budapest bans motor traffic from all but two streets in the downtown area during particularly polluted spells. In *Mexico City* and *Santiago*, one-fifth of all vehicles are

kept off the streets each weekday based on their license-plate numbers. *Florence* has turned its downtown into a pedestrian mall during daylight hours (see French 1990).

At least 11 Italian cities, including *Rome, Milan, Naples* and *Turin*, have imposed alternate-day driving rules on high-pollution days. Fines range from approximately $50 Cdn for driving with the wrong plate to $1000 for altering plates. On a single day in December 1991, police in Rome issued a record 12,983 such citations. In January 1992 the Italian Government abolished all the bans, saying cities did not have the power to impose them, and leaving it to regional governments - the Italian version of Canadian provinces - to act (see Associated Press 1991; Montalbano 1992).

Road Pricing

In February 1990 **Oslo,** Norway implemented a toll system. Oslo motorists are charged NKr 10 (US $1.50) to pass through one of the 18 gantries set up around the central business district. Prepayment coupons costing NKr 180 (US $27) for 20 trips or NKr 2,200 ($330) for an annual pass are also available. Coupons need to be displayed in the windshield. Prepayment lanes are enforced by a numberplate video surveillance and a 1:20 spot check to deter "sneak drivers." There were reportedly some 100,000 subscribers to the prepayment system in the first few months (see *PIA* 14(6), June 1990).

Parking Measures
• *Parking Offsets*

"Several cities have found that parking programs pay [...] *Sacramento,* California grants developers a 5% reduction in required parking for providing bicycle facilities, 15 % for providing marked car/van-pool spaces, and 60% for purchasing transit passes for tenants of new offices.

The Concealed Costs of Parking

"Ending the widespread employer practice of providing free or heavily subsidized parking to employees is a promising option for relieving congestion – and air pollution as well. One survey found that more than 90% of southern California employers provide free parking for their employees. A recent survey of 174,000 workers in downtown Los Angeles, an area with some of the region's best transit service, found that 61% drove to work alone, and 55% received subsidized parking with an estimated market value of $56 to $74 million annually [...] The effect of free parking on driving is significant; by one estimate it induces more travel than free gasoline would [...]

The concealed costs of parking are surprisingly large. A recent study by the Transportation Research Board estimates that residential parking requirements add more than $600 per year, or $50 per month, to the average cost of rental housing – regardless of whether or how much the residents need or use the parking facilities [...]

It is important to investigate variations of pricing policies which minimize regressive impacts, or to develop complementary policies which mitigate those effects [...] Studies of employer-paid parking indicate that middle- to upper-income groups are the principal recipients of these benefits. Even this is not a critical finding since the policy prescription for parking is simply to offer employees the cash equivalent of the parking space, which could be a progressive policy."

(Cameron 1991)

• *Preferential Parking*

Portland, Oregon and Seattle, Washington lead in on-street preferential parking programs for car-pools. Among the incentives: poolers are allowed to park downtown all

---

Environmentalists Plan Suit To Block Fare Rise
In Boston the Conservation Law Foundation (CLF)
announced it would sue the Massachusetts Bay Transit
Authority (MBTA) to block a scheduled increase in
bus and subway fares until the transit authority
completes an environmental impact report assessing
the traffic congestion and air quality likely to result
from higher fares. The MBTA plans to raise the price
of a subway token from 75¢ to $1 and a local bus trip
from 50 to 60 cents, which it estimates would force
43,000 commuters off the transit system and into their
cars. CLF projects a resultant increase in regional
ozone pollution of more than four-tenths of one
percent. The federal Clean Air Act mandates a 3
percent reduction in key pollutants. CLF contends
that increased automobile exhaust will force greater
anti-pollution measures by the region's industries.

(see Berg 1991)

---

day at specific metered locations, are exempted from
hourly parking limits and meter fees, and enjoy spaces
closest to building entrances.

• *Parking Pricing*

The [Federal] Government increased its parking rates for
federal employees in Ottawa, resulting in a 23 percent
reduction in employees driving to work, a 16 percent
increase in transit ridership among federal employees,
and an increase in average vehicle occupancy from 1.33 to
1.41 passengers.

Preferential high-occupancy vehicle pricing strategies
are also highly effective. Differential parking rates paid
by the employer are applied, with two-person car-pools
getting a 50 percent reduction, three-person car-pools 75
percent, and van-pools 100 percent. *Montgomery County,*
Maryland has achieved over 75 percent use of high-

occupancy vehicle spaces. *Seattle* has achieved 95 percent high-occupancy vehicle use in public spaces and 35 percent in private spaces." (Totten 1989)

Free or Inexpensive Transit

Experiments with eliminating systemwide fares in *Trenton*, New Jersey and *Denver*, Colorado in the late-1970s found that the costs of doing so were high relative to benefits. Based on experiments in *Seattle*, *Portland* (Oregon), *Syracuse*, and *Salt Lake City*, free fare programs limited to the downtown core have generally had better results. *Seattle* has had the most success. (see Cervero 1990)

Bicycle Transportation

Under a program called Bycyklen (City-Bike), *Copenhagen* plans to re-establish itself as a bicyclist's city by allowing residents and visitors to borrow bikes free of charge. Riders may borrow a City-Bike by inserting a 20-krone coin (about Cdn $3.20) in one of hundreds of special bike racks to be installed all over the city but concentrated in the downtown area. The bike can be returned to any rack and the coin will be refunded. Plans call to have 3,000 bikes available when the program is in full operation in spring of 1992. (see *Vancouver Sun* 1991)

Measures to make bicycling a better transportation alternative are currently under consideration in several North American cities. *Palo Alto* and *Davis*, California; and *Bordeaux*, France are "bikeable" cities where services and safety for bicycles are provided on a level comparable to that for automobiles. *Montréal* has built a 130-kilometre network of bicycle paths covering the whole city. (see Ville de Montréal 1991)

Figure 5

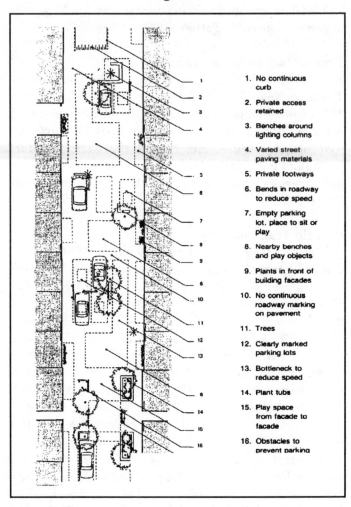

1. No continuous curb
2. Private access retained
3. Benches around lighting columns
4. Varied street paving materials
5. Private footways
6. Bends in roadway to reduce speed
7. Empty parking lot, place to sit or play
8. Nearby benches and play objects
9. Plants in front of building facades
10. No continuous roadway marking on pavement
11. Trees
12. Clearly marked parking lots
13. Bottleneck to reduce speed
14. Plant tubs
15. Play space from facade to facade
16. Obstacles to prevent parking

The Dutch *woon erf,* or "living yard," is a form of traffic calming. Cars are forced to navigate slowly around carefully placed trees and other landscaping.

Source: Royal Dutch Touring Club.

96

Traffic Calming

For more than two decades Dutch cities like *Delft*, *Groningen*, and *Maastricht* have calmed traffic by changing the layout of the residential street, transforming it into a *woon erf*, or "living yard." In the *woon erf*, cars are forced to navigate slowly around carefully placed trees and other landscaping. Since motor traffic cannot monopolize the entire breadth of the street, much of the space becomes more open to walking, cycling, and children's play. Automobiles are free to enter the *woonerf*, but only as "guests," while non-motorized traffic has priority. Experience with traffic calming has shown that it is most effective if widely implemented, so that motor traffic problems are not simply diverted to nearby streets. Traffic has been calmed on over 30% of residential roads in Maastricht.

West Germany's similar *Verkehrsberuhigung* ("traffic calming") schemes multiplied into the thousands since they were started in the seventies. Originally intended for residential areas, the technique is now spreading over whole cities. Traffic calming greatly improves the quality of life in neighbourhoods where it is implemented, and so is gathering popularity in many countries, including *Italy*, *Japan*, *Australia*, *Sweden*, and *Switzerland*. Such restraints are so well-received in *Denmark* that local residents themselves are often willing to pay for the measure. In the US, *Berkeley* is experimenting with a "slow streets" system.

Traffic calming is not just a set of engineering techniques – it is also a community process, a way to reclaim streets into more attractive public spaces. Wherever traffic calming has been conducted on a large scale the urban area has found, contrary to many economists' predictions, that the local economy has improved. This appears to be because people like to come to attractive, green cities; businesses

---

What Are We Transporting?
Transportation is a communications issue; often what is carried is nearly invisible, at the very least intangible. We move paper, and we move people about in order to move paper. The Postal System is an example of an arrangement that employs internal combustion engines and human backs to lug around information, an essentially weightless commodity.

(see RAIN 1981)

---

like to locate in cities with a high-quality urban environment; car access is not banned but it is not facilitated; and other modes are generally facilitated. (see Lowe 1991a; FOE/UK n.d.; Newman 1991)

Traffic Cells
Saarbrücken, the capital of West Germany's Saarland, along the French border, has a population of about 200,000. Saarbrücken now has plans which call for the entire municipal area to be a 30 km-per-hour zone, although a speed limit of 50 km/h will still apply on certain "priority roads" chosen according to their importance for traffic. The aim of this effort is to achieve the greatest possible restraint of traffic and to reduce accident figures, especially in residential areas, and mainly to reduce the number of accidents involving children, old people and bicyclists. It is anticipated that the 30 KPH speed limit will also stabilize traffic flow and thus result in a significant reduction of noise and exhausts in the residential areas. According to calculations performed by the Municipal Office of the Environment, the emissions released by car traffic alone now amount to between 50,000 and 60,000 tons of carbon dioxide. (see Leonhardt 1990)

Telecommunications

Portland's seven neighbourhood offices, several City bureaus and the Center for Urban Studies at Portland State University (PSU) are talking to each other via computers. The system enables the Office of Neighborhood Associations, neighbourhood offices, the Bureau of Community Development, the Planning Bureau, and PSU's Center for Urban Studies to exchange information about neighbourhood issues, meetings, mailing lists, resources, and statistics. (see City of Portland ONA 1990)

Transit Marketing

In *Frankfurt*, Germany transit operators have signed contracts with municipal administrators and private firms to allow their respective commuters free access to public transportation. The city and the employers consider the subsidized tab as a job benefit. The city led the way by signing an agreement to reimburse the regional transit authority for the issue of "job ticket" flash passes to all 26,000 municipal employees. The contract has been in force since May 1991 and is costing the city approximately US $8 million per year. The public employees union opted to drop its demand for an increase in a supplemental allowance to enable the city to fund the initiative out of current revenues.

The *Phoenix*, Arizona bus system has introduced a "transit credit card" which allows passengers' employers to be billed monthly for actual transit usage. The magnetic stripe Bus Card Plus is issued to employees of participating employers who fall under a county-imposed mandate to reduce by at least 5% commuter trips of single occupant vehicles. The order, imposed for air quality reasons, affects all companies with more than a hundred employees at a single work site. Employer contributions and employee payroll deductions defray the monthly cost of the system at specific firms. Employees are generally charged a fixed monthly fee through payroll deductions and the employer subsidizes the rest. Before the new system was installed, companies (or employees) paid $27 for a monthly pass, regardless of the number of trips taken. With Bus Card Plus, the company is only charged for trips actually taken up to the cost of the monthly pass. (*see PIA* 15 (9), September 1991)

Freiburg, Germany (pop. 172,000) introduced a public transit "environment pass" in 1985 which has since been adopted by more than 30 German communities. Freiburg's city council authorized the transit authority to lower season pass fares from the equivalent of US $34 to $22 a month to give people an incentive to switch from their cars to public transit in order to protect the environment. During the first year, ridership increased by as much as 23%; between 3,000 and 4,000 car owners switched permanently to the Freiburg streetcar system, and ticket revenues increased while expenditures remained constant. Revenues and ridership continued to increase in succeeding years, with more than 350,000 passes sold in 1988, about 100,000 more than in the first year. The upward trend continues. An agreement with the transit authority of neighbouring *Basel* (Switzerland) allows mutual acceptance of their respective environment passes. (*see PIA* 14 (6), June 1990)

The Swiss ski resort community of *Zermatt* has added two solar buses to its municipal fleet of battery-operated electric buses. Private vehicles are banned in the mountain resort. The solar buses get about half of their battery-stored energy from roof-mounted solar collectors. Their cost, about US $285,000, was shared equally between the local administration and the rail line which brings tourists to the mountain community. (*see PIA* 14 (9), September 1990)

> *[The car is] "a voracious beast which disfigures our cities."*
> HRH Prince Charles 1991

German transit authorities in *Hamburg* and *Frankfurt* have negotiated flash transit passes for hotel guests. Guests of one chain are offered an unlimited two-day transit pass good for all public transit in the city when they check in. The subsidized arrangement, negotiated between the hotel chain and the local transit authority, aims to make it easy for out-of-town hotel guests to use the city's transit system and leave their cars in the hotel garage or at home. (*see PIA* 14 (3), March 1990)

In the *Philadelphia* area, the Delaware Valley Regional Planning Commission's commuter benefit program enables employers to distribute tax-free transit vouchers, worth $15 a month, which employees can use to buy tickets, tokens, or passes on all public transit systems in the area, including Amtrak. (see Epstein and Driscoll 1991)

RESOURCES

CALIFORNIA DEPARTMENT OF TRANSPORTATION, *A Directory of Trip Reduction Ordinances* Second Edition (Sacramento: Division of Transportation Planning, 1990). Available from:

    Caltrans DOTP
    Technical Assistance Branch
    PO Box 942874
    Sacramento, CA 94274-0001
    Tel: 916/324-3692 or 322-9015

D. HOPE AND D. YACHUK, *Community Cycling Manual: A Planning and Design Guide* (Ottawa: Canadian Institute of Planners, 1990). Available from:

    Canadian Institute of Planners

404-126 York Street
Ottawa, Ontario K1N 5T5

CITY OF VANCOUVER, *Clouds of Change: Final Report of the City of Vancouver Task Force on Atmospheric Change, Volumes I & II* (Vancouver: City of Vancouver, 1990). Volume II contains a model trip reduction by-law. Available from:

Planning Department
City of Vancouver
453 West 12th Ave.
Vancouver, B.C. V5Y 1V4
Tel: 604/873-7344

DEBORAH GORDON, *Steering a New Course: Transportation, Energy, and the Environment* (Cambridge, MA: Union of Concerned Scientists, 1991). Gordon argues that the pollution, congestion, and damage to health caused by our dependence on motor vehicles are the hidden costs of our transportation system. As these costs continue to mount, we will pay them increasingly with our time, health, and welfare. In this report the Union of Concerned Scientists makes bold recommendations for policymakers seeking to ameliorate a host of problems associated with the US transportation sector. Issues addressed include greenhouse gases and other air pollutants, alternative transportation fuels, ultra-fuel-efficient vehicles, innovative transportation strategies, and public-policy options and recommendations. Comprehensive and well referenced, this book is a tremendous resource. Highly recommended. Available from:

Union of Concerned Scientists
26 Church Street
Cambridge, MA 02238
Tel: 617/547-5552

PETER NEWMAN AND JEFFREY KENWORTHY, *Cities and Automobile Dependence: An International*

Sourcebook (Brookfield, VT: Gower Technical, 1989). Based on extensive research, this landmark study examines urban form, transport and energy use in thirty-two cities in North America, Europe, Asia and Australia. The data cover approximately 100 parameters for 1960, 1970 and 1980 and include parking, car ownership and use, roads, congestion, public transport, modal split and energy consumption; city form is characterized by central, inner and outer area population and employment data. The study confirms that the shorter distances inherent in medium- and high-density urban areas correspond with much more walking and cycling. For example, in the West European cities in the study – with an average of some 85 people and jobs per hectare – more than 21% of workers walk or cycle to work. By contrast, in the study's U.S. and Australian cities, with about 20 people and jobs per hectare, only 5 percent of workers walk or cycle to their jobs.

LOCAL SOLUTIONS TO GLOBAL POLLUTION, **"Bicycle Legislation in U.S. Cities."** A packet of various cities' bicycle programs and policies. Available from:

Local Solutions to Global Pollution
2121 Bonar St., Studio A
Berkeley, CA 94702
Tel: 415/540-8843   Fax: 415/540-4898

MICHAEL CAMERON, *Transportation Efficiency: Tackling Southern California's Air Pollution and Congestion* (Boulder, CO: Environmental Defense Fund and Regional Institute of Southern California, 1991). The first report of a joint project to investigate economically sensible solutions to Southern California's vexing air and transportation problems. Available from:

National Transportation Program
Environmental Defense Fund
1405 Arapahoe Avenue
Boulder, CO 80302   Tel: 303/440-4901

PUBLIC INNOVATION ABROAD promotes "the international exchange of practical experience in dealing with common problems at the state, county and city levels of government." Particularly good on transportation and recycling initiatives. Available from:

> International Academy of State and Local Governments
> 444 North Capitol Street, N.W., Suite 349
> Washington, D.C. 20001
> Tel: 202/638-1445   Fax: 202/638-5109

THE TORONTO CITY CYCLING COMMITTEE, **"Bike to the Future: A Vision for a Bicycle-Friendly Toronto,"** (Toronto: City of Toronto Cycling Committee, 1990). Elaborates the set of proposals summarized in this chapter. Available from:

> The Toronto City Cycling Committee
> 19th Floor, East Tower, City Hall
> Toronto, Ontario M5H 2N2
> Tel: 416/392-7592

Transportation: An International Journal Devoted to the Improvement of Transportation, Planning and Practice devoted a special issue (Volume 17, No. 2, 1990) to Transportation Demand Management (TDM). TDM consists of efforts to induce behavioural changes on the part of travellers in order to maximize efficiency in the use of existing transport systems. Examples of TDM programs include employer subsidies of monthly transit passes in lieu of employer-provided parking facilities, encouragement of carpooling and vanpooling through financial incentives and preferential parking, and encouraging "telecommuting." Robert Cervero's article on "Transit Pricing Research: A Review and Synthesis" is essential reading. If your library doesn't have it, the journal is available in microform from:

> UMI
> Tel: 800/521-0600 toll-free in U.S.

Tel: 313/761-4700 collect from Alaska and Michigan
Tel: 800/343-5299 toll-free from Canada
Individual articles are available from:
UMI Article Clearinghouse
300 North Zeeb Road
Ann Arbor, MI 48108

THE INSTITUTE FOR TRANSPORTATION AND DEVELOPMENT POLICY, established in 1985, is a non-profit organization dedicated to promoting economically and environmentally sustainable global transportation policies and programs, particularly those that serve the needs of the poor. ITDP participates in a variety of projects concerning developing countries and international agencies. For example, ITDP's Bikes Not Bombs project sent some 2,100 bicycles to a variety of bicycle development projects in Nicaragua in 1990. In 1985 the World Bank issued a 400 page transportation sector study on China which did not even contain the word "bicycle" and produced an Urban Transport Policy paper which implied that bicycles were part of the problem and not a solution. ITDP's Transportation Alternatives Project, which campaigns to influence the World Bank to focus on sustainable transport principles, is showing some preliminary signs of success. In the U.S., ITDP helped organize the Campaign for New Transportation Priorities, a coalition of environmental, labour, and citizen organizations which advocates increased federal funding for energy-efficient, environmentally-safe alternatives to automobile dependence.

Institute for Transportation and Development Policy
1787 Columbia Road, N.W.
Washington, DC 20009
Tel: 202/387-1434   Fax: 202/387-1450
Telex: 155-217-437, Attn: Mobility
E-mail via PeaceNet, Attn: Mobility

MONTGOMERY COUNTY PLANNING DEPARTMENT, MARYLAND-NATIONAL CAPITAL PARK AND PLANNING COMMISSION, *Comprehensive Growth Policy Study, Volume II* (Silver Spring, MD: Maryland-National Capital Park and Planning Commission, 1989). This document describes how a set of alternative future growth scenarios were constructed and the results of applying two computerized impact assessment simulation models, TRAVEL and FISCAL, to the alternative growth scenarios. Available from:

Maryland-National Capital Park and Planning
     Commission
8787 Georgia Avenue
Silver Spring, MD 20910-3760
Tel: 301/495-4600

Also available from the above address is a short paper by Michael Replogle called "Computer Transportation Models for Land Use Regulation and Master Planning in Montgomery County, Maryland," Transportation Research Record 1262 (1990). This paper discusses the ways in which transportation models have been used for planning and growth management in Montgomery County, and describes preliminary work in combining Geographic Information Systems (GIS) technology with conventional regional transportation models. The paper describes the development of transportation models to support planning efforts such as reducing the ratio between jobs and households, clustering employment, providing a new light rail system connecting major regional centers, and bicycle- and pedestrian-friendly infrastructure improvements. The models show that much higher levels of urbanization could achieve acceptable levels of traffic congestion, and that GIS may be the best tool for dealing with transportation behaviour variables where the variance in the data within zones exceeds the variance between zones.

> **Family Transportation Expenditures**
> According to the Institute for Transportation and the Environment, many American families now spend more money on transportation than on food. With transportation expenditures at about 25% of household income, young families are often advised by banks to sell a second auto in order to qualify for a mortgage. Meanwhile, although most urban automobile trips are for distances of under 5 miles, our inefficient transportation infrastructure dictates that only one or two percent of our journeys are made by bicycle.

THE INSTITUTE FOR TRANSPORTATION AND THE ENVIRONMENT, incorporated in January 1991, has the mission of providing research, education and network services to concerned citizens, to environmental and community groups, to public agencies and to the media. Although its efforts focus on the Puget Sound region, the Institute is also committed to national transportation reform. The Institute intends to publish an annual journal of opinion and analysis on transportation and environmental matters.

Institute for Transportation and the Environment
85 E. Roanoke Street
Seattle, WA 98103
Tel: 206/322-5463

References

ASSOCIATED PRESS, "Traffic Controls Heeded Not By Hot-Blooded Commuters," *Vancouver Sun,* December 27, 1991, p. D18.

ASSOCIATION OF COUNTY COUNCILS (ACC), ASSOCIATION OF DISTRICT COUNCILS, and ASSOCIATION OF METROPOLITAN AUTHORITIES, *Environmental Practice in Local Government* (London: Association of District Councils, 1990).

BERG, M., "Environmentalists Plan Suit To Block Fare Rise," The *Patriot Ledger* (Quincy, MA), July 25, 1991, p. 28.

CALIFORNIA DEPARTMENT OF TRANSPORTATION, *A Directory of Trip Reduction Ordinances*, Second Edition (Sacramento: Division of Transportation Planning, 1990).

CAMERON, M., *Transportation Efficiency: Tackling Southern California's Air Pollution and Congestion* (Boulder, CO: Environmental Defense Fund and Regional Institute of Southern California, 1991).

CANADIAN URBAN INSTITUTE (CUI), "Cities Without Cars" (Toronto: CUI, 1991).

CERVERO, R., "Transit Pricing Research: A Review and Synthesis," *Transportation* 17:117-139, 1990.

CITY OF PORTLAND, OFFICE OF NEIGHBORHOOD ASSOCIATIONS (ONA), Press Release, January 9, 1990.

CITY OF VANCOUVER, *Clouds of Change: Final Report of the City of Vancouver Task Force on Atmospheric Change* (Vancouver: City of Vancouver, 1990).

DEAKIN, E., "Auto Disincentives, Transit Incentives," in Urban Ecology, Report *of the First International Ecological City Conference* (Berkeley, CA: Urban Ecology, 1990).

EPSTEIN, L.R. AND R.W. DRISCOLL, "Clearing the Air, Muddying the Water," Planning 57(8):24-25, August 1991.

FRENCH, H.F., "You Are What You Breathe," Worldwatch, 3(3): 27-34, May-June 1990

FRIENDS OF THE EARTH (FOE/UK), *Traffic Calming in Residential Areas* (London: FOE, n.d.).

GIULIANO, G., K. HWANG, D. PERRINE, AND M. WACHS, "Preliminary Evaluation of Regulation XV of the South Coast Air Quality Management District," unpublished paper, 1991.

GORDON, D., Steering a New Course: *Transportation, Energy, and the Environment* (Cambridge, MA: Union of Concerned Scientists, 1991).

HRH PRINCE CHARLES, quoted by Reuter in Vancouver Sun, May 3, 1991, p. A7.

HOPE, D. AND D. YACHUK, *Community Cycling Manual: A Planning and Design Guide* (Ottawa: Canadian Institute of Planners, 1990).

KENWORTHY, J.R., AND P.W.G. NEWMAN, "Cities and Transport Energy: Lessons From a Global Survey," Ekistics 57(344/

345):258-268, 1990.

KILCOYNE, R., "Auto Disincentives, Transit Incentives," in Urban Ecology, *Report of the First International Ecological City Conference* (Berkeley, CA: Urban Ecology, 1990).

LEONHARDT, W., "Integrated Urban and Transport Planning in Saarbrücken," presented to the World Congress of Local Governments for a Sustainable Future, United Nations, New York, September 7, 1990.

LOCAL GOVERNMENT COMMISSION, "Model Ordinances for Environmental Protection" (Sacramento: Local Government Commission 1990).

LOWE, M.D., "Rethinking Urban Transport," in Brown, L.R., et al, State *of the World 1991: A Worldwatch Institute Report on Progress Toward a Sustainable Society* (NY/London: W.W. Norton & Co., 1991a), pp. 56-73.

LOWE, M.D., "Shaping Cities: The Environmental and Human Dimensions," Worldwatch Paper 105 (Washington, D.C.: Worldwatch Institute, 1991b).

MONTALBANO, W., "A War on Urban Smog is Running Out of Gas," *Los Angeles Times,* reprinted in *Vancouver Sun,* February 1, 1992, p. B6.

MONTGOMERY COUNTY PLANNING DEPARTMENT, MARYLAND-NATIONAL CAPITAL PARK AND PLANNING COMMISSION, *Comprehensive Growth Policy Study, Volume II* (Silver Spring, MD: Maryland-National Capital Park and Planning Commission, 1989).

NEWMAN, P., "Greenhouse, Oil and Cities," *Futures,* May 1991a, pp. 335-348.

NEWMAN, P., "Suffocate City," *Consuming Interest,* June/July 1991b, pp. 13-18.

NEWMAN, P. AND J. KENWORTHY, *Cities and Automobile Dependence: An International Sourcebook* (Brookfield, VT: Gower Technical, 1989).

NEWMAN, P.W.G., AND J. R. KENWORTHY, "Transport and Urban Form in Thirty-Two of the World's Principal Cities," *Transport Reviews,* 1991, 11(3): 249-272.

ORGANIZATION FOR ECONOMIC COOPERATION AND DEVELOPMENT (OECD), *Environmental Policies for Cities in the 1990s* (Paris: OECD, 1990).

PENDAKUR, V.S., "City Center Traffic Restraint Schemes: The Singapore Experience" (Vancouver: UBC Planning

Papers, CS #14, 1986).

Public Innovation Abroad (PIA), various issues.

PUCHER, J., "Urban Travel Behavior as the Outcome of Public Policy: The Example of Modal-Split in Western Europe and North America," *Journal of the American Planning Association* 54(4): 509-520, Autumn 1988.

THE EDITORS OF RAIN, *Knowing Home: Studies for a Possible Portland* (Portland: RAIN, 1981).

REPLOGLE, M., "Computer Transportation Models for Land Use Regulation and Master Planning in Montgomery County, Maryland," *Transportation Research Record* 1262, 1990.

REPLOGLE, M., "Integrating Low and High Tech Transportation Strategies," presented to Second Annual Transportation 2000 Conference, Snowmass, Colorado, October 6-8, 1991.

ROCKY MOUNTAIN INSTITUTE (RMI) *Newsletter*, Vol. VII, No. 1, Spring 1991.

TOTTEN, M., *Energywise Options for State and Local Governments: A Policy Compendium* (Washington, D.C.: National Center for Policy Alternatives, 1989), draft.

THE TORONTO CITY CYCLING COMMITTEE, "Bike to the Future: A Vision for a Bicycle-Friendly Toronto" (Toronto: City of Toronto Cycling Committee, 1990).

U.S. DEPT. OF TRANSPORTATION (US DOT), Urban Mass Transportation Administration Office of Technical Assistance and Safety, "An Assessment of Travel Demand Approaches at Suburban Activity Centers" (Washington, D.C., U.S. Dept. of Transportation, 1989), cited in Totten 1989.

VANCOUVER BIKEWAY NETWORK GROUP (VBNG), "The Bikeway Solution: A Proposal to Vancouver City Council," (Vancouver: VBNG, 1991).

VANCOUVER SUN, "City of Bikes," *Vancouver Sun,* October 19, 1991, p. E1.

VILLE DE MONTRÉAL, *Montréal: The Sustainable Development Option* (Montréal: Ville de Montréal, 1991).

5

Land Use and Growth Management

To encourage people to use the transportation system more efficiently we need to adopt land use policies which reduce our needs for transportation and let us meet those needs in more energy-efficient ways.

Our needs for transportation arise directly from the way land is used in our communities. Through zoning and other techniques, land-use patterns and densities dictate travel volume, direction, and mode. In Canada and the US, our dispersed land use patterns are typified by the low density suburb.

> **Why Los Angeles Still Has Smog**
>
> "It is no wonder that Los Angeles still has smog more than 30 years after the battle to reduce it first began – the battle has concentrated on making vehicles cleaner and more efficient, it has done nothing to make them less needed. The principle that is often forgotten here is the Jevons principle. The Jevons principle was first enunciated in 1865 when an assessment was made that improving UK coal-burning efficiency would save coal – Jevons predicted that it would in fact lead to greater coal use as the efficiencies would lead to more economic uses for coal. The same principle seems to apply to our present assessment of transport fuel use. The price mechanism and urban sprawl ensure that for every increase in technological efficiency there is a rapid increase in the use of vehicles."
>
> **(Newman 1991a)**

The Costs of Sprawl

A recent Melbourne, Australia study suggests that it is cheaper for cities to pay developers to build near downtown cores than it is to pay for the costs of sprawl in terms of infrastructure development and remediating pollution from automobiles. Given its findings of lower road, sewer and education costs, the study showed a net benefit of Cdn $32,000 for every household created in downtown rather than suburban Melbourne. With three million residents spread over 2,500 sq km, Melbourne is considering a property tax holiday, bargain prices on city land and density zoning inducements to lure developers downtown. According to the Chief Executive of Melbourne's Planning Authority, "The net savings would be (Cdn) $130 million over 20 years for every 8,000 people who move downtown instead of the suburbs."

(see Neilson 1990; O'Brien 1990)

The problem with the low density land use pattern is not just its high energy use. Newman (1991b) notes that this settlement pattern has a complimentary set of environmental problems that all stem from its dispersed land use:

- High per capita auto emissions (both smog and greenhouse gases are directly related to the amount of gasoline used);
- High per capita water use (e.g., for lawn irrigation);
- High land requirements in both the block size and the road system required to service it (road provision is much greater in low density areas than in medium density areas);
- High stormwater pollution from the extra urbanized land (low density areas have double the stormwater pollution of medium density areas);

Misconceptions About Density

"Although denser land use could help solve the environmental, social, and aesthetic problems of sprawl, widespread misconceptions about increased density – even moderate density – often prevent communities from adopting compact land use strategies. Contrary to popular belief, augmenting the density of development does not create a harsh physical environment. For example, Copenhagen and Vienna – two cities widely associated with urban charm and livability – are of moderate density (measured by the number of residents and jobs in the city, including its central business district and outer areas), with 19 people per acre and 29 people per acre, respectively. By contrast, low-density cities such as Phoenix (5 people per acre) often are dominated by unwelcoming, car-oriented commercial strips and vast expanses of concrete and asphalt. People often assume that low density ensures more green space and easier living – yet with appropriate planning and design, dense urban areas can lend themselves to greater vitality, more inviting spaces, and even higher use of trees and other plants."

(Lowe 1992)

- High domestic heating energy due to the lack of a shared insulating effect when buildings are grouped (50% differences are found);
- Poor recycling rates due to the large cost involved in collection compared to a compact housing system (European cities have four to six times the recycling rates of North America);
- High physical infrastructure costs (utilities, pipes, poles, roads, etc.); and
- High social infrastructure costs (cars are required for participation in social life).

Land use planning initiatives are often motivated by the recognition that transportation planning and traffic management initiatives, as discussed in the previous chapter, will eventually be thwarted or simply overwhelmed by growth unless accompanied by long-term efforts to reduce the need for travel. Today there is also increasing recognition that to address problems such as air and water pollution, energy conservation, and infrastructure costs, land use planning initiatives are essential for moving toward sustainable communities.

The effectiveness of compact urban development can be fully achieved only if governments remove the conflicting incentives posed by other (often national) policies such as artificially low gasoline prices. For example, fuel taxes that more accurately reflect the true environmental and social costs of private vehicle use – from the health costs of air pollution to the military costs of policing the Persian Gulf – would give an enormous boost to more efficient urban land use and raise revenue for investment in a broader range of transport options (see Lowe 1992).

Despite the absence of supportive national policy frameworks, municipal and local governments can do a great deal to create more energy-efficient travel patterns by concentrating activities in specific areas and developing a mix of land uses in those areas. Our objectives should be to:

- create travel patterns that can be effectively served by more energy-efficient travel modes, such as public transit, bicycling, and walking; and
- reduce the average length of daily automobile trips where other modes are not feasible.

Comparing Three Urban Structure Concepts
A 1990 study of urban structure concepts for the Greater Toronto Area (GTA) detailed three different ways to manage

114

Reurbanization

In discussing energy-efficient land use, some analysts use the term reurbanization to refer to increasing the intensity of activity within present urban boundaries and "hardening" the urban fringe (reducing sprawl), thereby making more effective use of existing services, reducing infrastructure costs, and relieving pressures on adjacent agricultural lands.

"As the Canadian population becomes increasingly concentrated into urban areas, it is simultaneously becoming less concentrated within those areas. In other words, our cities and towns are not just growing in population, but at the same time they are spreading out and changing their structure into a looser, more widespread urban pattern."

Richardson 1991

"The New York metropolitan region, whose population has increased only 5 percent in the past 25 years, has expanded its developed area by 61 percent – consuming nearly one-quarter of the region's open space and farmland."

Lowe 1992

---

population growth over the next 30 years. The urbanized area of the GTA totalled 1,500 square kilometres (590 square miles) in 1986. Based on the three urban structures, that area could grow to between 1,890 square kilometres (730 square miles) and 2,400 square kilometres (940 square miles) in the next 30 years.

The study estimates that the cost of this growth would be approximately the same for each of the three concepts, about $79 billion, or approximately $23 billion more than would be spent on urban services in that period if there were no population growth. The three urban concepts were called Spread, Central and Nodal.

"The *Spread* model assumes that existing trends would continue and growth would occur largely in the suburban regions, resulting in an urbanized area of some 2,400 square kilometres (940 square miles) by 2021. This concept would be characterized by the lowest cost of acquiring parks and open spaces; ready availability of serviced land, with lower risks of sudden price increases; a more extensive road system, but increased traffic; and greater duplication of social services and facilities.

The *Central* concept would concentrate a great deal of growth in the central, built-up areas. It would result in an area of 1,890 square kilometres (730 square miles) and the least encroachment on greenlands; a more efficient and effective transit system; the lowest levels of air pollution and energy consumption from vehicle use; the greatest opportunity to reduce pollution of rivers and lakes through upgrading of existing storm sewers; and better use of existing health and education facilities.

The *Nodal* concept would have approximately the same number of residents living outside Metropolitan Toronto in the suburban regions as in the Spread concept, but they would be grouped in compact communities, or nodes. This would result in an area of approximately 2,124 square kilometres (820 square miles) in size. This concept would lead to greater preservation of green space than the Spread concept but less than the Central concept; a wider range of community sizes, housing types, densities, and population/employment patterns; expanded crosstown rapid transit; and potential integrating of social services on a community basis." (RCFTW 1990)

The study found that the *Spread* concept is the least compatible with sustainable development in that it would consume the greatest amount of rural land and related agricultural productivity and natural resources, would use the most energy and produce the most air pollution because of its higher travel effort and greater reliance on automobiles, and would provide less opportunity to enhance storm-water quality and dispose of toxic soils in central, built-up areas than would be the case for the other concepts.

While the *Spread* concept is the least risky in terms of change from the status quo, it carries the highest long-term risk since it would place greater negative pressures on the environment and on natural resources including energy sources and agricultural land.

The *Central* concept would provide the greatest likelihood of achieving sustainable development by making the most efficient use of resources (e.g., land, energy) and placing the least negative load on the environment. However, it would require the greatest change from the status quo in terms of population densities and housing types, automotive travel and transit, and growth management policies/ programs, and would require the greatest amount of government regulation in order to divert population growth from suburban areas to central, built-up areas.

The *Nodal* concept would be between the other two concepts in terms of its compatibility with sustainable development and the required level of government regulation. It would appear to provide the greatest range of choice in terms of population densities and housing types, community size and character, suburban and downtown living styles, available range of transportation modes, and integrated delivery of human services, while reducing per capita resource requirements and pollution levels relative to the *Spread* concept.

Because the study found that capital costs for the three concepts would be roughly the same, the authors concluded that the choices facing people and governments depend not so much on cost as on other factors such as environmental and economic considerations, lifestyle

> *"The amount of vacant and underutilized land in Portland,*
> *Oregon was estimated in 1989 at nine times the space needed*
> *to accommodate the city's projected growth for the next 20*
> *years."*
>
> Lowe 1992

preferences, and the quality of community and individual life. (see IBI Group 1990; RCFTW 1990)

Urban Form Policies

As described in the Transportation chapter, an Australian study of 32 major world cities shows that there are very clear relationships between transport and urban form. The data suggest that the primary urban form policy theme for sustainability should be *re-urbanization* – increasing the intensity of activity within present urban boundaries and "hardening" the urban fringe–emphasized mainly in Europe but with even greater application to North American and Australian cities, as detailed in the following set of policies. (Readers who wish to examine the data upon which these policies are based should consult the source document.)

"• *A policy to increase by stages the intensity of urban activity overall so that population densities of around 30 per ha to 40 per ha and job densities of around 20 per ha are obtained.* This will mean an immediate policy of restricting or at least slowing urban development at the urban fringe and concentrating on redevelopment; this consolidation generally has the added benefit of considerable capital savings due to better use of present urban infrastructure rather than requiring new infrastructure at the fringes.

• *A policy to build up the central city activity intensity so that job densities are maintained at more than 300 per ha and population densities are built up to over 50 to 60 per ha.* The provision of housing in central city areas seems to be harder than providing for jobs, though some outstanding successes have been achieved in recent years in Boston, Toronto, and San Francisco.

• *A policy to build up or maintain the inner area at population densities of 40 to 50 per ha and job densities of similar levels.* Most older cities have inner cities with these densities, although in many cases, particularly in the US, these have been declining in recent decades. Policies to contain inner city decline appear to have been relatively successful in Sydney, Melbourne and Toronto. In newer automobile-dependent cities like Houston, Denver, Brisbane, Adelaide and Perth there is enormous development potential in their inner areas.

• *A policy to build up outer area urban activity to population densities of around 20 to 30 per ha and job densities of around 15 per ha.* The way that this is most likely to be effective in transport and land use terms is (a) to slowly expand the present inner area type of development (i.e., mixed and more intensive) into the outer area, and (b) build up densities around rapid transit routes. For low density cities like Brisbane and Adelaide with present rail systems, and in cities like Los Angeles and Perth which are building new lines, this policy would appear to be of primary importance. Washington and Toronto are good examples where this policy has made major changes in transport and urban form in less than a decade.

[...] The time scale for such changes could possibly be gauged from cities like Detroit and Los Angeles which over a 30 to 40 year period were transformed from being compact rail-oriented cities to dispersed automobile-oriented cities." (Newman and Kenworthy 1991)

TOOLS

Cities and Automobile Dependence
Per capita gasoline consumption in US and many Canadian

cities is now more than four times that of European cities, and over 10 times greater than such Asian cities as Hong Kong, Tokyo, and Singapore. The biggest factor accounting for these differences in energy use appears to be not the size of cars or the price of gasoline, but the efficiency and compactness of land use patterns. Cities with low "automobile dependence" are:

- more centralized;
- have more intense land use (more people and jobs per unit area);
- are more oriented to non-auto modes (more public transit, foot traffic, and bicycle usage);
- place more restraints on high-speed traffic; and
- offer better public transit. (see Newman and Kenworthy 1989)

Policies for Energy-Efficient Land Use

"• encouraging greater density through multiple unit residential developments;
- integrating work, residence and shopping in mixed use development;
- encouraging residential clustering;
- zoning higher density development along established transit routes;
- decentralizing commercial and community services to reduce travel distances, creating self-contained communities with a better balance between employment and population;
- controls on outlying shopping centres, strip development and urban sprawl;
- encouraging the infilling [development] of existing vacant land in built-up areas;
- ensuring that major public facilities have provision for walking and bicycling access to transit;
- encourage the development of high quality walking

Garden Suburbs and Global Pollution
A recent Canada Mortgage and Housing Corporation study notes that the planning profession has been heavily influenced by various public health, housing, and environmental movements. Given the remarkable success of these types of neighbourhoods over the last four decades, these urban planning principles and practices have obviously accommodated an acute demand for millions of detached and semi-detached ground-oriented dwelling units. Ironically, however, while initially relieving the problems of local pollution and urban squalor, the mass implementation of these garden-oriented suburban communities has inadvertently contributed to today's more far-reaching environmental problems.

(see D'Amour 1991)

Jobs/Housing Balance
"The job/housing (J/H) balance is a useful developer's tool, although no rule of thumb or actual values are available. Basically, when jobs and housing are not in balance, transportation problems are the likely result. Land-use planners can look at the range of incomes and housing costs to determine how far people have to move away from their jobs to find housing they can afford. The farther they must move, the more congestion, energy use, and air-quality problems an area will have."

(Gordon 1991)

and bicycling facilities, [including development design guidelines to support transportation alternatives to private automobile use, such as provision of on-site lunchrooms, daycare facilities, automated bank teller machines and other facilities]." (Federation of Canadian Municipalities, 1990)

> *"Striking a 'balance' between jobs and housing is not enough, however, unless the people who work in a given area have the option of also living in that same area. This objective requires policies to encourage access by proximity."*
>
> City of Vancouver 1990

Population Density and Automobile Travel

Odometer readings taken during biennial auto emissions (smog check) inspections were used to calculate the annual mileages for five communities within the San Francisco region. The study found that doubling residential or population density reduces the annual auto mileage per capita or per household by 20 to 30 percent. These findings are consistent with studies in Toronto, Chicago, New York City, British cities, and major U.S. urbanized areas. Most striking were the differences between the San Francisco areas of Nob Hill (177 households per acre) and Danville-San Ramon (3.8 households per acre). Using the Hertz Corporation's estimates of auto ownership and operating costs per mile, the average Nob Hill area family annually spends nearly $14,000 less on autos, uses 66 percent less gasoline, and emits 14 kg less hydrocarbons, 12 kg less nitrogen oxides, and 98 kg less carbon monoxide than the average Danville-San Ramon family.

(see Holtzclaw 1991)

Selective Densification

"Attempting to start a city on a path of more disciplined, intelligent and efficient use of land does not imply widespread ruination of established suburban character. Every city has areas which are more suitable to redevelopment and densification than others. The initial goal in any automobile-dependent city should be to attempt to provide denser, more compact housing in selected areas. This will begin to diversify life style options and provide a small though significant portion of the population with opportunities to live where they are not so dependent on cars. It will also tend to minimize conflicts with established interests while beginning a tradition of denser housing which becomes progressively more acceptable as people become more familiar with it. These areas would typically include:

- underutilized or vacant land in central and inner areas, in particular government-owned land;
- waste or derelict land due to obsolete uses (warehouses, port installations, railway land, industrial land);
- residential areas that are run down and ripe for redevelopment – ensuring that provision is made in housing schemes for existing residents to remain but in new dwellings;
- areas within about 800m or half a mile radius of railway stations or significant bus transit terminals; and
- areas close to sub-regional centres.

In areas of established low density character, density may be gradually increased by building an extra dwelling (or perhaps more) on a single-family block without noticeably changing the area's character, though good design is essential." (Kenworthy and Newman 1990)

Rules of Thumb for Land Use Planning

The US Department of Transportation provides these rules of thumb for land-use planning tools to assist transportation planning. These numbers for residential and employment density are quite low in comparison with the more recent research of Newman and Kenworthy.

"• *Residential Density*

The higher the residential density, the higher the transit

ridership and the shorter the trip length. Result: improved cost recovery and better level of transit service. Two rules of thumb for residential density that promote transit ridership are: 1) density should exceed 2,400 persons per square mile and 2) a minimum of seven dwelling units per acre should be built.

• *Employment Density*

For significant transit use, there should be at least 50 employees per acre of business development (in areas with over 10,000 jobs). Densities of only 25 employees per acre result in ridership levels of only 1 percent of all employees, not enough to sustain transit services. At densities of 50-60 employees per acre, an estimated 6-11 percent of employees will ride transit.

• *Development Location and Proximity to Existing Transit*

All too often, access to mass transit and other alternative transport is a low priority in deciding where to locate development. Clustering new and existing development creates a concentration of trip destinations. Ideally, activity centers (areas of significant development – business parks, for example) in urban areas should be planned at distances of three to six miles from one another, allowing for shorter work and shopping trips. The rules of thumb for proximity to transit are as follows: People can be expected to walk up to 1,000 feet to a bus stop. Those over 45 years of age will not walk as far; senior citizens will not walk more than 750 feet to a transit stop (steep grades reduce these distances). Those with higher incomes are less inclined to walk any distance to mass transit. Bike&Rides attract cyclists from one-half to three miles away, while Park&Rides draw people from 1-10 miles away.

• *Mixed-Use Development*

Balanced residential and commercial/industrial

development in reasonably close proximity can lead to a reduction in transportation demand. Mixed-use development offers several benefits: reduced parking requirements, more open space, enhanced retail activity, reduced auto traffic, and increased safety during evening hours. For greatest benefits, the mix of housing should match the income structure of area employment in terms of affordability.

• *Land-Use Design Considerations*

Pedestrians are more likely to Walk&Ride if transit delivers them to their front door rather than to a parking lot they must walk through. Accordingly, new developments should be designed with parking in the rear. Provisions for on-site bus turnouts and passenger shelters also encourage transit use. Foot travel is enhanced when connecting complexes provide pedestrian arcades. And, of course, for safety reasons adequate lighting is critical.

• *Street Layout*

Designing transit routes early in the development process can minimize distances to stations and ensure that roads will support heavy buses, reducing maintenance costs. Improved road design can cut costs by reducing street size. Gridded systems provide the easiest pedestrian access, while cul-de-sacs, popular in suburban developments, restrict transit and pedestrian passage. Sidewalks, the need for which is often ignored, must be provided. They attract pedestrians and provide safety. For bicycles, wide curb lanes (14 feet minimum), striped bike lanes, or separate bike paths provide easier and safer access to transit centers, Bike&Ride lots, freeway-flyer stops, and major bus stops." (US DOT 1987)

Growth Management

"Growth management simply means *planning for the future*

[...] Fundamentally, all growth management systems involve the control of one or more of the familiar components of land use planning: the rate, location, type, density, amount and quality of development. Unlike traditional subdivision and zoning, which are two-dimensional (controlling the use of land and the density of permissible development), growth management adds and emphasizes a third dimension – timing. Managing growth does not mean stopping change or closing the doors to new residents. Properly designed and implemented, a comprehensive growth management system provides a framework that enables local governments to balance and accommodate diverse and competing interests while ensuring the quality of life expected by [their citizens]." (Stone and Freilich 1991)

Zoning Tools

"Zoning can encourage development that supports alternative transportation. A few of the many zoning tools available to land-use and transportation planners include:
  - planned unit development – gives developers incentives to meet pre-determined land-use goals
  - floating zoning – permits special uses within a jurisdiction in accordance with development criteria
  - bonus or incentive zoning – provides developers with bonuses and incentives to achieve increased development density
  - mixed-use zoning – requires a wide array of types of development aimed at reducing distances between houses and jobs
  - land banking – outright purchase of land by the public sector well in advance of any development to ensure appropriate land use
  - transit zoning districts – targeted development in areas with transit systems already in place." (Gordon 1991)

126

> *"The good news about these and other steps towards urban sustainability is that they fit very well together. More efficient structuring of urban growth, higher densities, better use of urban sites, and a shift from cars to transit, all work together to protect land resources, conserve energy, and improve air quality.*
>
> *The bad news, of course, is that all this is very difficult to do. You don't need to point out the problems to me, and I certainly don't need to point them out to you. But they aren't technical problems. In a technical sense we know pretty well what needs to be done, and how to do it. The problems of achieving urban sustainability arise out of the nature of our society and the way it is organized."*
>
> Richardson 1991

> ### The Pedestrian Pocket
> **"The Pedestrian Pocket is defined as a balanced, mixed-use area within a quarter-mile or a five-minute walking radius of a transit station. The functions within this 50 to 100-acre zone include housing, offices, retail, day care, recreation, and parks. Up to two thousand units of housing and one million square feet of office space can be located within three blocks of the transit station using typical residential densities and four-storey office configurations."**
>
> **(Calthorpe 1989)**

Residential Intensification

"Residential Intensification" means the creation of new residential units or accommodation in existing buildings or on previously developed, serviced land generally including:

- creation of rooming, boarding and lodging houses;
- creation of accessory apartments;
- conversion of non-residential structures to residential use;
- infill;
- redevelopment.

127

"One of the great mysteries of the American suburb is this: How, with such low-density development, have we produced such extraordinarily high traffic? How have we achieved the traffic of a metropolis and the culture of a cow town?"
Duany and Plater-Zyberk 1992

Transit-Oriented Developments

"Transit-Oriented Developments (TODs) are mixed-use neighbourhoods, between 20 and 160 acres in size, which are developed around a transit stop and core commercial area. The entire TOD site must be within an average one-fourth mile walking distance of a transit stop."

TODs offer different types of growth for different conditions. "Urban TODs" are located at light rail stops or bus transfer stations with an orientation to commercial and job development. "Neighborhood TODs" are located on feeder bus lines within 10 minutes travel time from light rail stops or bus transfer stations with an orientation to housing, retail and services. "Secondary Areas" of lower density housing, schools, community parks, and commercial and employment uses surround TODs within biking distance (one mile) of the transit stop.

"The TOD concept may be applied in four types of settings: Infill Areas on vacant parcels surrounded by urban development; Revitalization Areas in urbanized areas where the quality of development is significantly deteriorated or the land is underutilized; Reuse Areas for underutilized retail, office or industrial sites; and Urban Growth Areas in essentially undeveloped areas on the periphery of the developed portions of the county." (Calthorpe Associates 1990)

Traditional Neighbourhood Development Ordinance

General dissatisfaction with existing urban patterns motivated a group of architects and developers to draw on the lessons of the resort community of Seaside, Florida – designed by "neotraditional town planning" proponents Andres Duany and Elizabeth Plater-Zyberk – to devise a general system that could be applied to other towns and developments.

An illustrated chart called Traditional Neighborhood Development Ordinance (TND) lays out very simple guidelines for site and building design. These include the close proximity of houses and work places, well-defined public spaces, a variety of streets, and strategically placed civic buildings. The ordinance categorizes these features on a chart according to the needs of different types of buildings – for example, what percentage of public land shall be used for governmental versus retail or general use, how streets are to be arranged in residential areas, and so on.

The aim of the TND is to foster independence from cars by keeping the neighborhood's needs within walking distance. Moreover, by organizing neighbourhoods in ways proven to be effective in older North American towns, desirable social objectives automatically fall into place. As the ordinance states, "By walking instead of driving, citizens come to know each other and the bonds of an authentic community are established" (see Taylor 1990).

With increasing attention and publicity, the "neotraditionalists" have also earned their share of criticism. For example, Seaside does not employ ecological design techniques (e.g., passive solar) and infrastructure (e.g., provisions for reducing water consumption, such as recycling grey water systems or open rainwater drainage swales) (see Okamoto 1991). Seaside's design may reduce traffic congestion but does not reduce automobile dependence; the TND does not in itself create proximity or even balance between jobs and housing (see MacBurnie 1991). The TND is more suitable for a project under single

"The concept of sustainability is essential to our survival and should be viewed as the intent and central operating principle of planning [...]

If we are to achieve sustainable development, we will have to go beyond the notion that land is a mere commodity. Land is one of the fundamental components required for the continuation of human life. We should now recognize the rights of the ecosystem and the species, as well as the rights of individuals. Clearly, this principle holds numerous, significant implications for planners and land use planning."
Canadian Institute of Planners 1990

ownership than for a typical community trying to work with several developers (see Knack 1991). And although TNDs may be "designed" to encourage a mix of housing types and a diversity of income levels, they offer no mechanism to ensure any stock – never mind an adequate, permanent stock – of affordable housing. Even Duany admits that Seaside has in practice become a "resort community" for the wealthy (see Duany 1991).

Access information for the TND is in the Resources section of this chapter.

Principles for ecologically-sensitive land use planning

"• Expand the definition of land in land use planning to encompass the ecosystem, and expand the scope of land use planning accordingly

• Establish ecosystem maintenance and stewardship as important values in land use planning

• Undertake cooperative planning efforts to address the lack of coincidence between ecosystem and municipal boundaries

• Broaden the assessment criteria, procedures and techniques used in land use planning to include environmental factors and sustainability

considerations
 • Identify, protect and maintain key areas and processes
   in order to maintain ecological integrity." (Greater
Vancouver Regional District 1991)

Advantages of Cluster Housing to Specific Populations

"In a comparative study of residential satisfaction in a low-density U.S. suburb (Levittown, Pennsylvania) and a higher-density Swedish equivalent (Vällingby), sociologist David Popenoe concludes: 'With the percent of gainfully employed women in the U.S. sharply rising, the relative disadvantages of a Levittown-type environment for the working woman are increasing. For the woman who can't afford a second car, who has difficulty making child care arrangements, and who has specialized employment needs, Levittown can become a noose around her neck.'

Research shows that one of the most frustrated population groups in low-density suburbia is adolescents. When young people are entering a stage in which they are seeking more and more independence from their parents, they find themselves in an environment where getting together with friends is made difficult by distance, paucity of public transport, separation of housing from shopping centers, and so on. In his United States-Sweden study, Popenoe found American suburban teenagers more often bored and engaging in vandalism than their counterparts in Sweden living at higher density with easy access to shops, clubs, public transport, and so on. Teenagers in clustered housing are more likely to find others of the same age living within walking distance and may have access to shared facilities or hanging-out places where they can spend time together, out of sight of home, yet not far away.

Clustered housing in the inner city allows people to enjoy a green and quiet environment within easy access to city jobs. Similar housing on the city's fringes will, if repeated often enough, increase overall densities and render public transport more economical. As land costs continue to rise, clustered housing permits more dwellings on a given site. As ecological issues of natural drainage, solar access, and community gardens become more pressing, clustered housing permits the more rational use of any given site – the best soil saved for food growing, existing woodlot preserved for play or windbreak, natural drainage patterns preserved." (Cooper Marcus and Sarkissian 1986)

Transfer of Development Rights (TDR)

The right to develop a piece of land as allowed by zoning and land use controls is one of the rights that comes with property ownership under the "bundle of rights" theory. The ability to sever this right from one piece of property and transfer it to another piece of land is the central element in a transfer of development rights (TDR) program. This approach allows landowners to get development value from their land even if they choose not to develop it. All TDR programs include a sending zone, from which development rights can be severed, and a receiving zone, which can accept development rights and therefore can be developed more densely. TDR programs preserve or protect something in the sending zone, such as farmland, forest land, environmentally sensitive areas, open space, historic buildings, or landmarks; they can also steer development to areas best able to handle it.

At least fifty TDR programs have been established in the U.S. County programs include Montgomery County, Maryland; Collier County, Florida; and San Bernadino County, California. Municipal programs include New York City; Seattle; San Francisco; and Groton, Massachusetts. (see Heyerdahl 1991)

Conservation Land Trusts

Land trusts are local, regional, or statewide organizations directly involved in protecting important land resources for the public benefit. Land trusts are not "trusts" in the legal sense, but rather private, non-profit, tax-exempt organizations, funded largely through membership dues and donations from individuals, businesses, and foundations. Many refer to themselves as conservancies, foundations, or associations. Some are small and are run solely by volunteers, while others manage thousands of acres and have large, professional staffs.

Land trusts protect land permanently and directly. They accept donations of properties, buy land, or help landowners establish legal restrictions that limit harmful use and development. They protect land that has natural, recreational, scenic, historic, or productive value, depending on the needs of the community or region. Some preserve many different types of land, while others focus on a particular area or resource.

Land trusts are usually not adversarial, but work cooperatively with landowners and government agencies. Some own and manage nature preserves, recreation areas, or historic sites. Others monitor the development restrictions they have helped establish, but own no land at all. Some work in partnership with government conservation agencies, acquiring critical land that they later convey to the agencies.

As private organizations, land trusts offer quick response, flexibility, and confidentiality. They may be effective where government action falls short. Land trusts also provide a cost-effective approach to conservation. They often protect land at a cost far below its market value.

Nearly 900 land trusts in the US have protected over 2 million acres of farms, wetlands, wildlife habitat, urban gardens and parks, forests, ranches, watersheds, coastlines,

> *"It is impossible to halt further development; by prohibiting growth in their own jurisdictions, communities merely shift development to neighboring areas – where controls are looser, and more conducive to further sprawl. More importantly, future development presents an invaluable opportunity to remedy the status quo. If cities do not want to be frozen in their current automobile-dependent patterns, they need to exploit new growth to their advantage by filling in underused space to make the urban area more compact. In sum, cities would do well to focus their attention on controlling the pattern, not the pace, of growth."*
>
> Lowe 1991b

river corridors, and trails. New land trusts are forming at the rate of one per week. About half are operated exclusively by volunteers with operating budgets of less than $10,000. (see Land Trust Alliance, n.d.; Abberger 1991)

INITIATIVES

Proximity Planning
Vancouver's *Clouds of Change* report makes "access by proximity rather than access by transportation" a central focus of city planning.

The City and County of **Denver**, Colorado are investigating the possibility of offering new employees a financial incentive, in the form of a higher starting salary, to live close to their workplace. The amount of the adjustment would reflect the distance to be travelled and the relative costs of housing in the city as opposed to the more distant suburbs. (see City of Vancouver 1990; McCulloch 1991)

Energy-Efficient Land Use Planning
"Portland, Oregon provides an example of a larger city-region experimenting with land use policies to control

energy demand – in this case within the framework of a mandatory State planning goal which requires that land use should be managed in order to conserve energy. One of the main objectives of the Portland Energy Conservation Demonstration Project, completed in 1977, was to examine the links between energy saving and urban form. An energy zone map, dividing the city into five zones based on relative energy efficiency, was produced in order to guide new development to energy efficient locations, and an energy conservation policy was adopted by the city council after extensive public consultation in 1979. It included commitments to develop land use policies using density and location to reduce the need to travel, and to improve the efficiency of the transport system and reduce its consumption of non-renewable fuels. More specific objectives related to the location of new developments and encouragement of energy efficient transport modes. These strategies were then incorporated into the city's draft comprehensive plan.

One of the central features of the plan was a 'centers and corridors' concept, which would involve guiding new development into centers of existing commercial activity and along major streets (corridors). Emphasis was on energy conservation through compact high density development, using an urban pattern which combines nucleated centers with high linear densities. In theory, less travel would be required, essential travel would be carried out by energy-efficient modes and higher density development would permit more efficient use of fuel for space heating. During the public consultation phase, the energy related features of the plan were among the most controversial, winning strongest support from environmentalists, newspapers and heads of local government agencies, and opposition mainly from developers, industrial and union leaders and the Chamber of Commerce. Zoning was unpopular with development interests and landowners, while the emphasis on high-density corridors was opposed by neighborhood groups. Revisions were made to break up several corridors into 'development nodes' – clusters of commercial activity, surrounded by high-density housing. Any plan which tries to take energy considerations into account at this scale is likely to face intensive lobbying by interest groups, the power of which must be recognized as a constraint on 'pure' energy-related objectives." (Owens 1990)

Since the early 1970s, the volume of cars entering the downtown has remained the same, even though the number of jobs has increased by 50 percent. New development in Portland has been contained inside a regional "urban growth boundary" (UGB) surrounding the metropolitan area. Residential development, in particular, has been mandated at a high enough density to help support a nationally acclaimed public transit system that received top honours from the American Public Transit Association in 1989-90.

Today 43 percent of all Portland's commuters to downtown ride buses and a light rail system. This transit ridership rate is higher than most other U.S. cities its size. For example, Seattle has a rate of 38 percent, Denver 29 percent, and Buffalo 25 percent.

"The Portland experience demonstrates that it is possible to plan for greater energy efficiency in large, established urban centers, though it is difficult to establish how effective the policies will be in the longer term in modifying the spatial structure and in reducing energy requirements." (Owens 1990)

Unfortunately, Portland still has traffic woes. Local officials worry that already congested roads on the west side of town cannot accommodate expected growth in car traffic. The answer, according to state and regional transportation officials, is building a circumferential bypass road. (see Owens 1990; Kasowski 1991; and Lowe 1991a)

Compact Community Policies

In *Peterborough*, Ontario the Sustainable Development Task Force argues that Compact Community planning cannot happen without concerted effort by local governments, supported by the public at large. Specifically, Official Plans, Zoning By-Laws and local building or development by-laws should be amended to facilitate intensification.

"• Intensification should be made a *core* basis of housing policy in the Official Plan rather than a marginal component of traditional patterns of housing policy.

• Zoning By-Law matters relating to residential density, clustering, lot size, setbacks, basement apartments, etc., should also be amended to facilitate intensification.

• Design guidelines or standards (fitting into neighbourhood character, etc.) should also be established.

These policies should be developed with input from a broad range of stakeholders – from developers to affordable housing planners to environmental and community activists." (Peterborough Task Force on Sustainable Development 1991)

Urban Villages

"Urban villages provide a lifestyle with minimal car dependence and the kind of densities which make rail highly viable. The evidence would suggest that those cities which have tried to build urban villages have found them to be an extremely attractive lifestyle option. Recent examples appear to be succeeding and urban villages are now appearing such as Arabella Park, Zamilla Park and Germering in *Munich*, Der Seepark in *Freiburg* and Kista in *Stockholm*. These are nearly all private developments with very high popularity. Examples of urban village style developments in North America include False Creek in *Vancouver*, River Place in *Portland*, Oregon, and Mission Bay in *San Francisco*. The characteristics of these urban villages are:

- mixed land use, with commercial offices and shops on main spines, surrounded by residential;
- high density so that everything within the 'village' is within walking and cycling distance;
- considerable landscaping including gardens on top of buildings and on balconies;
- a mixture of public and private housing with an emphasis on families and hence quite large internal home spaces;
- extensive provision for children in good view of dwellings;
- community facilities such as libraries, child care, aged centres and in a few cases small urban farms;
- pedestrian links with car parks placed underground and traffic calming on any peripheral roads;
- public spaces with strong design features (water, street furniture, playgrounds, etc.);
- a large degree of self-sufficiency for the community but with good rail links to the rest of the city." (Newman 1991; see also 1991c)

Sustainable Urban Megaproject Planning

A 1990 sustainable development plan for *Toronto's* Waterfront Railway Lands (not adopted by the City) included several interesting recommendations in regard to urban megaproject planning:

"• That the City Council endorse the principles of:
    a) minimizing fossil fuel consumption
    b) producing no peak drain on Ontario Hydro power

from the railway lands development [...]
- That urban design principles maximizing solar access for heat and light be developed and included in a modified railway lands plan [...]
- That the Commissioner of Planning and Development in conjunction with the Commissioner of Parks and Recreation report on strategies to maximize shading within the railway lands including rooftop gardens. Such a strategy to be prepared in conjunction with strategies to maximize solar energy utilization.
- That landscape designs be developed to maximize the natural filtering of storm water.
- That strategies to use 'waste heat' be developed including the heating of greenhouses on rooftops or on atriums for food production, air filtration and humidity control [...]
- That a thorough study of 'solar aquatics' be undertaken in order to develop its eventual application within railway lands' development to achieve minimum or zero discharge and plant (including food) production [...]
- That proximity planning policies including appropriate ratios of residential to office space be established for the railway lands in order to minimize transportation per capita and greenhouse gases.
- That parking standards be set at an extremely low level for all development and at zero for many buildings.
- That a complete package of pro-cycling policies be adopted in the new plans [...]
- That composting factory space be provided in basements of some buildings, adequate to process all compostable waste generated within the lands. Methane by-products to be used locally for energy requirements [...]
- That an implementation strategy for the Greenplan be

139

developed, to include a team to be composed of developers' representatives; building industry representatives; environmental, alternative technology, and academic specialists; and civic staff including representation from the new Energy Efficiency Office." (Allen *et al* 1990)

Land Stewardship

The Regional Municipality of *Halton*, Ontario has advanced land stewardship as the *first guiding principle* for land use planning in Halton. "In this regard, we submit that the ownership rights of land are not absolute and the best and highest use of land is not an unfailing principle as there are other balancing factors to be considered. This is not meant as a denial of property rights, but an affirmation of a social responsibility.

The duration over which a particular individual has titles to a piece of real property is but a fleeting moment in the history of the land. Individual property owners shall be encouraged to consider themselves as stewards of the land and give proper regard to the long term environmental interests in proposing any change to their land. To be stewards, we have to develop a renewed respect for the land, knowing that the quality of our natural environment is as much a part of our quality of life as our jobs, wealth and health. *The extent to which an individual realizes the economic benefit of a land use change should be balanced by the community's desire in preserving the environment or certain land forms in the landscape.* As we said, we intend this to be a social responsibility and not a challenge to property rights [...]

Not only does the suburban form of development, with its attendant auto-dependency, consume land and energy, it also degrades the environment, segregates socio-economic classes, and reduces our opportunity of being more involved locally [...]

We should create a more integrated live-work environment through more compact and people-oriented urban development design [...] We should promote public transit, develop land uses that will support transit, create compatible jobs and housing, encourage mixed land uses, selectively increase urban densities, and make our daily activity functional without the absolute necessity of the private car." (Regional Municipality of Halton 1991)

Residential Intensification

Kingston, Ontario created a low-interest loan program in 1981 to encourage the conversion of vacant, obsolete second and third storey commercial space in the downtown area into residential units. The program, which provides financial assistance to property owners within the CBD, was funded by an initial allocation of $250,000 from Council to serve as a revolving fund for future loans. The program's advantages include business benefits to downtown merchants, cost-effectiveness, increased assessments; downtown revitalization; and easing a tight rental apartment situation.

St. Catherines, Ontario instituted a similar program in 1987, creating a $300,000 revolving fund to provide 8% conversion loans of up to $20,000 per dwelling unit.

The Metropolitan *Toronto* Planning Department has estimated that the conversion aspect alone of a residential intensification program could produce 39,000 new housing units, the equivalent of 11 years of rental housing production (both private and social units). (see Ministries of Municipal Affairs and Housing 1989; Kingston Planning Report 1987; St. Catherines Planning Report 1987; Metropolitan Toronto Planning Department 1987)

"Commute-sheds" for Jobs-Housing Balance

"Southern California has seized on the concept of balancing jobs and housing as a means of reducing traffic congestion and automobile emissions. In 1989, the South Coast Air Quality Management District and the Southern California Association of Governments, unveiled a plan that combines traditional approaches to air pollution abatement with strategies to reduce emissions by redirecting residential and commercial development. The plan establishes subregional 'commute-sheds' that are designated as either job-rich or job-poor. Planners estimate that by redirecting nine percent of new jobs from job-rich to job-poor areas and five percent of new housing in the other direction, the number of vehicle-miles travelled per day could be cut by 33.4 million, or nine percent." (APA 1991a)

Building Permit Allocation

In Florida, *"Key West's* 1986 growth management ordinance establishes the number of dwelling units that still can be constructed before the island is completely built out. Before the enactment of the ordinance, the city approved an average of 400 to 500 dwelling units annually. Under the ordinance, the city can allow either seven percent of the total units permitted or 300 units per year. Housing permits are allocated on a merit system that awards points for recreational amenities, landscaping and open space, design quality, impact on the local infrastructure, and energy efficiency.

The ordinance also requires that at least 40 percent of all residential housing units must be constructed as affordable housing. Affordable apartments have annual rental rates less than 30 percent of the median household income in the city, while affordable sale units have a sale price that is less than three times the city's median household income

[...] [Developers] must enter into a development agreement with the city. Deed restrictions guarantee that the unit will remain affordable for a period of five to 20 years, depending on the project. In addition, the ordinance contains provisions for the waiver of impact fees on affordable units. Developers can obtain waiver credits by offering the units at prices below those established by the affordability threshold and by ensuring that the project will remain affordable for at least five years. Usually, at least half of the impact fee is waived for affordable units." (APA 1991b)

RESOURCES

ROBERT D. YARO, ET AL, *Dealing With Change in the Connecticut River Valley: A Design Manual for Conservation and Development* (Amherst, MA: Center for Rural Massachusetts, University of Massachusetts at Amherst, 1988). This volume attempts to develop practical planning standards which rural New England towns can adopt to protect their distinctive character, while at the same time accommodating economic growth.

SIM VAN DER RYN AND PETER CALTHORPE, editors, *Sustainable Communities: A New Design Synthesis for Cities, Suburbs and Towns* (San Francisco: Sierra Club Books, 1986). Recently re-released in paperback, this is a stimulating collection edited by two forward-looking architects. See annotation in Chapter 2 of this book.

MICHAEL A. MANTELL, STEPHEN F. HARPER, AND LUTHER PROPST, *Creating Successful Communities* (Washington, DC: Island Press, 1990). Volume I is subtitled *A Guidebook to Growth Management Strategies;* Volume II is a *Resource Guide.* These books are particularly useful in regard to agricultural land, wetlands, historic and cultural resources, and open space. They also include useful information on easements and conservation restrictions, and on growth management tools and techniques.

MONTGOMERY COUNTY PLANNING DEPARTMENT, MARYLAND-NATIONAL CAPITAL PARK AND PLANNING COMMISSION, *Comprehensive Growth Policy Study, Volume I* (Silver Spring, MD: Maryland-National Capital Park and Planning Commission, 1989). Summarizes the major conclusions of a far-reaching technical study of congestion, affordability, policy-making and growth management. A good model, available from:

Maryland-National Capital Park and Planning
Commission
8787 Georgia Avenue
Silver Spring, Maryland 20910-3760
Tel: 301/495-4600

SAMUEL N. STOKES, ET AL, *Saving America's Countryside: A Guide to Rural Conservation* (Baltimore: John Hopkins University Press, 1989). This book was written for the U.S. National Trust for Historic Preservation. It focuses on protecting the entire spectrum of a rural community's resources—natural, historic, scenic, and agricultural. Twenty-eight recent case studies are documented. The chapter on land protection techniques that local governments can use is particularly valuable.

DOUG KELBAUGH, ED., *The Pedestrian Pocket Book: A New Suburban Design Strategy* (New York: Princeton Architectural Press, 1989). This little book documents a design charette with architect Peter Calthorpe at the University of Washington in 1988, testing Calthorpe's "Pedestrian Pocket" concept on a site next to a proposed rapid transit line. It shows that strategic interventions could affect the structure, legibility, and sense of place in suburbia. It contends that finite centers of community are achievable, and that affordability, traffic decongestion, open space, mixed population, and mixed use are all mutually compatible.

ALEX KRIEGER, ed., *Andres Duany and Elizabeth Plater-Zyberk: Towns and Town-Making Principles* (NY: Rizzoli International Publications, 1991). Based on an exhibition at the Harvard University Graduate School of Design in 1990, this volume consists of architectural plans and drawings woven together with essays by design theorists Alex Krieger, Leon Krier, William Lennertz, Patrick Pinnell, and Vincent Scully, Jr. As proponents of "neotraditional" town planning, Duany and Plater-Zyberk advocate designing suburban subdivisions in the manner of towns. They also challenge zoning conventions and write design codes that favour traditional patterns of placemaking. Duany and Plater-Zyberk are widely known for their design of the resort community of Seaside, on the Florida panhandle. This volume appears to be the first book-length treatment of their ideas.

The Traditional Neighborhood Development Ordinance (TND) discussed earlier in this chapter is available from:

Duany & Plater-Zyberk Architects
2949 Coconut Avenue
Coconut Grove, FL 33133

MICHAEL N. CORBETT, *A Better Place to Live: New Designs for Tomorrow's Communities* (Emmaus, PA: Rodale Press, 1981). Village Homes, Michael and Judy Corbett's 70-acre (28 ha), 270-unit solar subdivision in Davis, California is a pioneering example of sustainability by design which has received considerable attention. The development incorporates a wide range of innovative measures in a plan which satisfies three basic conservation objectives: reduction in total energy consumption, efficient use of energy, and conversion to renewable energy resource usage. The five main characteristics exhibited by this subdivision and neighbourhood design are: intensive land use, prominent use of solar energy, functional landscaping (e.g., trees were selected for maximum summer and minimum winter shading), energy-efficient transportation (all roads end in cul-de-sacs, making it faster to walk than drive from one area to another; a comprehensive greenbelt pathway is tied into the City bikeway network), and involvement of residents. The Corbetts attempted to facilitate "sense of community" through physical design, by establishing a homeowners association to participate in development and management decisions, and by becoming Village residents themselves. Michael Corbett later became mayor of Davis.

THE REAL ESTATE RESEARCH CORPORATION'S (1974) massive study for the US Government on *The Costs of Sprawl* still stands as a classic. Three community types were analyzed: the "low density sprawl" community (entirely single-family homes, 75 percent in traditional grid pattern typical of suburban development); the "combination mix" community (20 percent of each of five types of dwellings, half in planned unit developments, half in traditional subdivisions); and the "high density planned" community (40 percent highrises, 30 percent walkups, 20 percent townhouses, and 10 percent clustered single family homes, all clustered together into contiguous neighbourhoods). A major conclusion of the study was that sprawl is "the most expensive form of residential development in terms of economic costs, environmental costs, natural resource consumption, and many types of personal costs... This cost difference is particularly significant for that proportion of total costs which is likely to be borne by local governments."

THE LAND TRUST ALLIANCE is the US national organization of land trusts. Founded in 1982, the Alliance provides specialized services, publications, information, and training for land trusts and other conservation organizations, and works for public policies that advance land conservation. The Alliance recently published *Starting a Land Trust: A*

146

Guide to Forming an Land Conservation Organization (Alexandria, VA: Land Trust Alliance, 1990). For more information, contact:

The Land Trust Alliance
Suite 410
900 Seventeenth Street NW
Washington, DC 20006
Tel: 202/785-1410

TURTLE ISLAND EARTH STEWARDS (TIES) is a British Columbia-based international non-profit organization that helps place lands and forests in trust using the "land stewardship trust" model. TIES hosted the first West Coast Land Trust Conference in April, 1991. TIES publishes a quarterly newsletter and has introduced a non-profit real estate service to bring together private land owners, people seeking fellowship or community, and third party investors, financiers and philanthropists to establish land stewardship trusts. Access:

Turtle Island Earth Stewards
Box 39077 Point Grey RPO
Vancouver, B.C. V6R 4P1
Tel: 604/736-9221   Fax: 604/736-9218

References

ABBERGER, W., "Growth Management Through Land Acquisition," in DeGrove 1991.

ALLEN, G., ET AL, "Greenlands: A Sustainable Development Plan for Toronto's Waterfront Railway Lands," submitted to the City of Toronto, October 21, 1990.

AMERICAN PLANNING ASSOCIATION (1991a), "Solving Traffic Woes by Balancing Jobs and Housing," in DeGrove 1991.

AMERICAN PLANNING ASSOCIATION (1991b), "Taming the Exclusionary Effects of Growth Controls," in DeGrove 1991.

CALTHORPE ASSOCIATES, in association with MINTIER & ASSOCIATES, "Transit-Oriented Development Design Guidelines," prepared for Sacramento County Planning & Community Development Department, November 1990.

CALTHORPE, P., "Pedestrian Pockets: New Strategies for Suburban Growth," in Kelbaugh 1989.

CANADIAN INSTITUTE OF PLANNERS, *Reflections on Sustainable Planning* (Ottawa: CIP, 1990).

CITY OF VANCOUVER, *Clouds of Change: Final Report of the City of Vancouver Task Force on Atmospheric Change* (Vancouver: City of Vancouver, 1990).

COOPER MARCUS, C. AND W. SARKISSIAN, *Housing as if People Mattered: Site Design Guidelines for Medium-Density Family Housing* (Berkeley: University of California Press, 1986).

CORBETT, M.N., *A Better Place to Live: New Designs for Tomorrow's Communities* (Emmaus, PA: Rodale Press, 1981).

D'AMOUR, D., "The Origins of Sustainable Development and Its Relationship to Housing and Community Planning," Sustainable Development and Housing Research Paper No. 1 (Ottawa: Canada Mortgage and Housing Corporation, 1991).

DEGROVE, J.M., ed., Balanced Growth: A Planning Guide for Local Government (Washington, D.C.: International City Management Association, 1991).

DUANY, A., "Reinventing the Suburb," presentation to the Urban Development Institute, Pacific Region, Vancouver, B.C., September 24, 1991.

DUANY, A., AND E. PLATER-ZYBERK, "The Second Coming of the Small Town," *The Wilson Quarterly* (Winter 1992), reprinted in *Utne Reader* No. 51, May/June 1992, pp. 97-100.

FEDERATION OF CANADIAN MUNICIPALITIES, *A Guidebook on Transportation Energy Management* (Ottawa: Federation of Canadian Municipalities, 1990).

GORDON, D., Steering a New Course: Transportation, Energy, and the Environment (Cambridge, MA: Union of Concerned Scientists, 1991).

GREATER VANCOUVER REGIONAL DISTRICT (GVRD), "Creating Greater Vancouver's Green Zone" (Burnaby, B.C.: GVRD 1991).

HEYERDAHL, B., "TDRs: An Innovative Approach to Growth Management," in DeGrove 1991.

HOLTZCLAW, J., "Explaining Urban Density and Transit Impacts on Auto Use," presented to State of California Energy Resources Conservation and Development Commission, Docket No. 89-CR-90, January 15, 1991.

IBI GROUP, "Greater Toronto Area Urban Structure Concepts Study – Summary Report," prepared for the Greater Toronto Coordinating Committee (Toronto: IBI Group, 1990).

KASOWSKI, K., "Oregon: Fifteen Years of Land-Use Planning," in DeGrove 1991.

KELBAUGH, D., ed., The *Pedestrian Pocket Book: A New Suburban Design Strategy* (New York: Princeton Architectural Press, 1989).

KENWORTHY, J.R., AND P.W.G. NEWMAN, "Cities and Transport Energy: Lessons From a Global Survey," *Ekistics* 57(344/345):258-268, 1990.

KINGSTON PLANNING REPORT April 15, 1987, Item No. 213, File 60.73.70.

KNACK, R.E., "Tony Nelessen's Do-It-Yourself Neotraditionalism," *Planning* 57(12): 18-22, December 1991.

KRIEGER, A., ed., *Andres Duany and Elizabeth Plater-Zyberk: Towns and Town-Making Principles* (NY: Rizzoli International Publications, 1991).

LAND TRUST ALLIANCE, "Land Trusts" (Washington, DC: Land Trust Alliance, n.d.).

LOWE, M.D., "Portland Bypasses Progress," Worldwatch 4(5), Sept/Oct 1991a, pp. 9, 30.

LOWE, M.D., "Shaping Cities: The Environmental and Human Dimensions," Worldwatch Paper 105 (Washington, D.C.: Worldwatch Institute, 1991b).

LOWE, M.D., "City Limits," Worldwatch 5(1), Jan/Feb 1992, pp. 18-25.

MACBURNIE, I., "Reconsidering the Dream: Towards a Morphology for a Mixed Density Block Structure in Suburbia," paper presented to Colloquium on Sustainable Housing and Urban Development, Institute of Urban Studies, University of Winnipeg, Winnipeg, Manitoba, November 16, 1991.

MANTELL, M.A., S.F. HARPER, AND L. PROPST, *Creating Successful Communities* (Washington, DC: Island Press, 1990, 2 volumes).

MCCULLOCH, J.A.W., "Overview of International Conference on Cities and Global Change" (Toronto, June 1991), prepared for "World Cities and the Environment" Conference, Toronto, August 25-28, 1991.

METROPOLITAN TORONTO PLANNING DEPARTMENT, Policy Development Division, "Housing Intensification,"

Metropolitan Plan Review Report No. 4 (Toronto: Planning Department, 1987).

MINISTRIES OF MUNICIPAL AFFAIRS AND HOUSING, "Land Use Planning for Housing" (Toronto: Ministry of Government Services, 1989).

MONTGOMERY COUNTY PLANNING DEPARTMENT, MARYLAND-NATIONAL CAPITAL PARK AND PLANNING COMMISSION, *Comprehensive Growth Policy Study, Volume I* (Silver Spring, MD: Maryland-National Capital Park and Planning Commission, 1989).

NEILSON, L., "Economic Perspective on Better Urban Space," presentation to Globe '90 Conference, Vancouver, B.C., March 20, 1990.

NEWMAN, P., "Social Organization for Ecological Sustainability: Towards a More Sustainable Settlement Pattern" in P. Cook, ed., *Social Structures for Sustainability,* Fundamental Questions Paper No. 11 (Canberra: Centre for Resource and Environmental Studies, Australian National University, 1990).

NEWMAN, P., "Greenhouse, Oil and Cities," *Futures,* May 1991a, pp. 335-348.

NEWMAN, P., "Suffocate City," *Consuming Interest,* June/July 1991b, pp. 13-18.

NEWMAN, P., "Urban Villages – Concept for the '90s," Presentation to ECODESIGN Conference, RMIT, Melbourne, Australia October 18-20, 1991c.

NEWMAN, P.W.G., AND J. R. KENWORTHY, "Transport and Urban Form in Thirty-Two of the World's Principal Cities," *Transport Reviews,* 1991, 11(3): 249-272.

O'BRIEN, F., "Toward a Greener, Cleaner Planet and a New Environmental Perspective," *Canadian Building,* May 1990.

OKAMOTO, P., "The Neo-Traditionalists: Peter Calthorpe and Andres Duany/Elizabeth Plater-Zyberk," *The Urban Ecologist,* Fall 1991.

OWENS, S.E., "Land Use Planning for Energy Efficiency," in Cullingworth, J.B., ed., *Energy, Land, and Public Policy* (New Brunswick, NJ: Transaction Publishers, 1990), pp. 53-98.

PETERBOROUGH TASK FORCE ON SUSTAINABLE DEVELOPMENT, *Report of the Task Force on Sustainable Development for the Peterborough Area* (Peterborough, Ontario: Task Force on

Sustainable Development, 1991).

REAL ESTATE RESEARCH CORPORATION, *The Costs of Sprawl,* Volume I: Detailed Cost Analysis (Washington, DC: US Government Printing Office, 1974).

REGIONAL MUNICIPALITY OF HALTON (Ontario), *Land Stewardship & Healthy Communities: A Vision for the 90's and Beyond,* Official Plan Review Report B4 (draft), January 1991.

RICHARDSON, N., "Sustainable Development and Land Use Planning," presentation to Association of Municipal Clerks and Treasurers of Ontario (AMCTO) and Intergovernmental Committee on Urban and Regional Research (ICURR) Management Symposium, "Implementing Sustainable Development in Municipalities," Hockley Valley, Ontario, May 8-10, 1991.

ROYAL COMMISSION ON THE FUTURE OF THE TORONTO WATERFRONT (RCFTW), D. Crombie, Commissioner, *Watershed* (Toronto: RCFTW, 1990).

ST. CATHERINES PLANNING REPORT July 22, 1987, Item No. 433, File 60.80.1.

STOKES, S.N., *ET AL, Saving America's Countryside: A Guide to Rural Conservation* (Baltimore: John Hopkins University Press, 1989).

STONE, K.E. AND R.H. FREILICH, "Writing a Defensible Growth Ordinance," in DeGrove 1991.

TAYLOR, M., "Mashpee Commons and Seaside," in Urban Ecology, *Report of the First International Ecological City Conference* (Berkeley, CA: Urban Ecology, 1990).

UNITED STATES DEPARTMENT OF TRANSPORTATION (US DOT), *Encouraging Public Transportation Through Effective Land Use Actions,* DOT-1-87-35, 1987, cited in Gordon 1991, pp. 160-161.

VAN DER RYN, S. AND P. CALTHORPE, eds., *Sustainable Communities: A New Design Synthesis for Cities, Suburbs and Towns* (San Francisco: Sierra Club Books, 1986).

YARO, R.D., *et al, Dealing With Change in the Connecticut River Valley: A Design Manual for Conservation and Development* (Amherst, MA: Center for Rural Massachusetts, University of Massachusetts at Amherst, 1988).

6

Energy Conservation and Efficiency

> *"It has been calculated that increasing energy efficiency alone could reduce carbon dioxide emissions in several high-income countries by between 1% and 2% per annum. On this basis the United States could readily cut its emissions by 60% by the year 2050."*
>
> IUCN 1991

Current practices for the development, conversion and use of energy resources – especially the burning of fossil fuels – contribute to global warming, acid rain, health dangers through air pollution and residuals deposition, and depletion of natural resources. These problems already exert significant negative worldwide economic, environmental and social impacts.

Furthermore, if the less developed countries increase their consumption to match that of the industrialized world, global stocks of petroleum will drop perilously low (see Frosch and Gallopoulos 1989). Energy demand and use is a major contributor to the degradation of environmental resources, requiring far-reaching and far-sighted new management strategies if sustainable global development is to occur.

Urban areas in Canada and the US are significant users of energy. Local as well as senior governments should encourage energy conservation, energy efficiency, and a shift away from fossil fuels in favour of renewable fuel sources.

Energy conservation reduces utility bills, saving money for local government and for the consumer. Conservation

Energy Terminology

"Energy conservation" refers to changes in personal and organizational behaviour that result in lower energy consumption. "Energy efficiency" refers to technological changes that allow us to do what we already do while using less energy. "Energy substitution" refers to using the most environmentally appropriate source of energy to do a necessary activity.

Slowing Global Warming

According to a US Environmental Protection Agency study, energy efficiency and renewable energy sources could play a major role in helping to slow and eventually stop global warming. If nations took full advantage of opportunities to improve energy efficiency, global fossil-fuel use and carbon dioxide emissions would grow slowly, if at all. And if, in addition, renewable energy sources were developed to their full potential, fossil-fuel use and carbon dioxide emissions could be cut well below today's levels, eventually approaching the 50-80 percent reduction necessary to stabilize the global climate.

(see US EPA 1989)

measures are far more cost-effective than building new power plants. Money spent on conservation stays in the local economy and helps develop local business.

As described in earlier chapters on transportation and land use, energy conservation should be an explicit objective of urban design. Conservation strategies can also be targeted at the residential, commercial and industrial sectors where large energy savings in lighting, heating, ventilating and air conditioning systems are possible (see OECD 1990; Local Government Commission 1990).

"Buildings in industrial countries typically devour 35-50 percent of national energy budgets, mostly for space heating and cooling, water heating, refrigeration, lighting, and cooking."

Lowe 1991

Renewable Energy Sources

"Renewable energy sources are often regarded as new or exotic, but in fact they are neither. Until quite recently, in historical terms, the world drew most of its energy from the sun, either directly from sunlight or indirectly through the natural processes that generate winds, rivers, and plants... The advantages of renewable energy sources – particularly wind, solar, and biomass (plant) energy – are, if anything, more compelling today than ever before. The technologies that have been developed, ranging from wind turbines and photovoltaic cells to liquid fuels derived from biomass, are of startling versatility. Most produce little or no pollution and hazardous wastes. Drawing entirely on domestic resources, they are immune to foreign disruptions like the 1973 Arab oil embargo, and since their 'fuel' – sunlight – is free, they provide a hedge against inflation caused by the depletion of fossil-fuel reserves. Their development would almost certainly result in a net increase in employment, as renewable-energy industries generally require more labor, per unit of energy produced, than coal, oil, and natural-gas industries."

(Brower 1990)

"More than five-sixths of all U.S. coal consumption occurs in electric power plants. Two-thirds of all sulphur dioxide emissions and almost one-third of carbon dioxide emissions in the United States result from the operations of coal and oil-fired power plant boilers."

OECD 1990

TOOLS

City Energy Policies

City energy policy can promote more effective land use, energy efficiency, mass transit, and conservation of resources at the local level. To promote urban sustainability, cities can:

"• Set examples as model energy consumers in the operation of municipal facilities, vehicle fleets, and mass transit systems.

• Plan, finance, and operate energy-efficient infrastructures for major water, waste water, and solid waste management systems.

• Regulate and plan for energy use through local land use policies that effect the patterns of residential, commercial and industrial development.

• Promote policies that improve air and water quality.

• Enforce the energy efficiency standards of building codes more stringently.

• Institute energy efficiency service programs (such as weatherization or appliance efficiency) aimed at various community sectors.

• Educate local residents and businesses by providing information on energy-efficient technologies, service providers, and financing opportunities.

• Adopt site standards for renewable and alternative energy resources.

• Use renewable resources such as solar, geothermal, hydroelectric, biomass, and wind at City-owned facilities [...]

• Advocate and facilitate the development and implementation of energy policies and programs by utilities and other levels of government." (City of San Jose 1991)

Least Cost Utility Planning

Least Cost Utility Planning (LCUP) has been implemented in a number of cities in the US. LCUP for electricity supplies is a concept that allows the consideration of investments for energy conservation and demand management on an equal footing with investments for new generating capacity. It formally treats energy conservation as an alternative energy source (what Amory Lovins calls "negawatts" rather than "megawatts"), and will support assessments of non-conventional decentralized smaller generators to substitute for large central generating plants. Applications of this concept require close co-ordination among utility regulators, individual utilities and local governments. To ensure effectiveness, LCUP programs commonly combine technical support and financial incentives for energy efficiency improvements that are targeted to residential, commercial and industrial consumers.

Movements to implement principles of least cost planning are in process in the majority of US state utility regulatory commissions. Although there is wide recognition of the potential benefits of LCUP, for the vast majority of US electric utilities, conservation is not a "profit making" endeavour. Major efforts to define utility incentives for LCUP and to address questions of stability, reliability and equity are currently in progress. (see OECD 1990)

District Heating and Cogeneration

District heating pipes hot water or steam generated at a central facility to each building in a neighbourhood or community. The source is often a business (e.g., hospital, university, hotel, or factory) that has its own cogenerating system. Cogeneration systems make electricity and steam together with one-third less fuel than is needed to produce each on its own; they are also well-suited to sophisticated

> **Dense Development and Solar Energy**
> **Denser development does not necessarily hamper the
> potential for using solar technologies in buildings.
> With design ingenuity, passive solar systems could be
> compatible with densities of up to 50 dwellings per
> hectare, or three times the number permitted by
> zoning codes in many North American suburbs.**
>
> **(see Owens 1990)**

pollution control equipment. District heating requires a
certain level of density to be effective. For example, in the
UK, 44 dwellings per hectare is considered the minimum
density for economical operation. (see Lowe 1991)

Solar Access Ordinances
Many local governments have adopted and implemented
solar access ordinances. The ordinances provide and
protect solar access to the south face of buildings during
solar heating hours, taking into account latitude,
topography, microclimate, existing development, existing
vegetation and planned uses and densities. Solar access
ordinances may include, but are not limited to, standards
for:
(a) The orientation of new streets, lots and parcels;
(b) The placement, height, bulk and orientation of new
    buildings;
(c) The type and placement of new trees on public street
    rights of way and other public property; and
(d) Planned uses and densities to conserve energy,
    facilitate the use of solar energy, or both. (see Oregon
Revised Statutes 1989)

Comprehensive Energy Plans
Some municipal comprehensive plans are required to
include an energy plan. In the state of Vermont, the

energy plan must include an analysis of energy resources, needs, scarcities, costs and problems within the municipality; a statement of policy on the conservation of energy, including programs, such as thermal integrity standards for buildings, to implement that policy; a statement of policy on the development of renewable energy resources; and a statement of policy on patterns and densities of land use likely to result in conservation of energy. (see Vermont Statutes Annotated 1989)

Solar Reflection

"Cities can [...] counteract the heat island effect by mixing asphalt with light-coloured sand, which reflects heat instead of retaining it, and by encouraging the use of lighter-coloured paints and building materials. In temperate climates, the gains from lighter surfaces in summer are significantly greater than any corresponding losses in winter, because the amount of solar radiation in winter is much smaller; the US National Academy of Sciences has estimated that strategic use of white surfaces and vegetation could save $2.6 billion in energy costs." (Lowe 1991)

INITIATIVES

Least-Cost Utility Planning

Uncertainty about the future cost of regional hydro power electricity, concern over the environmental impacts of building large scale hydroelectric power dams, the 1973 OPEC crisis, and citizen opposition to nuclear power prompted the City of *Seattle*, Washington to conduct a major study to define its energy alternatives. "Energy 1990" included sophisticated load forecasts based on economic models and defining a menu of (non-generating) alternatives to serve future load growth. Results from this first "least-cost" planning study in the region recommended a strong emphasis on conservation and indicated that future loads could be met without participation and substantial investment in the development of two new nuclear generating plants. Seattle has established by City Council Resolution the goal of reducing the need to expand or develop new generating facilities through conservation. With leadership from Seattle's Mayor, Council and citizen committees, the city and its municipally-owned utility now produce a biennial Strategic Corporate Plan to guide cost-effective and environmentally-sensitive electric power provision (see OECD 1990).

Energy Efficiency Targets
In April 1990, the City of *Portland*, Oregon adopted an energy policy with the goal of "increasing energy efficiency in all sectors of the City by 10 percent by the year 2000 so as to enhance the livability, economic strength and well-being of the City's residents and businesses and reduce environmental problems, such as air pollution and emissions that contribute to global warming." The policy specifies that the City will advocate energy efficiency, promote energy efficiency in city-owned buildings and in residential buildings, promote energy efficiency through land use regulations, encourage energy efficiency in commercial and industrial facilities, provide energy efficient transportation, research and support telecommunications as an energy efficiency strategy, promote conservation as the energy resource of first choice, and promote waste reduction and recycling (City of Portland 1990). The city's Energy Office has already helped to weatherize more than 5,500 apartment units, and plans to complete 2,500 more by the end of 1992. It has also assisted over 1,300 of the city's poorest families to weatherize single family homes (see ICLEI 1991).

Energy Conservation Retrofit Ordinances

San Francisco, California enacted a comprehensive residential energy conservation retrofit ordinance in 1982, which has already resulted in the retrofitting of over 25,000 residential units. The San Francisco ordinance requires all existing residential buildings, including apartment buildings, to be brought up to an energy conservation standard at the time of sale. The cost of the conservation measures can be included in the financing of the residential unit. Cost-effective conservation measures required by the ordinance include ceiling insulation, weather-stripping, a water heater insulation blanket, low-flow showerheads, caulking and sealing of major cracks and joints, and insulation of heating and cooling ducts. Additional measures are required of multi-family units. San Francisco also has a commercial energy conservation retrofit ordinance, which is estimated to save San Francisco businesses over $50 million in energy costs after the first five years (see Local Government Commission 1990).

Local Energy Supply Concept

In reaction to the oil price shock of the 1970s, the *Saarbrücken* public utility company, Stadtwerke Saarbrücken, initiated a Local Energy Supply Concept in 1980. The program is based on a few simple premises: reduce energy consumption, exploit energy better through district heating and through innovative technologies, and focus on renewable energy sources. Some 40,000 homes are now supplied with district heating rather than individual heating, "at almost no cost to the environment." Stadtwerke Saarbrücken also set up the largest privately used photovoltaic system in Europe, as part of their campaign to develop "solar power from the roofs of Saarbrücken." Saarbrücken (pop. 128,000) enables citizens to sell back to its municipal utility excess power generated by solar rooftop installations. The city has offered to "buy back" solar power from individual suppliers at about 15 US cents per kilowatt hour. The local public utility will reward homes that install rooftop solar collectors by "sharing" its monopoly on power production. The subsidy scheme in effect underwrites part of the cost of household solar conversion. Loans are also provided, through a local partner savings bank, for any household improvements related to energy efficiency, energy conservation, or water conservation.

Since 1980 Saarbrücken has achieved substantial emissions reductions with respect to NOx (34%), SO_2 (76%), and CO_2 (15%). With continued effort to develop photovoltaics and further expansion of the district heating network, Saarbrücken expects to reach the target called for by the Toronto Conference on the Changing Atmosphere, namely a 20% reduction in CO_2 emissions by 2005, *10 years earlier*. Perhaps more significant is that this goal will be attained without nuclear energy (see Leonhardt 1990; *PIA* 14(4), April 1990; ICLEI 1992).

District Heating and Cogeneration
Helsinki, Finland's district heating program has used cogeneration to reduce Helsinki energy demand to 30% of early 1970s levels (see Helsinki Energy Board 1989).

Weatherization
Seattle provides free home weatherization inspections and advice, plus low-interest loans for weatherization. The city has also developed a list of qualified weatherization contractors who are authorized to do the work and to be paid from low-interest loans. Encouragement to participate in cost-effective conservation efforts is also provided to self-motivated customers through city-sponsored educational and pilot programs (see OECD 1990).

Energy Audits and Loans

Public utilities in the German state of *Schleswig Holstein* are providing households with free energy audits and low interest loans for the purchase of energy-saving domestic appliances. Households that can demonstrate lower energy consumption with their 1991 bills over their 1990 bills will get an "environment bonus" of DM 50 (US $35) (see *PIA* 15(5), May 1991).

Sacramento, California's Municipal Utility District promotes audits and arranges complete residential efficiency upgrades for their customers. Utility staff target the program to neighbourhoods through personal contact in church group meetings, ratepayer groups, and other avenues. Interested homeowners sign up on the spot for an energy audit. The utility arranges the audit, and the inspector recommends an appropriate package of measures to improve efficiency. This typically includes improved insulation, weatherstripping, insulating the hot water tank, installing compact fluorescent fixtures and replacement of electric resistance heating with a heat pump. For simply agreeing to the audit, the utility provides the homeowner free of charge with compact fluorescent light bulbs, a high performance showerhead, and 2 trees which, when planted, will reduce air conditioning energy requirements. If the customer decides to proceed with the full package, the utility arranges for one of the various qualified private contractors to come in and do the work. Part of the cost is an outright grant (about $800) from the utility, and the rest of the cost (typically $3400) is put on the customer's hydro bill, amortized over 15 years. This extra charge on the power bill is less than the immediate reduction in energy costs, so the customer comes out ahead with lower power bills (see Millyard 1992).

Municipal Energy Conservation Campaigns

The municipal utility in *Osage*, Iowa conducted a successful energy conservation campaign which included sending infrared photos of energy leakage to each home in the town. The utility's efforts have saved the citizens of Osage $1.2 million annually.

Research and pilot programs in *Seattle* are under way in conjunction with small private industrial plants to build energy conservation into their manufacturing equipment and processes. Several industrial firms have participated in pilot projects to retrofit for energy efficiencies, and then monitor such equipment as motor drives, heating and cooling systems and lighting (see OECD 1990).

Solar Oven Cookbook

The municipal utility in *Sacramento*, California published a solar oven cookbook to promote solar cooking and thereby reduce air conditioning in overheated kitchens.

RESOURCES

CENTER FOR RENEWABLE RESOURCES, *Renewable Energy in Cities* (NY: Van Nostrand Reinhold, 1984). This book supplies some of the information needed to develop local energy plans and policies based on the use of energy conservation and renewable energy technologies. It provides technical information to help city energy officials discriminate between appropriate and inappropriate technologies and options; explains constraints and opportunities with respect to land use patterns, building stocks, energy supply and distribution networks, and social and economic conditions; and examines the links between energy and housing, employment, and economic development.

REG LANG AND AUDREY ARMOUR, *Planning Land to Conserve Energy: 40 Case Studies From Canada and the United States* (Ottawa: Lands Directorate, Environment Canada, 1982). Although the case studies are dated, this volume contains a wealth of useful information. The case studies are in five categories: community energy profiles, municipal plans and policies, new communities and residential development, non-residential land use, and land use and development controls.

THE LOCAL GOVERNMENT COMMISSION, a California organization providing technical assistance to local governments, is developing energy efficiency guidelines for cities in the areas of land use, transportation, solid waste recycling, and energy conservation in buildings.

Local Government Commission
909 12th Street, Sacramento, CA 94814

THE ROCKY MOUNTAIN INSTITUTE (RMI) is a non-profit research and educational foundation which fosters the efficient and sustainable use of resources as a path to global security. Founded by energy policy analysts Amory and Hunter Lovins in 1982, RMI is particularly strong in renewable energy and conservation, and in demonstrating that understanding interconnections between resource issues can often solve many problems at once. RMI's work is focused in five areas – agriculture, economic renewal, energy, security, and water – and it carries on international outreach and technical exchange programs. RMI also publishes an excellent quarterly *Newsletter*.

Rocky Mountain Institute
1739 Snowmass Creek Road
Old Snowmass, CO 81654-9199
Tel: 303/927-3851   Fax: 303/927-4178

References
BROWER, M., *Cool Energy: The Renewable Solution to Global Warming* (Cambridge, MA: Union of Concerned Scientists, 1990).

CENTER FOR RENEWABLE RESOURCES, *Renewable Energy in Cities* (NY: Van Nostrand Reinhold, 1984).

CITY OF PORTLAND ENERGY OFFICE, "Draft Portland Energy Policy," City Heat 2:1, Winter 1990, pp. 1-8.

CITY OF SAN JOSE, Sustainable City Strategy 1991-1992 (San Jose, CA: City of San Jose, Office of Environmental Management, 1991).

FROSCH, R.A. AND N.E. GALLOPOULOS, "Strategies for Manufacturing," *Scientific American* 261(3): 144-152, September 1989.

HELSINKI ENERGY BOARD, *District Heating* (Helsinki: Helsinki Energy Board, 1989).

INTERNATIONAL COUNCIL FOR LOCAL ENVIRONMENTAL INITIATIVES (ICLEI), *The Urban CO$_2$ Project* (Toronto: ICLEI, 1991).

INTERNATIONAL COUNCIL FOR LOCAL ENVIRONMENTAL INITIATIVES (ICLEI), "Energy Conservation/Finance: Saarbrücken, Germany," Case Study No. 4 (Toronto: ICLEI, 1992).

INTERNATIONAL UNION FOR CONSERVATION OF NATURE (IUCN), THE UNITED NATIONS ENVIRONMENT PROGRAMME (UNEP), and THE WORLD WIDE FUND FOR NATURE (WWF), *Caring for the Earth: A Strategy for Sustainable Living* (Gland, Switzerland: IUCN/UNEP/WWF, 1991).

LANG, R. AND A. ARMOUR, *Planning Land to Conserve Energy: 40 Case Studies From Canada and the United States* (Ottawa: Lands Directorate, Environment Canada, 1982).

LEONHARDT, W. (Chairman of the Board of Directors, Stadtwerke Saarbrücken AG, West Germany), "Local Concepts for the Reduction of CO2," presentation to the World Congress of Local Governments for a Sustainable Future, United Nations, New York, September 7, 1990.

LOCAL GOVERNMENT COMMISSION, "Model Ordinances for Environmental Protection" (Sacramento, CA: Local Government Commission, 1990).

LOWE, M.D., "Shaping Cities: The Environmental and Human Dimensions," Worldwatch Paper 105 (Washington, D.C.: Worldwatch Institute, 1991).

MILLYARD, K., "A Preliminary Carbon Dioxide Inventory for the City of Ottawa" (Ottawa: Friends of the Earth, 1992).

OREGON Revised Statutes, Title 20, Chapter 215. ORS @ 215.044 (1989).

ORGANIZATION FOR ECONOMIC COOPERATION AND DEVELOPMENT

(OECD), *Environmental Policies for Cities in the 1990s* (Paris: OECD, 1990).

OWENS, S.E., "Land Use Planning for Energy Efficiency," in Cullingworth, J.B., ed., *Energy, Land, and Public Policy* (New Brunswick, NJ: Transaction Publishers, 1990), pp. 53-98.

Public Innovation Abroad (PIA), various issues

US ENVIRONMENTAL PROTECTION AGENCY (US EPA), *Policy Options for Stabilizing Global Climate,* Report to Congress, 1989 (draft), cited in Brower, 1990.

VERMONT Statutes Annotated, Title 24, Part 2, Chapter 117, Subchapter 5 @ 4382 (1989).

7

Solid and Hazardous Waste Reduction and Recycling

Most North Americans generate about five pounds of solid waste each day – 90% of which ends up in landfills. Small wonder that many urban areas are running out or have run out of land disposal sites for solid wastes. Furthermore, high capital costs, public opposition to site selection, and uncertainties concerning the risks associated with emissions make incineration alternatives difficult to implement. To deal with solid wastes, waste reduction and recycling strategies will require major initiatives in many communities (see OECD 1990).

Solid wastes which are not recycled contribute to incinerator emissions or to the production of methane in landfills. Either way, they contribute to atmospheric pollution. Much of these wastes are in the form of nondegradable, nonreturnable, and nonrecyclable food and beverage packaging. Household organic wastes which are not composted also contribute to the production of methane. In addition, our garbage represents the energy equivalent of millions of wasted barrels of oil and other nonrenewable natural resources.

Local governments need to develop comprehensive waste reduction strategies, focusing first on source reduction, then on reuse and recycling. Only when these approaches are exhausted should local governments turn to other, less environmentally sound alternatives.

Hazardous and toxic materials in the waste stream are also a great concern in many communities. Urgent action

> *"Although the exact ingredients of local garbage vary by place and time, the experts say our garbage consists of about 65% commercial wastes and 35% residential wastes. About 37% of the average waste stream is made up of paper and cardboard, 26% is yard and food wastes, 10% is glass, 10% is metals, 8% is plastics, and the remainder is miscellaneous wastes... Packaging materials account for a third of the volume of our waste."*
>
> Local Government Commission 1990

is needed to reduce the amount and increase the recycling of hazardous waste and to ensure the proper disposal of what is left. This has prompted some local governments to provide businesses with technical assistance to reduce their hazardous and toxic wastes.

An essential part of a comprehensive waste reduction strategy is a procurement policy to purchase recycled and/ or reusable products (see Chapter 12).

TOOLS

"Designing for Total Recycling
- 'Waste' is not waste until it's wasted.
- Recyclers handle discards, not wastes. Recyclers sometimes waste things, but their ultimate goal is to waste nothing.
- Recycling manages the supply of discards, not wastes. The term 'waste management' should be reserved for the garbage disposal industry.
- Recycling is a form of disposal.
- Gaining access to the disposal fee is the key to unlocking recycling's potential.
- All of what is now garbage can be sorted into twelve broad categories of recyclable material (see below).
- To plan a discard management system in which recycling is the preferred disposal technology, begin

with a composition study to establish the proportion and volume of each of the twelve master categories.

- Each locality should do composition studies, and results should be made public and shared. Observational studies that sort and weigh are preferable to 'desktop studies' that import data from other localities or use esoteric methodologies.
- A comprehensive recycling system is one in which there are opportunities to recycle all twelve of the master discard categories. Recycling systems should not be called comprehensive until all twelve of the master categories are provided for.
- The twelve master categories provide a way to estimate progress toward the goal of total recycling.
- We will move toward total recycling in incremental steps, not all at once.
- Banning and precycling (source reduction) are valid and useful tools for achieving the goal of total recycling.

The Twelve Master Categories for Recycling

1 *Reusable goods,* including but not limited to intact or repairable home or industrial appliances; household goods; clothing; intact materials in demolition debris, such as lumber; building materials such as doors, windows, cabinets, and sinks; business supplies and equipment; lighting fixtures; and any manufactured item or naturally occurring object that can be repaired or used again as is.

2 *Paper,* including but not limited to newsprint; ledger paper; computer paper; corrugated cardboard; and mixed paper.

3 *Metals,* both ferrous and nonferrous; including but not limited to cans; parts from abandoned vehicles; plumbing; fences; metal doors and screens; and any other discarded metal objects.

"In a 1989 survey of 100 licensed renovation firms, it was determined that during a 12 month period, over 8,000 reusable items were sent to landfill sites: [these included] 711 kitchen sinks; 455 bathtubs; 570 refrigerators; 3,777 interior doors; and 2,611 exterior doors. There are tens of thousands of licensed renovation firms across Canada plus countless informal operations adding to these numbers on an ongoing basis."

D'Amour 1991

4 *Glass,* including but not limited to glass containers and window glass.

5 *Textiles,* including but not limited to nonreusable clothing; upholstery; and pieces of fabric.

6 *Plastics,* including beverage containers; plastic packaging; plastic cases of consumer goods such as telephones or electronic equipment; and tires.

7 *Plant debris,* including but not limited to *leaves and* cuttings; trimmings from trees; shrubs; and grass.

8 *Putrescibles,* including garbage; animal, fruit, and vegetable debris; and offal.

9 *Wood,* including but not limited to nonreusable lumber; and pallets.

10 *Ceramics,* including rock; ceramic; brick; and concrete.

11 *Soils,* including but not limited to excavation soils from barren or developed land; and excess soils from yards.

12 *Chemicals.*

13 *(Garbage* – this category is reserved for unrecyclable mixtures of recyclable materials.)" (Knapp 1990)

Source Reduction Strategies for Local Governments

- Variable Can Rate (higher rate for more garbage cans)
- Second-Hand, Consignment, and Repair Shops (change zoning to encourage)
- Salvage Yards: Berkeley's salvage yard is connected

One Way to Reduce Packaging Waste
Half the food served by one major fast food chain is consumed inside restaurants where there is no need for disposable packaging of any sort, polystyrene or paper. Switching to china cups and plates for table service would immediately eliminate packaging waste by 50 percent.

(see Balcom 1990)

---

to its transfer station. The refuse workers remove salvageable materials like furniture, building materials, etc. from the tipping floor and independent haulers are encouraged to go to the salvage yard first to lighten their load. This reduces both the fee they pay at the transfer station and the amount of waste sent to the dump.

- Plastics and Packaging Reduction Laws (see Minneapolis description under Initiatives). Also, require that food eaten on the premises be served in washable reusables rather than disposable products.
- Taxes or fees on disposables: most U.S. cities can't do this, but counties can.
- Public Education: Berkeley's "Precycle" campaign encourages people to consider waste *before* they buy.
- Taxes or fees on disposal of large appliances
- Government and large office facility programs: two-sided copying; washable dishes in cafeterias and coffee rooms; air or cloth rather than paper towels/dryers; including durability in purchasing standards for tires and other products (see Skinner 1990.

Three Forms of Recycling

"The best form of recycling occurs when we re-use the original product. Refillable bottles, cloth diapers, refurbished appliances save virtually 100 percent of the energy, pollution, and materials required to make them in the first place – and the savings multiply with each reuse. Recycling materials into their original form is a second-best strategy. Recycling glass into glass, or newsprint into newsprint, saves 20 to 95 percent of the energy, water, mining wastes, and air pollution consumed or produced to process the product from virgin materials [...] The worst form of recycling transforms a material into a secondary form. Glass into 'glassphalt' for roads, paper into compost, plastic bottles into park benches do little to avoid the need to extract new materials and thus do little to reduce pollution."

(Morris 1989)

Pollution Prevention

In the US, state governments have led the transition to pollution prevention. Several states have passed laws which rest on a simple argument: the use of every toxic chemical should be reduced or eliminated. These new laws bypass debates over acceptable levels of toxicity and the risks of specific exposure levels or releases; they neither require risk assessments nor establish thresholds for chemical exposure. Instead, they set up reporting and planning responsibilities for firms that handle specified toxic substances. Many of the laws set a statewide goal for stemming the use of toxic chemicals or the amount of hazardous wastes generated, but they leave it up to firms to design their own "facility plans" for how to meet the goals. In other words, the plans give firms the responsibility

174

to reduce the use of toxics.

"These laws stretch the boundaries of pollution prevention in several significant ways. First, they focus on chemicals in use rather than on wastes. Second, firms must set goals and make plans, not just comply with an emissions limit. This emphasizes creativity and innovative technology. Third, the laws encourage continuous improvement, not simply reaching a regulatory threshold." (Geiser 1991)

Toxics use reduction foreshadows the idea of sustainable industry by focusing on materials policy as much as on environmental or waste policy. The "precautionary principle" contrasts with policies that simply seek to keep risks to a supposedly manageable level. "Precaution shifts the burden of proving safety from those who would protect the environment to those who would release chemicals into it. And like toxics use reduction, it bases decisions about releases on available options, not on the environment's assimilative capacity. The new adage is 'When in doubt, don't throw it out'." (Geiser 1991)

Toxics Use Reduction

There is only one effective way to prevent toxic contamination: by reducing the use of hazardous substances and the generation of hazardous wastes at the source of production. This can be accomplished through strategies such as:

- Shifting to a product where the manufacturing process requires less production of hazardous waste;
- Substituting a less hazardous substance as part of the production process;
- Conserving the use of hazardous substances by using more efficient housekeeping practices;
- Designing new processes and equipment that result in less waste production;

• Recycling hazardous waste, preferably at the site
where it is produced

Three basic strategies are available to local governments
to help industries reduce the amount of hazardous waste
they produce: educational programs, technical assistance
programs, and regulatory programs. (see Local
Government Commission 1990)

INITIATIVES

Waste Reduction Targets

In 1988 Seattle adopted a resolution establishing a goal of
reducing solid waste in the City by 60% by 1998 with
intermediate goals of 40% by 1991 and 50% by 1993 (City
of Seattle 1988). Recycling, composting, and avoiding
waste production are noted as the primary waste
management strategies. The resolution outlines specific
programs and a time line for implementation. Seattle also
operates a municipal compost operation and provides bins
and training to homeowners for backyard composting.

Packaging Restrictions

In 1989 *Minneapolis* placed severe restrictions on food
and beverage packaging – including national brands –
originating at retail food establishments. "The Council
therefore finds that the minimization of nondegradable,
nonreturnable and nonrecyclable food and beverage
packaging [...] is necessary and desirable in order to reduce
the City's waste stream, so as to reduce the volume of
landfilled waste, to minimize toxic by-products of
incineration, and to make our City and neighboring
communities more environmentally sound places to live."
(Minneapolis Code of Ordinances 1989)

Although the ordinance was initially opposed by the
Minnesota Grocers Association and the Council for Solid

Waste Solutions (a plastics industry group), it was passed unanimously by city policymakers. Rather than battle the ordinance, the plastics industry chose to work with local officials. The Council for Solid Waste Solutions offered to sponsor a six-month pilot recycling program to prove that plastics recycling was possible. The program impressed city environmental leaders, who now believe that recycling is a realistic option for certain products. As a result, the ban will not be as sweeping as originally proposed. However, to meet the new law's guidelines, an actual recycling system must be operating. McDonald's clamshell containers, for instance, have always been technically recyclable, but no one was actually doing it in Minneapolis prior to the new law (see Minneapolis Code of Ordinances 1989; Bulletin of Municipal Foreign Policy 1991).

Municipal Garbage Composting

As part of its waste reduction strategy, in 1991 *Portland* opened the first municipal garbage composting facility in the U.S. The facility is capable of handling 185,000 tons of garbage a year (see ICLEI 1991).

Hazardous Waste Reduction

The California cities of *Hayward, Santa Monica* and *Berkeley* have staff who provide businesses with technical assistance to reduce their generation of hazardous waste (see Skinner 1990).

Santa Monica distributes brochures to targeted small businesses which outline specific waste reduction measures. These include information for vehicle and equipment repair shops, machine toolers, the printed circuit board industry, metal finishing industry, general commercial printers, commercial dry cleaners, paint formulating industry, photographic processors, and automotive painting businesses.

Seven of *North Carolina's* POTWs (Publicly Owned Treatment Works) help industries reduce their regulated wastes by providing in-depth technical assistance to local companies through on-site waste reduction consultations as a routine part of compliance inspections (see Local Government Commission 1990).

Comprehensive Resource Recovery and Utilization
For a humbling perspective on even the most ambitious North American recycling programs, consider this Chinese example from *Shanghai.*

"The Shanghai Municipal Environmental Administration serves a 150 square-kilometre city (Shanghai) and 6035 square kilometres of suburbs and rural areas around the city core with a total population of some 12 million. Since 1957, it has developed a State complex retrieving materials and marketing the reclaimed products and now has some 29,000 full-time and many more part-time employees.

A network of 502 purchasing stations and 1500 purchasing agents in rural areas acquire material for reclamation or recycling and are paid on commission. Twenty-six integrated recycling centres reclaim or recycle material from industrial and consumer wastes and a network of sales departments and retail shops sell reclaimed products.

Among the materials recovered from wastes are ferrous and non-ferrous metals, rubber, plastics, paper, rags, cotton, chemical fibres, animal bones, human hair, broken glass, glass bottles, old machine parts, chemical residues and waste oil. The company has subsidiaries for copper refining, precious metal recovery and refining, iron and steel scrap recycling, plastics production, ferrous metal production and oil wastes recycling. In addition, there are over 3600 people employed to work with factories – for instance advising them on setting up containers for wastes and establishing systems by which the company can collect them." (Gunnerson 1989).

Recycling Land Use Controls

Several communities now set recycling space standards for all new buildings (see Canli and Gordon 1991). In *Santa Monica*, California, residential buildings with 10 or more units are required to provide 100 square feet for recycling facilities for the first 10 units and five square feet for each additional unit. Commercial buildings over 10,000 square feet must set aside 1,000 square feet for recycling for the first 10,000 square feet, then five square feet for each additional 1,000 square feet. The city is allowing its recycling program to mature before it specifies the types of bins required.

Davis, California requires the provision of at least three recycling carts for each trash enclosure in dwellings with 10 or more units. Building owners must submit collection plans for recyclable materials and provide occupants with information on the building's plan and the city's recycling program.

Developers in *Boulder*, Colorado seeking residential building permits must score at least 20 points among several categories of conservation measures. Providing a recycling facility and retrofitting for recycling each earn two points.

Orlando, Florida requires developers of large projects to agree to ensure that the development's tenants and future owners will participate in the city's recycling program.

Portland, Oregon requires new developments of three or more units to have recycling collection areas of at least 100 cubic feet for every 10 units, with specific requirements.

Apartment Recycling

The City of *North Vancouver*, British Columbia is providing curbside recycling to all apartments, townhouses and condominiums in North and West Vancouver. The city delivers big bins to apartment buildings and a local recycling firm collects the material weekly. The city has passed a bylaw requiring new buildings to provide space for the bins (see Gram 1990).

Redistributing Recycling Subsidies

An extra surcharge of A$ 1.50 per ton is being levied on Australian local governments in New South Wales which do not have recycling programs. Local governments with active recycling programs are expected to receive an average of A$ 17.50 per ton of reclaimed materials from the extra landfill charges, a subsidy of tens of thousands of dollars. The redistribution should provide a substantial incentive to start recycling, and officials hope it will double the estimated 100,000 tons currently recycled in the state (see *PIA* 15(4), April 1991).

Dishmobile

The German town of *Boeblingen* (pop. 42,000) has acquired a new "dishmobile" for food service at public festivals. Equipped with a commercial-size dishwasher and enough plates and silverware to serve 600 guests, the mobile facility is also available for a modest user charge to serve clubs and voluntary groups for their own festivities. Tens of thousands of non-biodegradable food containers will avoid the landfill as a result of the facility. The dishwasher on wheels, with its associated plates and equipment, cost approximately US $15,000 (see *PIA* 14(5), May 1990).

RESOURCES

LOCAL SOLUTIONS TO GLOBAL POLLUTION (LSGP) is a clearinghouse which provides technical assistance in developing pollution prevention programs on the community level and in the workplace. Their materials and information are directed toward local government officials, grassroots groups, citizens, businesses, and employees. LSGP is an outgrowth of an informal clearinghouse established by Berkeley City Councilmember Nancy Skinner in response to requests for information on polystyrene foam/plastics legislation and other innovative environmental programs. LSGP is particularly strong on "source reduction" – a concept which redefines "waste" to eliminate the unnecessary disposal of useful materials, promotes the reuse of materials now discarded, and challenges the use of those materials that are difficult to reuse or recycle, or that have significant polluting impacts in their manufacture and use. LSGP's source reduction focus has been on plastics, packaging, and single use disposable products. A variety of information packets containing fact sheets, ordinances, background articles, etc. are available from:

> Local Solutions to Global Pollution
> 2121 Bonar Street, Studio A
> Berkeley, CA 94702
> Tel: 415/540-8843   Fax: 415/540-4898

INSTITUTE FOR LOCAL SELF-RELIANCE, *Beyond 40 Percent: Record-Setting Recycling and Composting Programs* (Washington, D.C. & Covelo, CA: Island Press, 1991). This book offers ample proof that community recycling and composting operations can be our primary solid-waste management strategies. Case studies document the operating experiences of seventeen US communities – urban, suburban, and rural – all with materials recovery levels of over 30 percent. Fourteen have total, residential, or commercial materials recovery rates at or above 40 percent. The book discusses the advantages of mandatory recycling, its economic incentives, the collection of source-separated yard wastes for composting programs, and the benefits of extending programs beyond the residential sector to the commercial sector. It also provides specific examples of how your community can plan and implement recycling and composting programs that will work. The Institute for Local Self-Reliance is a non-profit organization promoting self-reliance for cities. Since 1974 ILSR has been providing research and technical assistance to citizens, local governments, and small businesses on waste utilization, closed-loop manufacturing, and materials policy. *Beyond 40 Percent* is part of an ongoing series of technical reports prepared by ILSR staff. For more information, contact:

Institute for Local Self-Reliance
2425 18th Street NW
Washington, DC 20009
Tel: 202/232-4108   Fax: 202/332-0463

Public Innovation Abroad is a monthly newsletter that promotes "the international exchange of practical experience in dealing with common problems at the state, county and city levels of government." Particularly good on transportation and recycling initiatives. Available from:

International Academy of State and Local Governments
444 North Capitol Street, N.W., Suite 349
Washington, D.C. 20001
Tel: 202/638-1445   Fax: 202/638-5109

THE NATIONAL ROUND TABLE ON THE ENVIRONMENT AND THE ECONOMY has published The *National Waste Reduction Handbook: An Introduction to Source Reduction and Recycling for Municipal Decision-Makers.*

For information contact:
The National Round Table on the Environment and
the Economy
1 Nicholas Street, Suite 520
Ottawa, Ontario K1N 7B7
Tel: 613/943-2055 or 0394

References

BALCOM, S., "Consumer Beat," *Vancouver Sun,* November 9, 1990, p. D8.

BULLETIN OF MUNICIPAL FOREIGN POLICY, "Working Together for a Cleaner Planet," *Bulletin of Municipal Foreign Policy,* Vol. 5, No.2, Spring 1991, p.16.

CANLI, S. AND S.W. GORDON, "New on the Recycling Scene: Land Use Controls," *Urban Land,* May 1991, pp. 34-35.

CITY OF SEATTLE, Resolution 27871 (1988).

D'AMOUR, D., "The Origins of Sustainable Development and Its Relationship to Housing and Community Planning," Sustainable Development and Housing Research Paper No. 1 (Ottawa: Canada Mortgage and Housing Corporation, 1991).

GEISER, K., "The Greening of Industry: Managing the Transition to a Sustainable Economy," *Technology Review,* August/September 1991, pp. 64-72.

GRAM, K., "North Shore Sets the Recycling Pace," *Vancouver Sun,* December 8, 1990, p. G11.

GUNNERSON, C.G., *Resource Recovery and Utilization in Shanghai,* UNDP/World Bank Global Programme of Resource Recovery (s.I., 1987), cited in United Nations Centre for Human Settlement (Habitat), *Urbanization and Sustainable Development in the Third World: An Unrecognized Global Issue* (Nairobi: United Nations Centre for Human Settlement (Habitat), 1989).

INSTITUTE FOR LOCAL SELF-RELIANCE, *Beyond 40 Percent: Record-Setting Recycling and Composting Programs* (Washington, D.C. & Covelo, CA: Island Press, 1991).

INTERNATIONAL COMMISSION FOR LOCAL ENVIRONMENTAL INITIATIVES (ICLEI), *The Urban CO$_2$ Project* (Toronto: ICLEI, 1991).

KNAPP, D., "Designing for Total Recycling," in Urban Ecology,

Report of the First International Ecological City Conference (Berkeley, CA: Urban Ecology, 1990).

LOCAL GOVERNMENT COMMISSION, "Model Ordinances for Environmental Protection" (Sacramento, CA: Local Government Commission, 1990).

MINNEAPOLIS CODE OF ORDINANCES, 1989, Amending Title 10, Adding a New Chapter 204, "Environmental Preservation: Environmentally Acceptable Packaging."

MORRIS, D., "The Materials We Need to Create a Sustainable Society Lie Close to Home," *Utne Reader* No. 36, Nov/Dec 1989, pp. 84-90.

ORGANIZATION FOR ECONOMIC COOPERATION AND DEVELOPMENT (OECD), *Environmental Policies for Cities in the 1990s* (Paris: OECD, 1990).

Public Innovation Abroad (PIA), various issues.

SKINNER, N., "Source Reduction Strategies: The Key to Reducing Waste," presented to the World Congress of Local Governments for a Sustainable Future, United Nations, New York, September 5, 1990.

8

Water and Sewage

The quality of water affects the quality of the life it touches. Both groundwater and surface water systems have deteriorated in quality in many urban areas. In cities, the rates of water use and water pollution are a primary concern. Urban water management requires a great deal of space and energy for both supply and wastewater treatment.

Water pollution in combination with a too rapid rate of water extraction can cause serious harm to hydrological systems. In the US, for example, the maintenance of adequate water supplies to urban areas in the western states and some of the major population centres of the northeastern states is emerging as a major issue, with rationing and curtailment of non-essential water use implemented in many of these areas during hot dry summers (see OECD 1990).

Wastewater treatment is a particular concern in many communities. Many municipal wastewater treatment facilities are designed to provide at least secondary treatment. At the community level, contemporary wastewater treatment technologies are major environmental polluters on at least three fronts:

- They produce an often-toxic by-product called sludge which is difficult to dispose of.
- They use hazardous compounds in the treatment process which end up in the environment.
- Without massive federal subsidies, most communities

Water Quality and Land Use
"While it is commonly recognized that specific activities such as sewage treatment or paper processing can be notorious water polluters, it is less widely understood that whole categories of land use, as well, are inherent threats to water quality. For example, car-dominated urban areas contaminate stormwater runoff with salt, oil, and toxic fluids from roads and parking lots. Suburbs allow large amounts of chemical fertilizers and pesticides to run off golf courses and large lawns. Construction sites from which trees and other natural vegetation are stripped add large amounts of eroded soil to runoff. Often, stormwater from cities and suburbs – together with agricultural runoff containing chemicals and animal wastes – constitute a greater hazard to water quality than factories and other specific sources do."

(Lowe 1991)

cannot afford to build and operate advanced wastewater treatment facilities; their huge, expensive infrastructure is also difficult to change or adapt.

Sustainable approaches to water management are urgently needed. Sustainable water management would aim to:

- treat water at its pollution source;
- discharge as high or higher quality water than is received; and
- prevent soil and land degradation (healthy terrestrial ecosystems purify water).

Many of the same land use principles that help urban and suburban areas to save energy – such as clustering development, discouraging automobile-oriented land use, and leaving natural vegetation intact – can help to assure that water resources will survive well into the future. (see Lowe 1991)

Negawatts from Negagallons
"Southern California Edison fixes toilet leaks. Connecticut Light and Power distributes faucet aerators. Pacific Gas and Electric funds irrigation improvements. What's going on here? Why should these companies, whose primary business is selling electricity and natural gas, care whether their customers waste *water*?

The answer is that providing water takes far more energy than most people realize. Before water reaches fields or taps, it generally must be pumped, sometimes across entire states. In our homes, water heaters add warmth for showers and baths. Flowing down the drain, water goes to a treatment plant to be pumped some more. Some water-short communities even face the prospect of using mammoth quantities of energy to transform saltwater into fresh. In a modern society, water is not just H_2O; it's a form of embodied energy. Over the past few years, growing numbers of utilities have begun to recognize that saving water saves energy. As a general rule, water efficiency is good for the environment and lucrative for farmers, consumers, and utilities. For a company like Southern California Edison, 10% of whose power is used to treat, heat, and pump water, negagallons equal negawatts equal megabucks. That's why they want to fix those leaky toilets."

(RMI 1991)

> "*In the Lower Fraser the major concern is related to municipal effluents originating from the three Greater Vancouver sewage treatment plants which only have primary treatment. More than 80% of all BOD, fecal coliforms, SS, nutrients, and trace metals (Cu) originate from the three sewage treatment plants. Stormwater inputs are of great diversity and highly variable depending on land use and rainfall events. The first hour of stormwater flush exceeds nutrient, metal and organic contaminant loads from all sewage treatment plants in the same time period.*"
>
> Schreier et al 1991

TOOLS

Some Sewage Definitions

"Sewage – The slurry that travels through municipal sewer pipes and includes mostly water from toilets, sinks, washing machines and dishwashers, but also human excreta, detergents, cleaners, decloggers, tampons, condoms, other miscellaneous items, and industrial wastes.

Septage – The truly disgusting stuff pumped out of septic tanks by 'honey wagons.' Often includes restaurant greases, toxic industrial byproducts, and hospital wastes.

Sludge – The thick slurry of 'solids' removed from sewage at treatment plants.

Biological Oxygen Demand (BOD) – The dissolved oxygen needed to decompose organic matter in water. BOD is used as a measure of pollution, since heavy waste loads need lots of oxygen to be broken down.

Nitrogen – A nutrient most commonly found in sewage in the form of ammonia and nitrates. Too much nitrogen in waterways causes algae blooms, and ammonia is toxic to fish.

Phosphorus – A nutrient most commonly found in sewage in the form of phosphates from detergents. A primary cause of algae blooms in waterways.

Suspended Solids – Tiny pieces of pollutants floating on or suspended in sewage.

Preliminary Treatment – The first thing that happens at any treatment plant: large objects (tampons and condoms) and "floatables" (plastic tampon applicators) are screened out and grit is removed.

Primary Treatment – The first stage of sewage treatment. The wastewater is held in settling tanks or basins so that roughly one-third of the biological oxygen demand and two-thirds of the suspended solids are removed.

Secondary Treatment – The second stage of sewage treatment, in which bacteria are used to treat the wastes. Removes about 90 percent of the biological oxygen demand and the suspended solids.

Tertiary Treatment – Advanced cleaning of wastewater that goes beyond the secondary stage and removes nutrients such as nitrogen and phosphorus and most suspended solids.

Wetlands – The trendy term for what used to be known as marshes, swamps, and bogs." (Marinelli 1990)

Land Applications of Municipal Waste Water
"A significant amount of research has been done over the past twenty years which has shown that forests can be used as land treatment systems to renovate secondary treated waste water for direct recharge to the groundwater table [...] A land application of municipal waste water provides many advantages to a community beset with waste water disposal problems [...] It provides an opportunity for water pollution abatement. It provides an opportunity for the recycling and beneficial use of the nutrients contained in the waste water. It allows for the replenishment of local groundwater supplies and for the preservation of open space or open greenbelts." (Sopper 1990)

"Comparing Sewage Treatment Technologies	
TYPE	**ADVANTAGES**
Conventional Sewage Treatment	Old technology, so engineers know exactly what to expect; doesn't require a lot of land
M a n - M a d e Marshes (with open water)	Cheap; no sludge; good removal of nitrogen, toxic chemicals, and trace organics; can survive toxic overload better than conventional treatment; can be used for secondary or advanced treatment without chemicals or a lot of energy; wastewater can be used to restore wetlands habitat; nice to look at
Man-Made 'Rock Marshes' (submerged flow systems	Efficient; can include showy ornamental plants; routine harvesting of plants unnecessary
Solar Aquatics	Virtually purifies water; effective in cold climates; creates substantially less sludge than conventional treatment; can treat extremely concentrated wastes such as septage; may cost significantly less than conventional treatment; sewage is treated as a resource not as a waste; produces potentially valuable plants and fish; nice to look at; requires less land than marshes

(Marinelli 1990)

LIMITATIONS	BEST FOR
Expensive; cranky; 'shock loadings' or sudden inflows of toxics (usually from industry) often upset the bacterial balance, sending barely treated sewage into the local waterway; energy intensive; advanced wastewater treatment often involves the use of toxic chemicals; hard to site [...]; sludge disposal is a major headache	**Big cities**
Require lots of land; plants may have to be harvested occasionally	**Small communities with a lot of land**
Rocks can be expensive; not as extensively tested as open-water marshes	**Small communities with extra land**
Leading-edge technology not as extensively tested as the other systems; requires a different kind of expertise; the greenhouse is an added cost and must be heated in winter	**Communities that have to meet stringent water-quality requirements; communities that have a septage problem; could prove to be a natural alternative for land-short cities"**

INITIATIVES

Water Offset Requirements
In the California cities of *Santa Barbara, San Luis Obispo*, and *Santa Monica*, water offset requirements on new projects require developers to replace old toilets in existing buildings with low-flow models in order to free up enough water to build (see Fulton 1991).

In Ontario, the Town of *Newmarket* requires water-saving devices in toilets as a condition of subdivision agreement, while the City of *Niagara Falls* requires low-flow bathroom basin faucets, showerheads, and toilets for any development subject to site plan control and for new plans for subdivision.

Tenant User Fees for Water
To protect water reserves and reduce the use of drinking water in the metropolitan area, the city government of *Hamburg*, Germany (pop. 1.8 million) has made tenants rather than property owners responsible for the water use fee. The ruling will lead to the retrofitting of water meters in apartments and end automatic billing of owners for water use based only on the size of their property and the number of occupants (see *PIA* 14(1), January 1990).

Grey Water Recycling
The *Los Angeles* county board of supervisors voted for a study on the safe use of "grey water" – recycled waste water from residential sources. Without objection, the board ordered the departments of health services and public works to issue recommendations within 60 days on how residents might use grey water from sinks, bathtubs and washing machines to irrigate trees and shrubs (see LADN 1991). *San Luis Obispo,* California allows the use of grey water (see Skinner 1990).

Natural Water Purification

A swamp pond system that purifies water by running it through some 125,000 plants of 11 species has turned an artificial lake on *Montreal's* Expo 67 site into an ecological preserve. The lake balances nature, recreation and public use. The three pond purification system on the Ile Notre Dame recreational lake has resulted in a wetlands preserve that has helped to make the lake safe for swimming without resort to chemical treatment such as chlorination (see *PIA* 15(2), February 1991).

Constructed Wetlands

Arcata, California (pop. 15,000) completed one of the first marsh-ecology sewage treatment systems in 1987. When Arcatans flush, gravity takes their wastewater to a conventional treatment plant on the edge of the bay, where it is screened and solids settle out. The effluent is piped to 50 acres of oxidation ponds, where algae work on the wastes and more solids are removed. The wastewater then flows into two 2-1/2 acre man-made marshes planted with bulrush and cattail, where the sewage effluent is "polished" (given advanced wastewater treatment). Next it flows into 45 acres of marshes constructed by the city and the California Coastal Conservancy to help restore fish, shellfish, waterfowl and other wildlife to the area. By the time it flows into Humboldt Bay, the effluent is cleaner than the water it meets there. Total cost of the system, including planning and environmental studies and acquisition of some land: $514,600 (see Marinelli 1990).

Denham Springs, Louisiana (pop. 20,000) runs its processed sewage through two shallow 40-acre ponds that have been lined, carpeted with stones, filled with water, and planted with lilies and other plants. Although it looks like a flower farm in summer, the facility can treat 3 million gallons of sewage per day. Compared with conventional treatment, the city saved $1 million in initial construction costs and will save $60,000 per year on operation and maintenance. Maintenance consists mostly of removing the dead plant tops in spring before new shoots start poking up (MacLeish 1990; Marinelli 1990).

Water Conservation Programs

Santa Monica, California and *Minneapolis* and *St. Paul*, Minnesota provide residents water conservation devices with free or low-cost installation (Skinner 1990). Santa Monica has installed low-flow toilets in one-quarter of the city's homes, saving almost a million gallons of water every day. The $2.8 million program, which offered free installation or rebates to cover installation costs of the low-flow toilets and shower heads, was financed by a conservation incentive fee (participants were exempt from this surcharge on their water bill), general water revenues, and money from the water wholesaler. The program has reduced per capita consumption for indoor use from 80 gallons to 50 gallons per day. It also eases demand on the municipal wastewater treatment system (see MacLeish 1990). Santa Monica has also installed treatment systems at drainage points for the city's storm drain system (see Skinner 1990).

The Metropolitan Water District of *Southern California* is promoting 16 "best management practices" for water conservation, including: installing low-flush toilets and other water-conserving fixtures; checking distribution systems for leaks and repairing them; installing meters with all new water hook-ups and billing by volume of water use; enacting water-efficient landscaping ordinances; providing incentives for reducing peak demand; and designating a water conservation coordinator to prepare and implement a conservation plan (see Schilling 1992).

Solar Aquatic Waste Treatment Facilities

Designed by Dr. John Todd of Ocean Arks International (see Resources), the first solar aquatic waste treatment facilities opened in **Providence**, Rhode Island in July 1989 and **Harwich**, Massachusetts in May, 1990. The Solar Aquatic System,™ or SAS, duplicates, under controlled conditions, the natural water purification processes of freshwater wetlands. Wastewater is circulated inside a greenhouse through a series of clear tanks, each with its own aquatic ecosystem, and marshes. In this treatment process, sunlight, oxygen, bacteria, algae, plants, snails and fish work together to purify the water. SAS uses aeration and mixing in the tanks to prevent sludge from settling. This enhances degradation of solids and results in fewer solids than conventional wastewater systems (see EEA n.d.).

The experimental Providence facility is an 11 by 40 metre (30 by 120 feet) greenhouse which treats up to 20,000 gallons of sewage per day, or about the amount from 150 households. To treat the whole city's wastes would require about 120 acres, comparable to the acreage now used to treat its wastes to secondary standards. Since the SAS waste doesn't stink, it can be disaggregated: each neighbourhood or community could have its own facility and use its own by-products, tree saplings, flowers, etc., to enhance the environment and urban landscaping, and as a source of income. The facilities are modestly more cost-effective than ordinary secondary treatment plants; for dealing with very concentrated wastes, like septage, which is 30-100 times more concentrated than sewage and hard to treat conventionally, the plants are far more cost effective than any other technology. They also create substantially less sludge than conventional treatment (see CBC 1990; Marinelli 1990).

The Solar Aquatic Waste Purification Research Facility Providence, Rhode Island

This facility is designed with four parallel raceways running the length of the greenhouse. Two raceways act as control systems and two as experimental streams. Each raceway consists of twelve 1,300-gallon translucent cylinders and two treatment marshes. The wastewater flows through the system by gravity. The treatment tanks are seeded with a commercial mixture of bacteria and planted with a selection of woody plants, aquatic plants and pond weeds. All of the tanks also contain microorganisms, snails, phytoplankton and zooplankton. The last few tanks in each raceway have been stocked with striped bass and tilapia. (Photo by the author, 1991).

RESOURCES

JOHN M. TEAL AND SUSAN B. PETERSON, "The Next Generation of Septage Treatment," *Research Journal Water Pollution Control Federation* (WPCF) 63(1): 84-89, January/February 1991. This paper describes the preliminary results of a pilot experiment run by Ocean Arks International in the town of Harwich, Massachusetts, in the summer of 1988 at the town landfill. The landfill held the lagoons, inlined pits in the sand, into which septage was pumped for disposal. Liquids seeped through the bottom of the lagoon or evaporated and the remaining solids were eventually placed in the landfill. During the experiment, septage was pumped from the active lagoon into the treatment system and the effluent was returned to the lagoon. Metals were sequestered in the system and all but lead met drinking water standards in the effluent. Metals in fish living in the last tanks met food standards except for antimony, cadmium, and lead. Methylene chloride, trichloroethene, and toluene were high in the influent but met drinking water standards in the effluent.

THE CENTER FOR THE PROTECTION AND RESTORATION OF WATERS @ OCEAN ARKS INTERNATIONAL is a not-for-profit global center for water awareness and action founded in 1989. Dr. John Todd of OAI originally developed the Solar Aquatics System,™ or SAS, a biologically integrated technology which treats septage, sludge, sewage, and industrial process wastewater to high quality specifications at low cost. Membership in OAI is available from:

The Center @ OAI
1 Locust St.
Falmouth, MA 02540
Tel: 508/540-6801   Fax: 508/540-6811

ECOLOGICAL ENGINEERING ASSOCIATES purchased the rights to the SAS technology and markets the system.

They provide wastewater treatment plant design, engineering, construction and operating services. For further information, contact:

Ecological Engineering Associates
13 Marconi Lane
Marion, MA 02738
Tel: 508/748-3224   Fax: 508/748-9740

NANCY JACK TODD AND JOHN TODD, *Bioshelters, Ocean Arks, City Farming: Ecology as the Basis of Design* (San Francisco: Sierra Club Books, 1984). This book extends the work of design pioneers such as R. Buckminster Fuller and Gregory Bateson in developing renewable energy and systems based on natural cycles in agriculture, aquaculture, fuel resources, and general design. It describes a spectrum of innovative experiments integrating small, self-adapting systems with 21st-century biotechnologies. Includes sketches of a neighbourhood sewage treatment facility, a solar sewage wall, rooftop farming, sidewalk gardening, warehouse farming, and bus stop and sidewalk aquaculture.

References

CANADIAN BROADCASTING CORPORATION (CBC), "The Age of Ecology," *IDEAS* (Toronto: CBC Ideas, Part Five, June 25, 1990).

ECOLOGICAL ENGINEERING ASSOCIATES (EEA), "Solar Aquatic Systems: Greenhouses That Grow Clean Water" (Marion, MA: EEA, n.d.).

FULTON, W., "How Dry We Are," Planning 57(5):30, May 1991.

Los Angeles Daily News (LADN), "Rain Helps Out Thirsty Californians," *Vancouver Sun,* March 6, 1991, p. A5.

LOWE, M.D., "Shaping Cities: The Environmental and Human Dimensions," Worldwatch Paper 105 (Washington, D.C.: Worldwatch Institute, 1991).

MACLEISH, W.H., "Water, Water, Everywhere, How Many

Drops to Drink?" *World Monitor,* December 1990, pp. 54-58.
MARINELLI, J., "After the Flush: The Next Generation," *Garbage,* Jan/Feb 1990, pp. 24-35.

ORGANIZATION FOR ECONOMIC COOPERATION AND DEVELOPMENT (OECD), *Environmental Policies for Cities in the 1990s* (Paris: OECD, 1990).

Public Innovation Abroad (PIA), various issues

ROCKY MOUNTAIN INSTITUTE (RMI) *Newsletter,* "Negawatts from Negagallons," VII(III):4, Fall/Winter 1991.

SCHILLING, E., "The Big Thirst," *Planning* 58(2):18-19, February 1992.

SCHREIER, H., S.J. BROWN AND K.J. HALL, "The Land-Water Interface in the Fraser River Basin," in A.H.J. Dorcey and J.R. Griggs, eds., *Water in Sustainable Development: Exploring Our Common Future in the Fraser River Basin* (Vancouver: Westwater Research Centre, 1991).

SKINNER, N., "Ecocity Legislation," in Urban Ecology, *Report of the First International Ecological City Conference* (Berkeley, CA: Urban Ecology, 1990).

SOPPER, W., "Forests as Living Filters for Urban Sewage," in Gordon, D., ed., *Green Cities: Ecologically Sound Approaches to Urban Space* (Montreal: Black Rose Books, 1990).

TEAL, J.M. AND S.B. PETERSON, "The Next Generation of Septage Treatment," *Research Journal Water Pollution Control Federation* (WPCF) 63(1): 84-89, January/February 1991.

TODD, N.J. AND J.TODD, *Bioshelters, Ocean Arks, City Farming:Ecology as the Basis of Design* (San Francisco: Sierra Club Books, 1984).

9

Greening the City

Greening the city refers to a spectrum of ideas and techniques ranging from edible planting and indigenous landscaping to community organizing to protect urban open space and restore creeks. These activities are motivated by awareness of factors such as the need to reduce the urban heat island effect, reduce our use of pesticides, conserve energy, clean urban air, and absorb carbon dioxide from the atmosphere.

Our urban ecosystems serve as indicators of ecological health. Especially in urban areas, there is a fine line between ecological health and public health. No one wants their children to play in water that kills fish.

Beyond this, if we accept the argument that sustainability requires cities to become more urban, they need also to become more pleasant. One sure way of enhancing the quality of urban life is through "greening" the city. Greening the city means emphasizing an environmental perspective that begins with the city. It means combining urbanism and nature to create cities that are healthy, civilizing, and enriching places to live (see Hough 1990).

Perhaps the most important aspect of greening the city is that cities are where most of us live, and therefore cities are where most of us learn about the interplay between society and nature. It is a truism that many urbanites think food comes from supermarkets, water comes from faucets, and wastes are simply taken "away." In a democratic society, we cannot expect people to support

Transforming Our Cities

"There needs to be a profound shift in the fundamental premises and activities of city living. Urban people have to adopt conservationist values and carry out more responsible practices in wide areas of daily life. Municipal governments need to restructure their priorities so that long-term sustainability can become a feasible goal. With such a large portion of the population removed from the land and from access to resources, ways to secure some share of the basic requirements of food, water, energy, and materials will have to be found within the confines of cities. Cities need to become 'green.' They must be transformed into places that are life-enhancing and regenerative."

(Berg 1990)

"We need to consider ways in which people can relate more closely to nature in cities either by protecting the surviving vestiges of the natural world, or by creating completely new opportunities for nature to exist within an urban setting. By examining the ecology of cities, there is much that we can learn about natural processes within the urban environment: which species are able to survive and what restoration is possible. By applying that knowledge we could alter the face of many cities to a great extent."

Goode 1990

sustainability policies if they have no experience of the ecological basis of life – our urban areas should demonstrate our dependence on ecological health. Nor can we expect people to support more ecologically appropriate urban lifestyles (e.g., more compact communities, less use of private automobiles) unless our urban areas themselves become healthier.

The "Green City" Concept

"The green city concept is as much a way of thinking as it is a physical reality. It brings together notions of urbanism and nature, ideas that most people have normally separated into water-tight compartments. There has been an overwhelming propensity to focus on the problems of the larger environment while ignoring the one where most of us live. Putting urbanism and nature together provides us with an opportunity to create cities that are healthy, civilizing, and enriching places in which to live... at its broadest level, the green city means an environmental perspective that begins with the city. This makes sense since all environmental decisions are made by urban people with urban attitudes in urban places. Solutions to the environment as a whole have to begin, therefore, at home."

(Hough 1990)

Shopping Malls or Genuine People-Places?

"Given the failure of many urban areas to offer humane, welcoming spaces, it is no wonder so many people flock to suburban shopping malls. These vast structures are an attempt to recreate, artificially, the amenities of a hearty city: a profusion of different activities; sunlight, trees and fountains; and inviting benches and cafes – all designed for the convenience of pedestrians. But like most imitations, malls are, in the long run, far less viable than the real thing. The creation of genuine people-places lies not in despoiling the countryside with new shopping centers, but in more humanely planning the city's existing spaces and streets."

(Lowe 1991)

"It is in some senses climatically now considered to be very much more valuable to plant an urban tree rather than a rural one. The difference being, both take about six kilograms of carbon dioxide out of the air per year. But the urban tree has the extra benefits that it shades hot urban surfaces, which need energy in the form of air conditioning to cool them off... It turns out that the urban tree is worth 15 times as much as your rural tree. And that's a very important need for the planet right now."

Dr. Tim Oke, urban climatologist
quoted in McMartin 1990

"A 100 year-old beech tree, 25 m tall with a 15 m crown diameter, produces enough oxygen in a year to meet the needs of ten people. If that tree dies, 2700 young trees, each with a crown volume of 1 m, would have to be planted to achieve the same oxygen benefit."

City of Toronto 1990

Urban "Heat Island" Costs

"Calculations suggest that, in Los Angeles, for each degree Fahrenheit of temperature increase, the energy demand goes up by 1.6%, which translates to 300 megawatts of electricity. In terms of cost, the five-Fahrenheit-degree temperature rise over the last 50 years (due largely to the urban heat island phenomenon) accounts for US $100 million per year. Moreover, for a city with severe air-quality problems, a 30% increase in smog days has been associated with that rise; this comes about because of the temperature dependence of the process which creates ozone from the other components of the smog."

(McCulloch 1991)

TOOLS

Benefits of urban planting

- More livable cities. Trees, bushes and grasslands are beautiful and can relieve the barrenness of the concrete and asphalt that covers many cities.
- Improved drainage. Properly planted land absorbs the rain that falls on it, eliminating excessive run-off that otherwise requires expensive storm sewers that often overflow and flood.
- Closer-knit communities. Sidewalk planting projects present an opportunity for residents to work together on bettering their neighbourhoods. (see Berg et al 1989)

Integrated Pest Management

"In response to these severe problems with pesticides, integrated pest management concepts have been developed. Put very simply, integrated pest management is the use of all available tools and methods to suppress, but not to control, insect populations and keep damage to acceptable levels using the safest, most effective and most economical means. That is rather a tall order, and it requires thought about all the kinds of controls that can be used. There is no one magic chemical or one magic bullet, or one magic predator, or one magic technique. We have to think about using many techniques together." (Gilkeson 1990)

Planting Trees to Save Money and Energy

A recent study examines the use of vegetation and high albedo materials in Toronto, Montreal, Edmonton, and Vancouver to modify the urban microclimate, thus saving on residential energy for heating and cooling. It shows that simply planting trees can produce significant savings of money and energy. The annual household savings range, depending on the structure, from $30 to $180 in urban areas and from $60 to $400 in rural zones. (see Akbari and Taha 1991)

Benefits of Urban Wild Habitat
- *Improved quality of life.* The existence of urban wild habitat makes undomesticated animals a visible reality, especially for children, instead of just something to read about in books.
- *An indicator of ecological health.* The vigour and robustness of native animals and plants indicate how clean the air and water are, and can help us assess the health and life-supporting capacity of the entire ecosystem.
- *An awareness of the natural cycles of the life-place.* By having wildlife close at hand, city-dwellers can be in closer touch with the natural systems of which they are a part. (see Berg et al 1989)

Conservation Commissions
Many local governments establish a conservation commission to protect the natural resources and the watershed of their community. In the state of New Hampshire, conservation commissions may receive gifts of money and property, both real and personal, in the name of the city or town. They may also "acquire in the name of the town or city by gift, purchase, grant, bequest, devise, lease or otherwise the fee in such land or water rights, or any lesser interest, development right, easement, covenant, or other contractual right including conveyances with conditions, limitations or reversions, as may be necessary to acquire, maintain, improve, protect, limit the future use of or otherwise conserve and properly utilize open spaces and other land and water areas within their city or town, and shall manage and control the same," although they do not have the right to condemn property for these purposes. (see New Hampshire Title III)

INITIATIVES

Creek Raising

"In our cities, we have tended to bury or modify streams beyond all recognition, in the process neglecting the power of these waters to renew the human spirit, just as they renew the life of the land. Stream corridors [...] represent one of the most varied ecosystems. This richness can enable us to re-create our relationships to creeks. The restoration of urban streams thus takes on an ecology of meanings: they are a vehicle which permits us to 're-inhabit' where we live and to cultivate a sense of place; provide an organizing principle for community building and a means to revitalize neighborhoods and commercial areas; give us a way of finding the child again (who loved to play by them); and offer a forum for environmental art, dance, and poetry. Conceiving creek work in this way can serve to infuse community activism with a creative and inspirational dimension that has profound implications for grassroots efforts to revitalize our cities." (Steere 1990)

Communities that have raised and restored their creeks include *San Luis Obispo* and *Berkeley*, California. *Burnaby*, British Columbia passed a resolution in 1972 that its streams must be "preserved and conserved." Housing developments must incorporate existing streams into their landscaping, and individual homeowners are not allowed to build right down to the bank (see Sarti 1992).

Green Guerrillas

"People's needs and involvement in their own neighbourhood open space is what the Green Guerrillas is all about. Our organization began in 1973 with a group of neighbours on the lower east side of *Manhattan*. They had decided that they were tired of the disinterest in and

destruction of their community. They cleaned and greened
[...] a vacant lot on the corner of Bowery and Houston
streets, an area some of us know as Bum's Row. Today that
lot is lush with plants during the growing season, and the
small Metasequoia tree they planted there is now forty feet
tall. The garden has meandering paths, a grape arbour, a
pond, and all kinds of flowers, fruits, and vegetables.
Anything that will grow in an urban environment is there.
It even has a bee hive. That the garden is in an area known
for its urban blight holds important significance." (Keller
1990)

Tree Replacement Bylaws
Vancouver's 1991 tree-replacement bylaw requires the
replanting of trees affected by development. It requires
builders to file site plans showing existing trees with
trunks over 20 centimetres (eight inches) in diameter
measured 90 centimetres (three feet) above the ground. A
tree that is removed must be replaced somewhere on the
property by a tree of a type and size approved by the city.
Vancouver had originally asked the provincial government
to amend the city charter to give it the authority to fine
people who destroy trees, but that was not granted. The
penalty for those who break the new bylaw is that their
occupancy permit will be withheld (see Fayerman 1990,
1991).

Natural Planting
In a critical aquifer district in the town of *Southampton*
on Long Island, ordinances require that at least 80 percent
of each lot be kept in its natural state, and no more than 15
percent of any lot (and in no case more than 1,900 square
meters) can be planted in fertilized lawns or plants. These
restrictions still leave landowners with ample landscaping
choices; sites that are not left in woodland vegetation can

be planted in meadow grasses, perennial wildflowers, ivy, or other dense plantings that need little or no fertilizing (see Lowe 1991).

"Green" Roofs

The German cities of *Mannheim* and *Frankfurt* are now granting planning permission for structures with flat or gently sloping roofs only if they are designed to be of the "living" variety. The German League of Cities has noted that flat "green" roofs save energy and increase residents' comfort by limiting the temperature spread, thus reducing heating and air conditioning requirements. Current technology allows flat roofs to be retrofitted for vegetation economically without any danger that plant roots will perforate roof surfaces. "Green" roofs have 60% less runoff than gravel or asphalt tiles, reducing the costs of drainage systems and, in sufficient numbers, improving the urban micro-climate (see *PIA* 14(5), May 1990).

Integrated Pest Management

Burnaby, British Columbia uses integrated pest management (IPM) wherever possible to maintain its green areas.

RESOURCES

GARY MOLL AND SARA EBENRECK, editors, *Shading Our Cities: A Resource Guide for Urban and Community Forests* (Washington, D.C.: Island Press, 1989). This valuable reference, published under the auspices of the American Forestry Association, explains how to preserve and extend urban forests. The authors argue that beyond the aesthetic benefits of parks and tree-lined streets, trees can also reduce energy demand (by providing cooling shade), improve air quality, protect water supplies, and signal community stability. The book includes practical measures to save existing trees, information on how to start an urban forestry program, and profiles of successful projects in Los Angeles, Philadelphia, New York, Atlanta, and other cities.

HASHEM AKBARI AND HAIDER TAHA, *The Tree-House Effect: The Impact of Trees and White Surfaces on Residential Energy Use in Four Canadian Cities* (Ottawa: Friends of the Earth, 1991). A technical report by scientists with the Heat Island Project of the University of California-Berkeley and the Lawrence Berkeley Laboratory of the US Department of Energy. Available from:

Global ReLeaf Program   Global ReLeaf Program
Friends of the Earth   American Forestry Assoc
251 Laurier Ave. West   PO Box 2000
Ottawa, Ontario   Washington,
K1P 5J6   DC 20013
Tel: 613/230-3352   Tel: 202/667-3300

US ENVIRONMENTAL PROTECTION AGENCY (EPA), *Cooling Our Communities: A Guidebook on Tree Planting and Light-Colored Surfacing* (Washington, D.C.: US EPA, 1992, S/N 055-000-00371-8). This guidebook was developed specifically for reducing summer heat in cities. It discusses ways of reducing the effects of urban "heat islands," and the likely environmental and economic benefits of taking appropriate measures. Includes resources, references, sources of support, descriptions of mitigation efforts already underway, and technical appendices. Available from:

Superintendent of Documents
PO Box 371954
Pittsburgh, PA 15250-7954

INTERNATIONAL SOCIETY OF ABORICULTURE, *Municipal Tree Manual* (Urbana, Ill: International Society of Aboriculture, 1990). A municipal ordinance to control the planting and care of trees is a critical tool for improving the health of a city landscape. This report is a comprehensive guide to drafting or revising such an ordinance. It includes three sample ordinances as well as additional ordinance sections and commentary. Also included is a useful and well-illustrated section on management standards and specifications that can be developed as an appendix to a tree ordinance or as a separate management document. Contains examples from the field and useful advice on contract specifications and standards. Available from:

International Society of Aboriculture
PO Box 908
Urbana, Ill 61801

PETER BERG, BERYL MAGILAVY AND SETH ZUCKERMAN, *A Green City Program for San Francisco Bay Area Cities and Towns* (San Francisco: Planet Drum Books, 1989). This intriguing book arose from a set of symposia on urban sustainability in the San Francisco Bay Area in 1986. The premise of the participants was that cities must be transformed into places that are life-enhancing and regenerative, and that enormous changes in a society can come from a handful of citizen planners who restructure how they live and actively influence others. Topics include urban planting, transportation, planning, energy, neighbourhood character and empowerment, recycling and reuse, celebrating life-place vitality, urban wild habitat, and socially responsible small businesses and cooperatives. Each chapter includes a section on "What can cities do to promote ...?," long-term visions for municipal action, a "fable" to illustrate the way beneficial changes could occur, and a section on "... in Green City: what's possible?"

DAVID GORDON, ed., *Green Cities: Ecologically Sound Approaches to Urban Space* (Montreal: Black Rose Books, 1990). What is the Green City? This anthology begins with a series of attempts to articulate ideas on culture, globalism, international economics, and local

211

initiative. The bulk of the book is devoted to strategies and techniques for "naturalizing" and "greening" urban areas. The final section describes how some local organizations have overcome institutional and social barriers in their attempts to realize visions of the green city. Appendices include a list of horticultural services and suppliers; a bibliography on urban wilderness and ecological landscaping, edible landscaping, groundcovers and herbs, and urban agriculture and gardening; and a listing of selected organizations and demonstration projects.

GERALD F.M. DAWE, editor, *The Urban Environment: A Sourcebook for the 1990s* (Birmingham, UK: Centre for Urban Ecology, Nature Conservancy Council, and World Wide Fund for Nature, 1990). This 636 page book contains 1,768 abstracts of articles, papers, reports and books on various aspects of urban ecology. Each abstract is classified by means of key words which tie into the main indexes (plant and animal, town and city and subject indexes), as well as with graphic symbols designed to give a first-glance impression of the emphasis of each abstract. The book is a useful guide to work carried out in the 1980s on urban landscape, wildlife, climate, pollution, and ecosystems. This is an expensive volume, but may be worth asking your library to order. Available from:

Centre for Urban Ecology
318 Summer Lane
Birmingham B19 3RL, United Kingdom
Tel: 021 - 359 7462   Fax: 021 - 359 6357

URBAN ECOLOGY, a California non-profit organization founded by *Ecocity Berkeley* author Richard Register, publishes a newsletter *The Urban Ecologist*. Although primarily focused on the San Francisco Bay Area, this group organized the First International Ecocity Conference in 1990. The conference emphasized the need to rebuild our cities in harmony with nature, and the newsletter includes vignettes of ecological rebuilding around the world. *The Report of the First International Ecological City Conference* and the newsletter are both available from:

Urban Ecology
P.O. Box 10144
Berkeley, CA 94709
Tel: 415/549-1724

References

AKBARI, H. AND H. TAHA, *The Tree-House Effect: The Impact of Trees and White Surfaces on Residential Energy Use in Four Canadian Cities* (Ottawa: Friends of the Earth, 1991).

BERG, P., B. MAGILAVY AND S. ZUCKERMAN, *A Green City Program for San Francisco Bay Area Cities and Towns* (San Francisco: Planet Drum Books, 1989).

BERG, P., "Developing the San Francisco Green City Plan," in Gordon 1990.

CITY OF TORONTO, "The Greening of Toronto: An Environmental Greenprint for the Future" (Toronto: City of Toronto, Department of Parks and Recreation, 1990).

DAWE, G.F.M., ed., *The Urban Environment: A Sourcebook for the 1990s* (Birmingham, UK: Centre for Urban Ecology, Nature Conservancy Council, and World Wide Fund for Nature, 1990).

FAYERMAN, P., "Tree Replacement Bylaw Canada's First," *Vancouver Sun,* December 27, 1990, p. B1.

FAYERMAN, P., "Tree Bylaw Successful, Author Says," *Vancouver Sun,* May 17, 1991, p. A12.

GILKESON, L., "Integrated Pest Management," in Gordon 1990.

GOODE, D., "A Green Renaissance," in Gordon 1990.

GORDON, D., ed., *Green Cities: Ecologically Sound Approaches to Urban Space* (Montreal: Black Rose Books, 1990).

HOUGH, M., "Formed by Natural Process: A Definition of the Green City," in Gordon 1990.

INTERNATIONAL SOCIETY OF ABORICULTURE, *Municipal Tree Manual* (Urbana, Ill: International Society of Aboriculture,

1990).

KELLER, T., "The Greening of the Big Apple," in Gordon 1990.

LOWE, M.D., "Shaping Cities: The Environmental and Human Dimensions," Worldwatch Paper 105 (Washington, D.C.: Worldwatch Institute, 1991).

MCCULLOCH, J.A.W., "Overview of International Conference on Cities and Global Change" (Toronto, June 1991), prepared for "World Cities and the Environment" Conference, Toronto, August 25-28, 1991.

MCMARTIN, P., "Our Future: To Live and Die, Like LA?" in *Vancouver Sun*, March 14, 1990, p. A11.

MOLL, G. AND S. EBENRECK, eds., *Shading Our Cities: A Resource Guide for Urban and Community Forests* (Washington, D.C.: Island Press, 1989).

STATE OF NEW HAMPSHIRE, New Hampshire Title III, Chapter 36-A:2, A:4.

Public Innovation Abroad (PIA), various issues

SARTI, R., "Alderman's Stream of Consciousness Fount for Burnaby," *Vancouver Sun*, March 12, 1992, p. D1.

STEERE, J., "Creeks Alive!" in Urban Ecology, Report of the First International Ecological City Conference (Berkeley, CA: Urban Ecology, 1990).

US ENVIRONMENTAL PROTECTION AGENCY (EPA), *Cooling Our Communities: A Guidebook on Tree Planting and Light-Colored Surfacing* (Washington, D.C.: US EPA, 1992).

10

Economic Development

Conventional approaches to economic development often produce enormous amounts of pollution and consume huge quantities of energy and materials while failing to deliver sufficient jobs. A host of existing government policies that encourage pollution and discourage job creation need to be overhauled. While many of these policies, e.g., taxation, are primarily within the jurisdiction of senior governments, municipal and local governments can begin to point the way toward a sustainable economy (see Renner 1991).

A sustainable economy will emphasize two factors: sustainable employment, and economic demand management. Sustainable employment includes turning "wastes" into resources (e.g., recycling); improving efficiency with regard to energy and materials; converting to greater reliance on renewable energy sources; increasing community self-reliance (e.g., food and energy production); and sustainable management of natural resources (e.g., community forestry).

Several kinds of community-oriented enterprises have proven valuable in the pursuit of sustainable employment. Community Development Corporations (CDCs), for example, have been active in rehabilitating or constructing affordable housing, creating jobs and businesses in economically disenfranchised areas, engaging in commercial and industrial real estate development to promote economic development in their communities, and providing job training and placement services. Likewise, community finance institutions such as community development credit unions, revolving loan funds, and housing trust funds have helped communities experiencing disinvestment and/or a lack of investment capital create their own financial institutions to retain or gain access to capital.

The other factor to emphasize in a sustainable economy is managing economic demand. In Chapter One we noted that "development" can no longer simply mean economic "growth," but requires instead that we learn to live on the "interest" generated by remaining stocks of "natural capital." Just as sustainability has prompted a shift in our transportation and energy planning away from the traditional concerns with increasing supply to the new focus on managing demand, we must also shift our economic development emphasis from the traditional concern with increasing growth to the new focus on reducing social dependence on economic growth, or what we might call Economic Demand Management (EDM). A primary focus of EDM should be reducing the need for paid work (see Schor 1991). Local governments can promote EDM by, for example, land-use planning that links trip reduction with affordable housing, and by developing partnerships with institutions such as community land trusts to provide an expanding stock of permanently affordable housing.

Local Self-Reliance
"Self-reliance in socioeconomic systems has its analogue in natural systems. As a general rule of natural process, energy (and subsequent action) are captured or expended as close to the point of origin as possible. The diversity of ecosystems is a reflection of the diversity of local conditions and ways of responding to them. Our built systems often impose homogeneity upon highly diverse natural systems.

Sustainability as Public Policy
"The sooner we embrace the principles of sustainability as an essential goal of public policy, the less traumatic the transition will be. An early decision to alter or abandon environmentally destructive practices is likely to cause fewer economic problems or job losses than a reactive policy. Although the short-term costs of redesigning products and production technologies can be high, delaying a response until it is dictated by sheer ecological necessity would be even more costly [...] A sustainable society will have to give greater emphasis to conservation and efficiency, rely more on renewable energy, and extract nominally renewable resources only to the degree that they can regenerate themselves. It will need to minimize waste, maximize reuse and recycling, avoid the use of hazardous materials, and preserve biodiversity. And it will need to develop more environmentally benign production technologies, and design products to be more durable and repairable."

(Renner 1991)

This results in dislocations of materials and disruption of system dynamics, leaving us with what we call waste or pollution.

Local self-reliance does not mean isolation, either in natural or built systems. It means creating an organizational system that enhances the internal economy and cohesiveness of a place, reduces entropy, and provides the base for import/export relationships with other communities. It is an integrative process that links the consumer sector of the local economy with the producer sector and through the relationship strengthens both.

One way to enhance the self-reliance of a community is

> ### *Miniaturizing the Economy*
> "The primary benefit of local self-reliance is [...] [that] it improves decision making because the costs of the decision and the benefits from the decision begin to fall on the same community. We do not separate the productive process over long distances. Psychologically, we improve the self-confidence and the security of our communities by miniaturizing the economy." (Morris 1990)

to identify the imports and, where possible, substitute local products. Import substitution can dramatically improve the 'balance of payments,' but its real value lies in creating momentum. As communities organize to find substitutes for imports, they begin to think consciously about self-reliance – and this releases a certain inventiveness and drive for efficiency. Inventiveness and efficiency help a community reduce imports still more, but they also allow the community to develop exports – and in our information-laced society, ingenuity itself is exportable [...]

Communities that recover materials from the trash stream and use them as resources for local production will realize the full potential of waste recycling as a tool for economic development. Colonized nations often point out that colonizers extract raw materials cheaply, refine them at home, and then sell them back to the colonized countries for a large profit. U.S. cities are like colonized countries in that they export what little recycled material they do collect. The two leading exports from the port of New York are scrap metal and paper. Other countries are importing these materials, processing them, and then often exporting them back to the U.S. For example, Japan imports scrap paper from us and turns it into boxes for exports." (Martin 1988)

Introducing Economic Diversity and Self-Reliance
"A greater degree of economic diversity and self-reliance can be introduced in several ways. Community organizations can be formed to create, nurture, and assist worker self-managed firms. This will involve a social approach to entrepreneurship, an economic function usually left to the private sector in capitalist countries, or to the state in socialist ones. Local governments can help by structuring social services and support systems to enable self-reliance rather than creating dependency."

(Bruyn 1987)

"Invariably people come up and talk to me about comparative advantage and, invariably, the argument of 'bananas' comes up. The argument is that perhaps we should be locally self-reliant, but surely Canada should not, because of the climate, be raising its own bananas. Surely it is cheaper to import those bananas. Perhaps, but, once again, what is the price and the cost? Bananas that come from Central America come from countries that do not permit unions, through companies that do not pay any taxes, and by production methods that have no environmental regulations [...] if you calculated the amount of dollars that have been spent by the United States in military intervention in Central America and divided that by the number of bananas that are imported into the United States, you would find that it is very costly to import bananas rather than to grow them by yourself."

Morris 1990

Employment Impacts of Sustainability Policies
"The employment impacts of sustainability policies are a frequent concern and highly variable. For example, mandatory container reuse and recycling, many energy conservation measures, and enhanced public

transportation may involve more rather than fewer job opportunities, while energy efficiency standards for appliances and automobiles may be employment neutral. Where there are significant dislocations, special job training programs and new forms of social safety nets may have to be implemented to serve those people in transition from unsustainable forms of employment.

Many other sustainability measures are inherently positive in their distributive effects. For example, more efficient land use and tax policies to discourage land speculation will increase the affordability of housing in the city and enable people to live closer to work. Shifting some of the public subsidy from automobile use to improved public transit will improve access to the city for lower income groups while attracting more riders from all social strata. All such effects are much in need of further research. However, in the final analysis, to the extent improving the health, access, and livability of our cities contributes to the long-term survival of society, we all benefit in equal measure." (Rees and Roseland 1991)

Sustainable Industry

Sustainable industry means converting the material basis of society. While the shape of sustainable industry is still emerging, several features will be critical:
"• Technologies appropriate to the desired ends.
• Safe and environmentally compatible materials.
• Products that meet basic social needs and some individual wants.
• low- and no-waste production processes.
• safe and skill-enhancing working conditions.
• energy efficiency.
• resource conservation to meet the needs of future generations." (Geiser 1991)

Sustainable industry encompasses the entire social,

economic, and technological system by which we produce goods. This systems-wide perspective unites prevention policies, the precautionary principle, and clean technology into an integrated view that regards economic and environmental goals as equal determinants in a healthy society.

"From this point, it is a short jump to considering the entire industrial system as an environment and health issue. The design of new production processes would take into account both occupational and community health. The consumption of materials, water, and energy would be evaluated in determining efficiencies.

In short, policies to promote sustainable industry would consider the risks of materials throughout their full life cycle – from synthesis or extraction through processing, distribution, and application to final disposal. The use of existing materials would be carefully tailored to fit into natural ecological systems. The design and selection of new materials would be consciously directed toward enhancing the quality of the environment and public health." (Geiser 1991)

Community Economic Development

"Whether CED (community economic development) is practised in hinterland resource towns, urban ghettos, obsolescent manufacturing cities, or Native communities reserves, the general objective is the same: to take some measure of control of the local economy back from the markets and the state. Within this common objective, CED practice is variously oriented to controlling the local economy for narrow ends (increasing the capacity of a community to make money), for broader purposes (e.g., to increase economic stability and control of resources) or to serve fundamental goals of economic justice. That is to say, CED varies according to whether 'economic,'

221

> ### A New Community Constitution
> "There are risks in empowering people in the local community. We are reminded of the provinciality, bigotry, and local elitism that existed in small towns at the turn of the century and how the rise of the big city, created largely through free market forces, eliminated that rigidity. But big cities substituted their own problems of anonymity, impersonality, delinquency, crime, drug addiction, prostitution, slums, and class divisions between the wealthy and the poor. We are talking about a new social-economic constitution to the local community."
>
> (Bruyn 1987)

'development,' or 'community' is emphasized." (Boothroyd 1991)

Market Development
"Policies adopted by local governments can play a strong role in market development. For example, prior to the passage of local government regulations on ozone-depleting compounds, there were few manufacturers and few models available of CFC "vampire" units – machines that remove freon from refrigerators and air conditioners to enable the freon to be recycled. Since local governments started passing CFC regulations in 1989, more manufacturers have begun producing the vampire units, making available a variety of models at lower, competitive prices. Energy conservation and renewable energy incentive measures adopted by local governments can spur similar market development in these areas and set new standards for senior government policies." (Skinner 1991)

"Local governments should promote balanced development by applying development control laws stringently, implementing local plans that have been developed through wide community participation... Plans should also broaden the economic base by encouraging new sustainable activities that will create employment and income."

IUCN 1991

Redefining Labour
"As we move toward an economy based on the principles of local self-reliance, we may see a significant reduction in the trade of products or raw materials, accompanied by a rapid expansion in the trade of information, knowledge, entertainment, and culture. As we move toward a steady-state society with respect to raw material consumption, we may begin to redefine the nature of labor itself."

(Morris 1986)

TOOLS

Sustainable Employment
Community Development Corporations

Community Development Corporations (CDCs) are democratic firms designed to be accountable to *all* the residents of the community, not just special interests like producers and consumers. Residents become members for a small fee and may participate equally with one vote in shaping community policy.

"The CDC is a planning and governance vehicle organized in the private sector to help meet local needs. It has an overall responsibility to help develop land, labour, and capital and, by implication, the responsibility to help

223

redress any imbalance of power within the exchange system... It is like a municipal government, except that its task is simply to coordinate local economic development... The CDC does not replace the local government in any real sense, but it can reduce the need for services (and thus for taxes) by encouraging local corporations to meet the needs of their stakeholders. Where possible, it can help reduce the need for competitive motives serving as the driving force of the local economy and increase the possibility for cooperative motives and mutual aid to become the basis of local economic organization." (Bruyn 1987)

Community Development Credit Unions

"A credit union is a cooperative, non-profit corporation created by and for people affiliated by a common bond, for the purpose of promoting thrift among its members and of loaning funds to its members at reasonable interest rates [...] A Community Development Credit Unions (CDCU) is a specific type of credit union. CDCUs are based on a residential common bond and serve low-to moderate-income communities and individuals. Of the 19,000 credit unions in the US, approximately 400 are community development credit unions. CDCUs share two common themes: All CDCUs serve people who need financial services but cannot get them readily from banks, and all CDCUs are motivated by a vision of community economic empowerment." (Swack 1987)

Community Loan Funds

"A community loan fund (CLF) is a not-for-profit corporation, or a program within a not-for-profit corporation, that accepts loans from individuals and institutions and uses this capital to make loans for community development projects within its own geographic area. A CLF typically borrows and lends at below-market interest rates, and places a high-priority on making loans to community-based organizations that are unable to get them from conventional sources. With its specialized knowledge of local housing and other community economic development activities, a CLF is able to evaluate loan requests from local groups in a way that most investors and investment professionals cannot. A CLF is also able to help these groups develop sound financial plans and identify and approach other sources of capital. As both lender and technical assistant, a community loan fund is a bridge between investors and community groups in need of capital." (Swack 1987)

Trust Funds

One source of public capital for local governments is a dedicated, renewable trust fund.

"Trust funds are characterized by the establishment of a permanent endowment, dedicated to the investment of capital assets in housing or other community economic development activities. A trust fund's endowment may be capitalized by one-time contributions, or by annually renewable revenue sources. Trust funds established by one-time allocations of funds provide for loans from their endowment or grants from the endowment's investment earnings. Those capitalized by annually renewable revenues can afford to grant or lend funds from the trusts principal [...] Trust fund capital assets are stable and predictable, and may be relied upon for long-term financial commitments necessary for capital development, particularly housing development." (Rosen 1988)

Reinvestment Policies

Reinvestment policies are a source of public capital for local governments.

"Reinvestment policies address the issue of available credit and insurance for community economic development. [US] depository institutions which extract capital from communities in the form of deposits have an obligation to reinvest significant portions of their assets in those communities. Reinvestment policies apply most directly to commercial banks and savings and loan associations. However, reinvestment principles may be applied to the insurance industry as well, which not only extracts capital from communities, but whose own self interest dictates that communities remain economically stable. Community economic stability is largely dependent on the availability of investment capital. Thus, the insurance industry can simultaneously serve its self interest and the public interest by assuring that a significant portion of its capital assets is reinvested in community economic development for the benefit of low income areas." (Rosen 1988)

Recycling vs. Incineration Employment
"Recycling in the U.S. may already be as important a source of jobs as coal mining. Compared with incineration and landfilling, recycling offers more employment and is still the cheaper alternative, due to its lower capital requirements. The construction of waste-burning plants and the manufacturing of the machinery they use create more temporary jobs than the more modestly equipped recycling centers do, but recycling offers a large number of permanent jobs in operations and maintenance activities. In New York City, the cost of building an incinerator (about $500 million) is three times that of recycling facilities that can handle the same amount of trash. Boosting the city's recycling rate from 18 percent to a modest 25 percent – as mandated by law by April 1994 – would create about 1,400 jobs, or more than four times the number generated if the same volume of waste were incinerated."(Renner 1991) These jobs would be in addition to the jobs created by the remanufacturing process – taking the recycled materials and turning them into new goods.

Community Supported Agriculture
Community Supported Agriculture (CSA) is catching on as

a way for city dwellers to supply themselves with fresh vegetables while supporting small local organic farms. Some 100 CSAs were in operation in the US during 1991. Urban families or individuals typically pay a yearly fee of $200 to $600, and in return receive a weekly supply of fruits and vegetables. Buyers either pick up the produce at the farm itself or receive weekly shipments delivered to the city. Purchasers share the risks of farming with farmers – they may receive less of one vegetable than expected, but more than another – but gain a sense of connection with local farmers and the bioregion (see Urban Ecologist 1991).

Community Forestry

"There are several examples of community forests in Canada, including the county forests in southern and central Ontario, and the Mission Tree Farm and the North Cowichan Municipal Forest, both in British Columbia [...]

There are several ways of administering a community forest, including the use of cooperatives, regional trusts, and public or private ownership. Each has its own strengths and weaknesses, and success depends on the political attitudes and economic realities prevailing in the locality. However,[...] there is a set of fundamental principles that are applicable in most community forest projects.

First of all the principle of local control in order to produce and retain local benefits, is paramount. Next, this local control has to be based on a very good knowledge and understanding of what the local people want, what will work in their area now, and what could be tried to develop new ideas and outputs [...] Finally, the community forest should be developed and managed in order to promote economic diversification, rather than stifle it by placing a continued reliance on only one commodity output such as raw timber for export away from the locality." (Ontario Conservation News 1989)

> ### Ecological and Economic Linkages
> "Maintaining ecological capital requires making appropriate linkages among seemingly unrelated economic activities. This in turn makes it possible to finance new kinds of employment. For example, revenue to finance many aspects of rehabilitation forestry should come in part from carbon taxes imposed on fossil fuel combustion. This is both economically efficient in that it 'internalizes' the costs of CO_2 emissions and ecologically sound in that the growing forest absorbs the CO_2, reducing the rate of atmospheric change [...] Forest rehabilitation and harvesting is best undertaken by local people with a direct stake in the outcome and familiarity with the management area [...] Local control of the forest will clearly require a reassessment of the present forest tenure system."
>
> **(Rees 1991)**

Economic Demand Management
Trip Reduction and Affordable Housing
A 1990 paper drafted by the staff of the Maryland-National Capital Park and Planning Commission as part of the Planning Department's Comprehensive Growth Policy Study examined the links between trip reduction and affordable housing. Below is the abstract of that three-part paper. (Access information is provided in the Resources section of this chapter.)

"Trip Reduction, Surplus Surface Parking, And Provision Of Housing Near Jobs
Trip reduction measures can reduce the need for parking, and free land from surface parking for new development opportunities. That land could be used for both market rate and affordable housing. The housing would also be

> ### *Reducing the Need for Paid Work*
> "Although many people prefer to spend less time in the factory or at the office, working fewer hours is often not a practical option for them, because in a commodity-intensive economy they are compelled to seek full-time employment. Yet, a key component of sustainability, the production of more durable goods, provides a crucial underpinning for such a move. When goods do not wear out rapidly, they need not be replaced as frequently. More durable goods are likely to be more expensive than throw-aways; but over time, people will spend less money on purchases of furniture, appliances, and clothing. Hence there is less need for paid work to achieve a given material standard of living.
>
> A more sustainable economy promises great environmental and economic benefits, though the transition will not be without pain. It will produce many losers, particularly among extractive and heavy industries. But the evidence is strong that the winners will outnumber the losers: more jobs will be created in energy efficiency, recycling, and public transportation than will be lost in the oil and coal industries, car manufacturing, and waste disposal. In fact, automation is a much more important cause of job loss than environmental protection is. And while extractive industries tend to be geographically concentrated, jobs arising out of energy conservation, renewables, and recycling are likely to be more evenly spread."
>
> (Renner 1991)

near jobs, which would both reduce vehicle trips and shorten average vehicle trip lengths, reducing demand for road capacity. The profit potential of market rate housing on land freed from surface parking would provide owners of existing office and research developments with the incentive to implement trip reduction measures and provide some affordable housing.

Making Housing Affordable By Giving Up The Second Car
Second car ownership costs about $3000/year. By giving up a second car and using public transportation, an entry level household would save between $150 and $250 a month which could be spent on housing. Means are proposed to help County residents turn savings from single car ownership into increased buying power for housing. These means include designing subdivisions in ways that make second car ownership unnecessary, County provided private mortgage insurance to increase borrowing power for single car households, and public education that buying where two cars are necessary is buying into a $3000 a year habit.

Charging Separately For Parking To Lower Housing Costs, Car Ownership, And Trip Generation
Most residents of multi-family housing do not know that they are paying approximately $50 a month for each parking space. Requiring landlords and condominium associations to price housing and parking separately would spur some people into giving up cars. It would also make the average rental unit in the County 8-9% more affordable for those without cars. As a result of lower car ownership, it should also result in lower trip generation rates." (Maryland-National Capital Park and Planning Commission 1990)

Community Land Trusts

Although similar to the conservation land trusts described in the Land Use chapter, a community land trust is not simply a land trust that happens to be in a community. As developed by the Institute for Community Economics, a community land trust (CLT) is *an organization created to hold land for the benefit of a community and of individuals within the community. It is a democratically structured non-profit corporation, with an open membership and a board of trustees elected by the membership.* The board typically includes residents of trust-owned lands, other community residents, and public-interest representatives. Board members are elected for limited terms, so that the community retains ultimate control of the organization and of the land it owns (see ICE 1982).

The CLT acquires land through purchase or donation with an intention to retain title in perpetuity, thus removing the land from the speculative market. Each land trust writes its own bylaws and defines its own goals, priorities and structure. Appropriate uses for the land are determined in a process comparable to public planning or zoning processes, and the land is then leased to individuals, families, cooperatives, community organizations, businesses, or for public purposes.

CLTs in rural areas are working to provide access to land and decent housing for low-income people, to preserve family farms and farmland, and to facilitate sound, long-term land and forest management. Urban CLTs have formed to combat speculation and gentrification, to preserve and develop low- and moderate-income housing, and to maintain useful urban open spaces (see ICE 1982).

Given their community-wide scope and varied memberships, CLTs tend to be, and should be, expansive organizations, taking on new projects at the same time that they perform a stewardship role in relation to past projects (see ICE 1989).

Government Partnerships With Community Land Trusts

Local governments are recognizing the advantages of partnerships with community land trusts (CLTs). These include quick response, flexibility, cost-effective protection of historic or environmentally significant land, and increasing the stock of permanently affordable housing. Governments have formed several kinds of partnerships with CLTs, including: allocating funds to CLT programs; allocating city-owned lands to CLTS; using "linkage" programs to foster CLT development; using municipal zoning powers to negotiate commitments from developers to make donations of land and to build affordable housing for a CLT; and placing publicly owned lands, such as bike paths, conservation areas, and community gardens, under the care and management of a CLT.

INITIATIVES

Sustainable Employment

"A city plan drawn up by *San Jose*, California would create 170 jobs over 10 years with an initial investment of just over $645,000. The program includes educational campaigns to show consumers how to save energy, and technical assistance, such as energy audits and the development of a home energy rating system. Prominent in the San Jose plan are initiatives to reduce energy use in government buildings and transportation, in effect providing an example for the community. The city investment, which would spur nearly $20 million in private spending, is expected to pay for itself in two-and-a-half years, and result in reduced carbon dioxide emissions." (Flavin and Lenssen 1991)

Community Land Trusts

There are now more than 125 community land trusts (CLTs) in operation or development throughout the U.S. Although most are quite young, these CLTs have acquired or developed several thousand units of permanently affordable housing and provided land for family farms, shelters and health centres.

The United Nations International Year of Shelter for the Homeless (1987) cited three CLTs in the U.S. for its Special Merit Award. For one of these, in *Burlington*, Vermont, the city provided an initial seed grant for a CLT, and staff people in the city's Community and Economic Development Office took the lead in encouraging local residents to establish the Burlington Community Land Trust (an independent non-profit corporation) in 1984. Other US cities with CLTs include *Philadelphia*, *Atlanta*, and *Providence*.

Linkage Programs

For community land trusts and related institutions to have a truly appreciable effect on sustainable development, public powers and public funds will be required for their expansion. At the local government level, a good model would be the "linkage" programs which have been used in several cities to provide funds for affordable housing, job development, and day-care. Linkage works by taking a portion of the value created by investment in areas undergoing substantial development, and directing that value to build affordable housing, provide job training, and fund social services in less fortunate neighborhoods. Linkage policies represent "a new social contract to build lasting bridges of economic opportunity between areas of the city experiencing rapid growth, and the people [...] who, historically, have not shared in the benefits of that growth" (BRA 1988).

Linkage programs for sustainable community development, modelled after these existing programs, could provide a means for the environmental costs of conventional development to be balanced by conservation and ecologically appropriate development. While linkage programs have operated for several years in US cities such as *Boston* and *San Francisco,* they are also becoming more common in Canada. In December 1990 *Vancouver* approved its first agreement with a commercial developer in which the capital costs of a day-care centre are financed as a condition of rezoning.

New Product Development

"In *Gothenberg,* Sweden's most industrialized city, the municipal government established the Gothenberg Environment Project (GEP) to demonstrate a more contemporary and effective approach to environment-economy integration. GEP researched the toxic chemicals in Gothenberg's harbor and discovered most of them originated from ordinary household detergents. Rather than the conventional attempt to regulate emissions, the GEP instead challenged the soap manufacturers to change the product. A truly environment-friendly detergent is being developed. The city also recognized that environmental responsibility is global as well as local. Powerpipe AB wanted to set up a factory in Gothenberg to manufacture pipes. These pipes are normally insulated with a CFC-based foam (CFCs are chemicals which destroy the ozone layer). The city allowed the company to operate only on the condition that they not use CFCs. Reluctant at first, the company discovered it was able to obtain government funds to develop a foam made without CFCs. The new pipes cost about 10% more, but are the world's first CFC-free pipes. The company will benefit as the chemicals are phased out world-wide. Powerpipe AB's President, Rune Engvall, agrees that 'we have a promising market.' And senior government officials are learning from the GEP that unless government sets rules, these kinds of technical developments will not come about." (Public Broadcasting System 1990)

234

> "*Manufacturers want to come to Gothenberg, and we do like that, and want them here, but we have to think about the environment. And if we know that they are using something which is not good for the environment, we have said 'no.' And then, usually, the factory says: 'It's impossible! We must use it! We don't know anything else! The technique isn't there yet!' But if you have the guts, and say it must be like that, I have seen many, many times, if you stand by, to be firm, they will come with something else. It was a factory who want to come to Gothenberg and start producing pipes. And they were using CFCs. And then we made a decision in this government, in Gothenberg, you might come here, you're welcome, but you mustn't use CFCs.*"
> Kerstin Svenson, Gothenberg City Councillor, 1990

Increasing Affordable Housing Supply

"The *Portland* metropolitan region has enhanced the supply of affordable housing by replacing zoning codes that require each house to occupy its own spacious lot with controls that promote a variety of housing types, including smaller and multi-family homes. Because of changes in local zoning plans, 54 percent of all recent residential development in the region consists of apartments, duplexes, and other affordable housing types, compared with the 30 percent maximum allowed by previous zoning. This policy has been a leading factor in keeping the city's housing prices affordable. In relation to household income, housing in Portland is two to three times as affordable as in Seattle, San Jose, San Francisco, and other West Coast cities." (Lowe 1992)

Local Self-Reliance

St. Paul, Minnesota's "Home-Grown Economy" project experimented with a number of attempts to establish closed-loop, self-sustaining economic networks. Rubber tires, for example, are ordinarily a disposal nuisance. St.

Paul learned that tires can be recycled by freezing them in liquid nitrogen, pulverizing them, and using them as a filler for repairing potholes, another nuisance for which the city is responsible. The recycling costs were $1 per tire; the disposal costs were $3.25 per tire (see Meehan 1987).

Greenmarkets

New York City's Council on the Environment – a citizens' organization that works out of the mayor's office – initiated a system of "Greenmarkets" in 1976. Currently operating at 10 sites year-round and 20 in summertime, the Greenmarkets aim to preserve farmland and help struggling upstate farmers, while making fresh fruits and vegetables available in city neighborhoods. The markets offer many New Yorkers their only chance to get local produce without journeying to the suburbs (see Lowe 1991).

Local Currencies

In 1988 the local Energy Commission in *Lester Prairie,* Minnesota (pop. 1,229), developed an innovative way to invest state energy grant money for long-term local development: a "Prairie Buck." Residents and businesses who signed up for an energy audit received fifteen "Prairie Bucks," good for the purchase of a compact fluorescent lamp at local hardware stores. Instead of flowing out to distant energy suppliers, local dollars stay in town and bolster the local economy. To encourage carpooling to Hutchinson (15 miles) or the Twin Cities (45 miles), the town began offering "Rideshare Bucks" according to the number of passengers in the car and the number of gallons required for their commute. During the first eight months of the program, 75 participants earned a total of $1,239. After two years, the citizens of Lester Prairie saved an estimated 600,000 miles of travel and prevented 200,000 pounds of carbon dioxide from polluting the atmosphere (see RMI 1991).

RESOURCES

Sustainable Employment

FRANK T. ADAMS AND GARY B. HANSON, *Putting Democracy to Work: A Practical Guide for Starting Worker-owned Businesses* (Eugene, OR: Hulogos'i Communications, 1987). This is a comprehensive "how-to" guide for setting up a worker-owned organization. As a changing economy forces many businesses to the brink, more workers are considering buying them. This book tells how to do it and how the worker-owner edge can make a difference. Topics include organizing, managing, participating, assessing, technical assistance, capital, taxes, law and the business plan, with examples from the U.S. and Europe. Also includes examples and models on the decision-making process, by-laws, board and officer roles, legal structure, membership, meeting process and voting.

EDWARD J. BLAKELY, *Planning Local Economic Development: Theory and Practice* (Newbury Park, CA: Sage Publications, 1989). This comprehensive volume, combining theoretical and practical information, is indispensable for local economic development planning. Topics include the planning process, analytical techniques, selecting a strategy, locality and business development, human resource development, community-based economic and employment development, preparing project plans, and institutional approaches.

KEITH M. COSSEY, *Co-operative Strategies for Sustainable Communities: Community-Based Development Organizations* (Sackville, N.B.: Mount Allison University, 1990). This paper focuses on the role of community development corporations as a vehicle for sustainable community development.

FLOYD W. DYKEMAN, ed., *Entrepreneurial and Sustainable Rural Communities* (Sackville, N.B.: Mount Allison University, 1990). This collection links theory and action by focusing on rural community adaptation/innovation and support systems for rural community development. Dykeman's introductory essay discusses a range of alternative organizational structures for community development, from development corporations to local government committees.

DAVID MORRIS, *An Environmental Policy for the 1990s: Fashioning the Molecular Basis for a Green Economy* (Washington, DC: Institute for Local Self-Reliance, 1990). Morris is well known for his work around the concept of local self-reliance. The Institute for Local Self-Reliance's Carbohydrate *Economy Project* is researching the feasibility of moving toward a plant matter based economy, with the objective of substituting plant matter for a third of our current consumption of fossil fuels. In this essay Morris argues that all environmental and economic development policies should be guided by a molecular accounting system, with the goal of extracting the maximum amount of useful work on a sustained basis from every molecule. A fascinating, forward-thinking piece on creating a new economy that integrates concerns about democracy, equity, economic development, and the environment, with attention to the role of local as well as senior government. Access information below.

INSTITUTE FOR LOCAL SELF-RELIANCE, *Waste to Wealth: A Business Guide for Community Recycling Enterprises*. A how-to guide for community groups and small businesses interested in establishing recycling programs. Available from:
Institute for Local Self-Reliance
2425 18th Street NW

Washington, DC 20009

Tel: 202/232-4108   Fax: 202/332-0463

THE CANADIAN MANUFACTURERS' ASSOCIATION, *Sustainable Development: A Policy Paper* suggests that embracing the concept of sustainable development offers "our best opportunity to work in a spirit of cooperation with governments and members of the public to achieve practical and cost-effective solutions to our environmental problems." Available from:

Doreen C. Henley
Director, Environmental Affairs
The Canadian Manufacturers' Association
130 Albert St., Suite 302
Ottawa, ON K1P 5G4
Tel: 613/233-8423   Fax: 613/233-6048

THE WESTCOAST DEVELOPMENT GROUP is the project arm of the Centre for Community Enterprise. Westcoast conducts community economic development (CED) research, planning and training. It also publishes and distributes a wide range of resources to assist in CED training, research, and analysis. Of particular interest is *Making Waves*, a quarterly newsletter for CED practitioners in Canada. Available from:

Westcoast Development Group
Suite 337 - 163 West Hastings
Vancouver, B.C. V5B 1H5
Tel: 604/685-5058   Fax: 604/685-5363

THE INDUSTRIAL COOPERATIVE ASSOCIATION provides a wide range of consulting services to employee-owned businesses, unions, state agencies, and economic development organizations. ICA helps create employee-owned firms in three situations: 1) in response to a plant closing, when employees threatened with job loss purchase the enterprise; 2) when the retiring owner of a business sells to his or her employees; and 3) when individuals start an entirely new employee-owned firm. ICA can train local government staff, assess the feasibility of employee buyouts, and advise on economic development policies that promote local ownership and control of businesses. For more information contact:

Industrial Cooperative Association
58 Day Street, Suite 200
Somerville, MA 02144
Tel: 617/629-2700

Economic Demand Management

SEVERYN T. BRUYN AND JAMES MEEHAN, eds., *Beyond the Market and the State: New Directions in Community Development* (Philadelphia: Temple University Press, 1987). Part One of this fascinating and informative collection of essays explores new community-oriented enterprises such as CLTs, CDCs, worker and consumer coops, and community financial institutions. Part Two examines local, regional and national strategies to enhance local self-reliance, including education and legislation. Of particular note is Karl Seidman's essay, "A New Role for Government: Supporting a Democratic Economy."

THE INSTITUTE FOR COMMUNITY ECONOMICS is a non-profit corporation providing technical and financial assistance to community land trusts, limited-equity housing coops, community loan funds, and other grassroots organizations, as well as providing information and educational material to the general public. The Institute authored *The Community Land Trust Handbook* (Emmaus, PA: Rodale Press, 1982), and also publishes a quarterly journal, *Community Economics*.

The Institute for Community Economics
57 School Street
Springfield, MA 01105-1331
Tel: 413/746-8660

WARD MOREHOUSE, ed., *Building Sustainable Communities: Tools and Concepts for Self-Reliant Economic Change* (NY: Bootstrap Press, 1989). The three major sections of this book deal with community land trusts and other forms of community ownership of natural resources; worker-managed enterprises and other techniques of community self-management; and community currency and banking. Also included are a lexicon of social capitalism and a bibliography of key works on self-reliant economic change.

MARYLAND-NATIONAL CAPITAL PARK AND PLANNING COMMISSION. To follow up on the links between *trip reduction and affordable housing* contact:

Pat Hare
Maryland-National Capital Park
    and Planning Commission
8787 Georgia Avenue
Silver Spring, MD 20910-3760
Tel: 301/495-4559

Community Forestry

THE VILLAGE OF HAZLETON in British Columbia produced in 1991 *Framework for Watershed Stewardship*, a key document for forest communities struggling to gain some measure of control over the local forest base. The Framework is based upon Hazleton's 1990 "Forest Industry Charter of Rights," which was adopted wholly or in principle by at least eleven municipalities and regional districts in British Columbia. The original Charter was revised to reflect growing understanding of the principles of "new forestry" at the Community Options Forestry Conference at the University of Victoria, February 15-17, 1991. Although the *Framework* is focused on British Columbia, it could serve as a model for communities in other jurisdictions where forest resources are primarily controlled by senior government agencies.

The *Framework* argues that forests are unique resources which should be stewarded to maintain ecological diversity and integrity; guarantee biologically sustainable levels of resource harvest and extraction; require maximum value-added manufacturing of all resources; provide stable, fairly paid, and challenging employment; support a fair return on natural resource industry investments; and allow stable growth of regions whose communities control management of their local watersheds. Available from:

The Corporation of the Village of Hazleton
P.O. Box 40
Hazleton, B.C. V0J 1Y0

Note: The 1991 Community Options Forestry Conference at the University of Victoria was sponsored by the New Perspectives Forestry Society.

New Perspectives Forestry Society
158 Joseph St.
Victoria, B.C. V8S 3H5

ORVILLE CAMP, The Forest *Farmer's Handbook: A Guide to Natural Selection Forest Management* (Ashland, OR: Sky River Press, 1984). This book describes a sustainable all-age, all-species forest management system that does not involve clearcuts, burning, or herbicides. It also includes an appendix on designing appropriate access roads for a kinder, gentler forestry. Visitors to Camp's 160-acre Forest Farm can seen how the author has successfully practised sustainable forestry since 1967. Available from:

Camp Forest Farm
2100 Thompson Creek Road
Selma, OR 97538

ECOTRUST is a private, non-profit organization created by and affiliated with Conservation International. Its mission is to help conserve ecosystems, biodiversity, and the ecological processes which support life on Earth, and to support conservation-based human development in the Pacific Northwest, British Columbia and Alaska. Ecotrust has expertise in community development, ecosystem science, ecological economics, policy, fund raising and institution building. It helps to bridge the supply and demand of technical, scientific, financial and political resources for sustainable development. According to Ecotrust, "Every community is full of entrepreneurial creativity in people who are trying to improve the quality of both their lives and the environment. Our hope is to help them develop a new strategy to get rich slow."

Ecotrust
Suite 470, 1200 NW Front
Portland, Oregon 97209
Tel: 503/227-6225   Fax: 503/222-1517

RUTH LOOMIS, *Wildwood: A Forest for the Future* (Gabriola, B.C.: Reflections, 1990). Describes the sustainable forest management practices of Vancouver Islander Merv Wilkinson.

CHRIS MASER, *The Redesigned Forest* (San Pedro, CA: R. and E. Miles, 1989). Maser is a consultant on sustainable forestry and was formerly a researcher for the US Bureau of Land Management. This book has won unqualified praise for its clarity and relevance to current issues in forestry.

Forest Planning Canada is a bi-monthly which rightly describes itself as "Canada's community forestry forum." Available from:

Forest Planning Canada
PO Box 6234, Stn. "C"
Victoria, B.C. V8P 5L5

The Trumpeter: Journal of Ecosophy is a quarterly which addresses serious discussions of ecophilosophy, but also includes good coverage of books and developments in community forestry. Available from:

Toward Sustainable Communities

The Trumpeter
PO Box 5853 Stn B
Victoria, B.C. V8R 6S8

References

ADAMS, F.T. AND G.B. HANSON, *Putting Democracy to Work: A Practical Guide for Starting Worker-owned Businesses* (Eugene, OR: Hulogos'i Communications, 1987).

BLAKELY, E.J., *Planning Local Economic Development: Theory and Practice* (Newbury Park, CA: Sage Publications, 1989).

BOOTHROYD, P., "Community Economic Development: An Introduction for Planners" (Vancouver: UBC Centre for Human Settlements, 1991).

BOSTON REDEVELOPMENT AUTHORITY (BRA), "Linkage" (Boston: BRA, Winter, 1988).

BRUYN, S.T., "Beyond the Market and the State," in S.T. Bruyn and J. Meehan, eds., *Beyond the Market and the State: New Directions in Community Development* (Philadelphia: Temple University Press, 1987).

CAMP, O., *The Forest Farmer's Handbook: A Guide to Natural Selection Forest Management* (Ashland, OR: Sky River Press, 1984).

COSSEY, K.M., *Co-operative Strategies for Sustainable Communities: Community-Based Development Organizations* (Sackville, N.B.: Mount Allison University, 1990).

DYKEMAN, F.W., ed., *Entrepreneurial and Sustainable Rural Communities* (Sackville, N.B.: Mount Allison University, 1990).

FLAVIN, C. AND N. LENSSEN, "Designing a Sustainable Energy System," in Brown, L.R., et al, *State of the World 1991: A Worldwatch Institute Report on Progress Toward a Sustainable Society* (NY/London: W.W. Norton & Co., 1991), pp. 21-38.

GEISER, K., "The Greening of Industry: Managing the Transition to a Sustainable Economy," *Technology Review,* August/September 1991, pp. 64-72.

INSTITUTE FOR COMMUNITY ECONOMICS (ICE), *The Community Land Trust Handbook* (Emmaus, PA: Rodale Press, 1982).

INSTITUTE FOR COMMUNITY ECONOMICS, *Community Economics* (No. 18, Summer 1989).

INTERNATIONALUNION FOR CONSERVATION OF NATURE (IUCN), THE UNITED NATIONS ENVIRONMENT PROGRAMME (UNEP), AND THE WORLD WIDE FUND FOR NATURE (WWF), "Caring for the Earth: A Strategy for Sustainable Living" (Gland, Switzerland: IUCN/UNEP/WWF, 1991).LOOMIS, R., *Wildwood:A Forest for the Future* (Gabriola, B.C.: Reflections, 1990).

LOWE, M.D., "Shaping Cities: The Environmental and Human Dimensions," Worldwatch Paper 105 (Washington, D.C.: Worldwatch Institute, 1991).

MARTIN, L., "Resources from Waste and Self-Reliant Investment," in S. Meeker-Lowry, *Economics as if the Earth Really Mattered: A* Catalyst *Guide to Socially Conscious Investing* (Philadelphia: New Society Publishers, 1988).

MARYLAND-NATIONAL CAPITAL PARK AND PLANNING COMMISSION, "Trip Reduction and Affordable Housing," staff document, March 15, 1990.

MASER, C., *The Redesigned Forest* (San Pedro, CA: R. and E. Miles, 1989).

MEEHAN, J., "Working Toward Local Self-Reliance," in S.T. Bruyn and J. Meehan, eds., *Beyond the Market and the State: New Directions in Community Development* (Philadelphia: Temple University Press, 1987).

MOREHOUSE, W., ed., *Building Sustainable Communities: Tools and Concepts for Self-Reliant Economic Change* (NY: Bootstrap Press, 1989).

MORRIS, D., "Local Self-Reliance," in Van der Ryn, S. and P. Calthorpe, *Sustainable Communities: A New Design Synthesis for Cities, Suburbs, and Towns* (San Francisco: Sierra Club Books, 1986).

MORRIS, D., "The Ecological City as a Self-Reliant City," in D. Gordon, ed., *Green Cities: Ecologically Sound Approaches to Urban Space* (Montreal: Black Rose Books, 1990), pp. 21-35.

MORRIS, D., *An Environmental Policy for the 1990s: Fashioning the Molecular Basis for a Green Economy* (Washington, DC: Institute for Local Self-Reliance, 1990a).

ONTARIO CONSERVATION NEWS, "Geraldton: A Sustainable Community," Ontario Conservation News 16(10), September 1989.

PUBLIC BROADCASTING SYSTEM, *The Race to Save the Planet* (Boston: WGBH, 1990), Part Eight.

REES, W.E., "Vital Communities and Sustainable Forests," presented to Transitions to Tomorrow: Community Options Forestry Conference (Victoria: New Perspectives Forestry Society, February 15-17, 1991).

REES, W.E. AND M. ROSELAND, "Sustainable Communities: Planning for the 21st Century," *Plan Canada 31(3):15-26,* May 1991.

RENNER, M., "Jobs in a Sustainable Economy", Worldwatch Paper No. 104 (Washington, D.C.: Worldwatch Institute, 1991).

ROCKY MOUNTAIN INSTITUTE (RMI) *Newsletter,* VII(1), Spring 1991.

ROSEN, D., *Public Capital* (Washington, DC: National Center for Policy Alternatives, 1988).

SCHOR, J.B. "Global Equity and Environmental Crisis: An Argument for Reducing Working Hours in the North" *World Development* 19(1): 73-84, 1991.

SKINNER, N., "Making Energy Policy, Not War," *Bulletin of Municipal Foreign Policy,* 5(2):14, Spring 1991.

SVENSON, K., on Public Broadcasting System, *The Race to Save the Planet* (Boston: WGBH, 1990), Part Eight.

SWACK, M., "Community Finance Institutions," in S.T. Bruyn and J. Meehan, eds., *Beyond the Market and the State: New Directions in Community Development* (Philadelphia: Temple University Press, 1987).

URBAN ECOLOGIST, "Ecological Rebuilding in the United States," *The Urban Ecologist,* Fall 1991.

11

Community Development

Although some people confuse development with mere growth, development is actually a much more complex, rich term. This chapter explores sustainable community development both in terms of local community livability and also in terms of responsibility to the global community.

The environmental advantages of urban areas – such as compact development, shorter travel distances, economically viable public transit, and per capita energy conservation – can only be realized if our communities are livable. Perhaps the most important indicator of "livability" is that livable communities are *communities people want to live in*. Municipal and local governments therefore need to address those issues that cause people to stay in their communities - e.g. employment and educational opportunities, accessible healthcare services, vibrant arts and culture, and a thriving non-profit sector as well as those that cause people to leave - e.g. crime, dissatisfaction with existing housing choices and lack of opportunity to participate in decisions affecting their lives and well-being.

In many cities with good public transit systems, for example, a substantial proportion of the population is afraid to use the system after dark. The obvious consequences are that those who can afford it will drive or take taxis, those who cannot will either travel in fear or lock themselves up at home, and the public transit system will lose revenue.

Public and Private Space
"Mobility and privacy have increasingly displaced
the traditional commons, which once provided the
connected quality of our towns and cities. Our shared
public space has been given over to the car and its
accommodation, while our private world has become
bloated and isolated. As our private world grows in
breadth, our public world becomes more remote and
impersonal. As a result, our public space lacks identity
and is largely anonymous, while our private space
strains toward a narcissistic autonomy. Our
communities are zoned black or white, private or
public, my space or nobody's. The automobile destroys
the urban street, the shopping center destroys the
neighborhood store, and the depersonalization of
public space grows with the scale of government.
Inversely, private space is taxed by the necessity of
providing for many activities that were once shared
and is further burdened by the need to create identity
in a sea of monotony. Although the connection between
such social issues and development is elusive and
complex, it must be addressed by any serious theory
of growth."

(Calthorpe 1989)

Sustainable community development implies that we
address not only the "hard" urban environmental issues
such as transportation, land use, air quality, and energy
conservation, but also the "soft" issues such as public
health and safety, gender equity, environmental education,
and global environmental responsibility.

Healthy Communities

Public health has been among the traditional responsibilities of local government. A century ago, municipalities were instrumental in improving public health by preventing the spread of disease through slum clearance, community planning, water treatment, and the provision of certain health services. These early interventions were based on the view of health as the absence of disease, and disease prevention as the main challenge for local government. In the last decade a new, broader conception of public health has been developed and adopted by municipal governments in Europe and North America. Although the name "healthy communities" implies a focus on medical care, the Ottawa Charter for Health Promotion (1986) recognizes that "the fundamental conditions and resources for health are peace, shelter, education, food, income, a stable eco-system, sustainable resources, social justice, and equity."

Local governments play a big role in all these areas through their impact on public hygiene (waste disposal and water systems), food handling and other public health regulations, recreational facilities, education, transportation, economic development, and land use planning.

The Canadian Healthy Communities Project was jointly sponsored by the Federation of Canadian Municipalities, the Canadian Institute of Planners, and the Canadian Public Health Association to create healthy public policy at the community level. The Project was funded by Health and Welfare Canada from 1988-1991. (For further information contact the Canadian Institute of Planners - see "Resources.")

"*Planners and citizens, particularly in North America, often assume that moderate and high-density land use are synonymous with crime and unhealthy conditions. Yet there is no scientific evidence of a link between these social problems and density per se... where density and crime coincide, other, more powerful forces are at work; there is no inherent relationship between population density and urban social ills.*"

Lowe 1991

One Reason Transit is Under-utilized

Fifty-six percent of Canadian women say there are areas near their homes where they are afraid to take an evening walk, according to a Gallup poll. Combined male-female statistics indicate 37 percent of the public are hesitant about walking in their neighbourhood in the evening.

(see Canadian Press 1991)

"*Every first-world city has within it a third-world city of malnutrition, infant mortality, homelessness and unemployment. Every third-world city has within it a first-world city of high tech, high fashion, and high finance. Seeing the cities of the world as a global laboratory breaks down the stereotype North / South technology transfer, and opens up the rich possibilities of South / North and South / South exchange, vastly increasing the number of potential solutions.*"

Perlman 1990

"*The sustainable city is one that achieves a steady improvement in social equity, diversity and opportunity and 'quality of life,' broadly defined. Economic, fiscal and sectoral policies, however, often have the unintended effects of reducing all of these and increasing social polarization and cultural and economic barriers between groups.*"

Institute for Research on Public Policy 1989

TOOLS

Safety Audits

Metro Action Committee (METRAC), which evolved out of a 1982 Toronto panel on public violence, developed the idea of "safety audits" of city streets, lanes, and parks. Informal groups of four to six people, mostly women, evaluated lighting, access to emergency phones, overgrown shrubbery near bus shelters, and so on. The information collected was given to the appropriate authorities (transit, parks, engineering, etc.), which began to take steps to improve safety within their jurisdiction. Lighting in public places such as railway stations has been improved, landscaping around universities and schools has been designed with security in mind, and buses will stop anywhere along their routes after dark so women have shorter distances to walk. Safety audit programs are now being used in Hamilton, Ontario and on several university campuses. (see Hamilton Spectator 1991; Taylor 1991; Canadian Press 1991b)

Urban Design and the Elderly

An Australian study highlighted the vulnerability of the elderly in a car-dependent city by showing that they are:
• less transport independent due to a much higher proportion who do not drive;
• more isolated due to the physical distances and poor public transport in low density suburbs; and
• more prone to injury from vehicles while walking.

Solutions to these problems, as part of a wider agenda of urban reform, include enhanced transit (especially light rail), traffic calming and urban villages. The study suggests that the time to provide these improved urban design options for the elderly is before the aging of the "baby boom" generation is felt in 20 years. (see Newman 1991)

Cohousing Developments

Cohousing is a grass-roots movement that grew directly out of people's dissatisfaction with existing housing choices. Its initiators draw inspiration from the increasing popularity of shared households, in which several unrelated people share a traditional house, and from the cooperative movement in general. Yet cohousing is distinctive in that each family or household has a separate dwelling and chooses how much they want to participate in community activities.

Cohousing developments are unique in their extensive common facilities and in that they are organized, planned, and managed by the residents themselves. Pioneered in Denmark some 20 years ago, there are now over 100 cohousing developments in *Denmark*, plus many more in *The Netherlands, Sweden, Norway, France,* and *Germany*. In *North America* over 40 cohousing communities are now in the planning stages.

Cohousing developments vary in size, location, type of ownership, design, and priorities, but all share four common characteristics:

"Participatory Process: Residents organize and participate in the planning and design process for the housing development, and are responsible as a group for all final decisions.

Intentional Neighbourhood Design: The physical design encourages a strong sense of community.

Extensive Common Facilities: An integral part of the community, common areas are designed for daily use, to supplement private living areas.

Complete Resident Management: Residents manage the development, making decisions of common concern at community meetings." (McCamant and Durrett 1988)

> *Environmental Policy and Environmental Education*
> "Environmental policy and environmental education
> must be seen as mutually dependent and supportive.
> Hence an environmental policy will not work without
> an informed population, while environmental
> education will not be effective if it is contradicted in
> wider society through environmental policy being
> weak or absent."
>
> (U.K. Council on Environmental Education,
> in ACC 1990)

> *"All education is environmental education. By what is
> included or excluded we teach students that they are part of
> or apart from the natural world. To teach economics, for
> example, without reference to the laws of thermodynamics or
> those of ecology is to teach a fundamentally important
> ecological lesson: that physics and ecology have nothing to do
> with the economy. It just happens to be dead wrong. The
> same is true throughout all of the curriculum."*
>
> Orr 1991

Aims of Environmental Education

"The aims of environmental education apply equally well
in both schools and the community more generally.
Environmental education aims to develop:
- a greater awareness of the environment and the
  consequences of human interactions with it;
- an understanding of how life is sustained and supported
  on earth both locally and globally;
- a wide range of knowledge and skills from different
  fields to assist in investigating environmental issues
  and choosing appropriate courses of action;
- an appreciation of the range of perspectives that
  impinge upon environmental issues – for example, the
  biological, the economic and the technological aspects;

- an environmental ethic which clarifies and enhances environmental values, leading to the appreciation of natural and human-made beauty, valuing a healthy environment, concern for the welfare of people and other living things, and belief in the wise use of resources;
- a commitment to work, personally and cooperatively, for a better physical and social environment and a willingness to apply the knowledge and skills acquired in action programs to improve or protect students' own environment;
- an understanding of the need to balance development and conservation to meet the needs of society."

(Ministry of Education, Victoria, Australia, 1990)

Environmental Education in Schools

"To be fully effective, environmental education in schools needs to be covered in a diversity of ways. For example:

- an appropriate environmental education dimension needs to be included in every area of the curriculum (the arts and humanities have just as crucial a contribution to make as the sciences);
- all students need at some stage to be involved in studies which bring the range of subject areas together to focus on environmental issues of clear importance to the students' own lives;
- a specialist environmental education subject is needed at senior level for students intending environment-related careers." (VEEC 1991)

> *"We have a compulsory school course called Consumer Education – and we hate it. This course teaches us how to spend money, how to use credit cards, how to be materialistic, how to be consumers. That's exactly what we don't need. [We] came up with a new course. We call it Environomics. In it we would learn how to be environmentally aware when we buy. It would teach us that the environment and the economy interact and that a balance needs to be found and maintained. It would stress the holistic approach to learning by taking students out of the classrooms, through field trips and work experience, to discover the issues first-hand."*
>
> Affolter and Biagi (both age 17), 1991

INITIATIVES

Worker Safety
San Francisco passed the first US municipal ordinance to regulate the use of video display terminals (VDTs) in private businesses. The ordinance is intended to reduce the risk of ailments caused by prolonged use of a computer terminal, including eye strain, muscle fatigue and carpal tunnel syndrome, an injury that can incapacitate the hand and that often requires surgery. The law requires that workers be provided with adjustable chairs and adequate lighting and that computer terminals be equipped with detachable keyboards and adjustable screens. Employees without regularly scheduled rest breaks are to be given 15 minutes of alternative work after every two hours at a terminal if such work is available. The law also requires employers to provide training on safe use of VDTs and recommends that pregnant VDT users be shifted to other work if they request it (see New York Times 1990; Associated Press 1990).

Healthy Community Projects

In Europe the World Health Organization has directed the successful creation of a 30-city network known as the Healthy Cities Project. In Canada, there have been approximately 100 active healthy community projects, and interest has been growing in *Seattle* and other US cities. Several Canadian cities, including *Vancouver, Toronto, Edmonton, Montreal,* and *Québec City,* have adopted healthy community platforms. *Toronto* City Council has established a Healthy City Office.

Smoking Disincentives

New York City Council's health committee unanimously passed a bill that would ban cigarette vending machines from apartment buildings, gasoline stations, coin-operated laundromats and restaurants where the sale of alcoholic beverages is incidental. Taverns and many bars would be exempted. As many as 75 percent of the city's estimated 36,000 cigarette machines would be affected (see LADN 1990).

Integrated Environmental and Social Policy

The Dutch municipality of Zutphen (pop. 31,000) has integrated environmental aspects into its social policies through its "disassembly line" (*Sloopstraat*) project, an apprentice shop for young people. In the "disassembly line" discarded but still serviceable equipment is repaired and sold, usable parts are taken out of equipment and sold, and polluting substances are removed. Mostly washing machines and refrigerators are handled. The work is done by long-term unemployed people who have fallen into arrears socially and economically (see Association of Netherlands Municipalities 1990).

At the Southeast Regional Correctional Center in

Bridgewater, Massachusetts, an innovative pilot program provides food for the prison and the community while training inmates for future employment. Situated in a prison greenhouse, the program uses an integrated fish culture and hydroponic vegetable production system. Within each 5-by-5 foot 675-gallon fibreglass tank fish swim in the lower portion and lettuce or other plants grow on top. The Bridgewater program, sponsored by the MIT Sea Grant College Program, began in 1987. By 1990 the inmates were managing some 20 tanks and growing a weekly crop per tank of about 100 heads of lettuce, plus a seasonal crop of up to 100 pounds of fish. They were also experimenting with watercress, basil, and flowers. The produce and fish were sold to the culinary arts program at the prison, to prison staff, to a regional high school, and to a local health-food store. The inmates are learning valuable skills which they may be able to transfer to careers such as horticulture and aquarium management after release. In 1990 the Massachusetts Horticultural Society presented the program with a gold medal for the best use of horticulture in therapy and a silver medal for best example of education (see Zweig 1990; Levi 1991).

Gender Equity
"Delagacias da Mulher" in *Sao Paulo*, Brazil are all-female police stations responsive to the special needs of women victims, while creating new career paths for women at every level (see Perlman 1990).

Urban Environment Platforms
In May 1989 over two hundred *New York City* organizations – from local chapters of prominent national groups to the smallest block associations – agreed upon "Environment '90: A Platform for the Future of New York City." With its 49 recommendations, the Platform addresses

parks, gardens and open spaces; air quality; water quality; energy conservation; garbage, sewage and toxic wastes; environmentally sound development; and environmental education for all age levels. Political candidates were asked to state their positions on the recommendations.

Green City *Philadelphia*, a coalition of more than 60 businesses, government agencies, academic institutions, and community organizations, issued an "Urban Environment Platform" in 1990 which sets out detailed lists of "green" political principles in 13 issue areas, including parks, open space, housing, water, energy, air quality, transportation, environmental health, historic preservation, solid waste, and recycling. The program includes specific consideration of the social environment, and in 1991 received additional support from 70 community organizations, including many in minority neighbourhoods. The coalition secured endorsements from both major party mayoral candidates for the 1991 elections, and organizers developed a short list of 10 cost-effective "green" steps the new mayor can take within 100 days of taking office (see *Urban Ecologist* 1991).

In *Victoria, B.C.* in 1990, Voters for a Responsible Community, a non-partisan group, was formed to raise voter awareness on a wide range of social, economic and environmental issues. With the support of more than 30 community and environmental organizations, the group distributed a pre-election questionnaire of some 100 questions to candidates throughout the Capital Regional District.

Topics ranged from waste management and transportation to public involvement, affordable housing, and global responsibility. In Victoria, 70 percent of the candidates responded, including seven of the nine who were elected to office. At least five – a majority vote on council – indicated they would support a broad range of sustainable community initiatives (see Dauncey 1990).

Global Environmental Responsibility
In an effort to save tropical rainforests, local community groups associated with Friends of the Earth have convinced hundreds of city councils in the *United Kingdom, West Germany, The Netherlands,* and *Belgium* either to restrict or to ban altogether the use of tropical timber within municipal boundaries (see Towns and Development, n.d.).

City-to-City Sustainable Development Partnerships (Twinning)
The city-state of *Bremen*, Germany has established innovative "sustainable development" partnerships with villages and communities in India and Africa, providing safe water and appropriate energy sources. Bremen has an overall program covering development education, support for liberation movements and the development of alternative energy sources. Within this program Bremen works with NGOs to support the installation of bio-gas plants in *India, Mali* and *Rwanda*. In this way Bremen helps to alleviate the firewood crisis and to restore ecological balance in these countries (see SODC 1990).

The Austrian town of *Leibnitz* has an official link with *Pedra Badejo*, a little village on a barren island of Cape Verde. Within the city link a dozen projects have been set up, in fields such as carpentry, fishing, sewing, city-planning and restoration. Craftsmen and women from Leibnitz worked side by side with the local population to improve life in Pedra Badejo (see Towns and Development, n.d.).

The municipality of *Amsterdam* detached two civil servants to help and train colleagues in the Dutch capital's sister city of *Managua*, Nicaragua for two years (see Towns and Development, n.d.).

The link between the municipality of *Campbell River,* British Columbia and the Kenyan village of *Kivi* (pop. 3,500) was first forged by World Vision Canada, an international relief agency, as a pilot project for young people. Kivi has no electricity or running water. With support from the municipal council, schools, local offices of government agencies, and various community organizations, Campbell River is now sending cows, bicycles, and clothing to Kivi. With help from the Rotary Club of Campbell River and the Federation of Canadian Municipalities "Africa 2000" program, an earthfill dam was completed in July 1991, providing drinking water and irrigation. A photocopier for the regional government and wheelbarrows are next on the list. "Some people ask, 'What's in it for you?' But I think we learn a lot from sharing and our children learn there are many people in the world who need help," said Mayor Mary Ashley (see Farrow 1991).

RESOURCES

K. MCCAMANT AND C. DURRETT, *Cohousing: A Contemporary Approach to Housing Ourselves* (Berkeley: Habitat Press, 1988). McCamant and Durret are an American husband-wife design team, and leading experts on cohousing. After an extensive study of cohousing in Denmark, where they lived in or visited 60 communities, they introduced cohousing to North America through this book. *Cohousing* is written in three sections. The first introduces cohousing and explains how it works. The second is an inside look at eight cohousing communities. The third, "Creating Cohousing," considers the evolution of cohousing, the development process, design considerations, and translating cohousing to North America.

DORIT FROMM, *Collaborative Communities: Cohousing, Central Living, and Other New Forms of*

Housing with Shared Facilities (NY: Van Nostrand Reinhold, 1991). This volume focuses on housing forms characterized by residents taking the initiative to plan and manage their neighbourhoods. It includes case studies of Dutch, Danish, Swedish, and U.S. prototypes, and offers guidelines on transplanting European models to North America. Issues and obstacles are addressed, and a variety of tenure and management styles are discussed. The book features models for urban, suburban and rural environments. The appendices include community diagrams, comparisons of ownership types, sample design programs and bylaws, and definitions of housing terms.

MEDEA BENJAMIN AND ANDREA FREEDMAN, *Bridging the Global Gap: A Handbook to Linking Citizens of the First and Third World* (Cabin John, MD: Seven Locks Press, 1989). This book launched Global Exchange, a non-profit research, education and action centre focusing on US-Third World internationalism. Global Exchange's version of internationalism recognizes that the interests of the Third World coincide with the interests of the majority of North Americans. For example, less poverty abroad would mean fewer companies abandoning the US and Canada in search of cheaper labour; higher standards of living in Third World countries would mean more markets for our goods; greater democracy overseas would mean less US tax dollars wasted on military aid to repressive regimes. Includes information on municipal foreign policy and an extensive Resource Guide. For further information, contact:

Global Exchange
2940 16th St., Rm. 307
San Francisco, CA 94103
Tel: (415) 255-7296

THE INSTITUTE FOR SUSTAINABLE COMMUNITIES was founded in 1990 by former Vermont Governor Madeleine M. Kunin to promote sustainable development, environmental protection, and participatory democracy in Central and Eastern Europe. ISC is interested in developing community-based approaches to solving and preventing environmental problems by emphasizing activities that reinforce and complement the region's move toward economic restructuring and democratic decision-making. In partnership with the Independent Ecological Center in Hungary and Ecoglasnost in Bulgaria, ISC's Community Environmental Action Project is working with one community in Bulgaria and two in Hungary to demonstrate the benefits of environmental priority setting, democratic decision making, and citizen initiated action.

A second project assists elementary schools in Hungary in developing environmental curriculum and teaching methods, while a third project provides comprehensive environmental training to NGOs, government officials, businesses and universities in Poland, Bulgaria, Czechoslovakia and Hungary. For more information contact:

The Institute for Sustainable Communities
c/o The Environmental Law Centre
Vermont Law School
South Royalton, Vermont 05068
Tel: 802/763-8303   Fax: 802/763-2920

THE MEGA-CITIES PROJECT is a network of professionals and institutions in the world's largest cities, committed to promoting urban innovations for the 21st century. Its focus is reducing poverty and environmental degradation, and encouraging popular participation. Mega-cities are cities with over 10 million inhabitants – by 2000 there will be 23 of them. The North American mega-cities are New York, Los Angeles, and Mexico City. The project gives particular attention to urban innovations that empower women. For more information, see the special issue of *Cities* on "Urban Innovation for the 21st Century" (Volume 7, Number 1, February 1990) or contact:

Dr. Janice Perlman, Director
Mega-Cities Project
4 Washington Square North
New York University
New York, NY 10003
Tel: 212/998-7520   Fax: 212/995-3890

AFRICA 2000: THE MUNICIPAL RESPONSE is a multi-phase project to facilitate direct cooperation between Canadian and African municipalities. This project combines the effort and skill of elected officials, municipal administrators and community members in exchange of municipal officials, small capital expenditures, municipal environmental assessment, community-based projects, and new initiatives.

Africa 2000 is funded by the Canadian International Development Agency (CIDA) and implemented by the Federation of Canadian Municipalities (FCM). FCM's International Office also co-ordinates a twinning program. More than 100 Canadian municipalities are twinned with sister cities around the world. For more information, contact:

Federation of Canadian Municipalities
24 Clarence Street
Ottawa, Ontario K1N 5P3
Tel: 613/237-5221   Fax: 613/237-2965

Healthy Communities

BRIJESH MATHUR, editor, *Perspectives on Urban Health* (Winnipeg: University of Winnipeg, Institute of Urban Studies, 1991) is a collection of essays on urban health and wellness and the implications of healthy cities for urban planning. Available from:

The Institute of Urban Studies
University of Winnipeg
515 Portage Avenue

Winnipeg, Manitoba R3B 2E9

Tel: 204/786-9409   Fax: 204/786-1824

PETER BOOTHROYD AND MARGARET EBERLE, *Healthy Communities: What They Are, How They're Made* (Vancouver: UBC Centre for Human Settlements Research Bulletin, 1990) explores the meaning of healthy communities and how they can be created. The authors define a healthy community as "a community in which all organizations from informal groups to governments are working effectively together to improve the quality of all people's lives." Available from:

UBC Centre for Human Settlements

2206 East Mall

Vancouver, B.C. V6T 1W5

Tel: 604/822-5254   Fax: 604/822-6164

THE CANADIAN INSTITUTE OF PLANNERS For more information on the future of the *Canadian Healthy Communities Project,* contact:

Canadian Institute of Planners

126 York Street, Suite 404

Ottawa, Ontario K1N 5T5

References

AFFOLTER, M., AND I. BIAGI, "Forum Gave Us Confidence To Act," *Vancouver Sun,* December 9, 1991, p. A3. Based upon presentation to British Columbia Round Table Youth Forum.

ASSOCIATED PRESS, "San Francisco Law Helps VDT Workers," *Vancouver Sun,* December 28, 1990, p. A7.

ASSOCIATION OF COUNTY COUNCILS (ACC), ASSOCIATION OF DISTRICT COUNCILS, AND ASSOCIATION OF METROPOLITAN AUTHORITIES, *Environmental Practice in Local Government* (London: Association of District Councils 1990).

ASSOCIATION OF NETHERLANDS MUNICIPALITIES, *Municipal Environmental Policy in the Netherlands: Setting out for Sustainable Development* (The Hague: Association of Netherlands Municipalities, 1990).

BENJAMIN, M. AND A. FREEDMAN, *Bridging the Global Gap: A*

Handbook to Linking Citizens of the First and Third World (Cabin John, MD: Seven Locks Press, 1989).

BOOTHROYD, P. AND M. EBERLE, *Healthy Communities: What They Are, How They're Made* (Vancouver: UBC Centre for Human Settlements Research Bulletin, 1990).

CALTHORPE, P., "Pedestrian Pockets: New Strategies for Suburban Growth," in D. Kelbaugh, ed., *The Pedestrian Pocket Book: A New Suburban Design Strategy* (New York: Princeton Architectural Press, 1989).

CANADIAN PRESS, "Women Fear Walking, Poll Finds," *Vancouver Sun,* October 11, 1991, p. A8.

CANADIAN PRESS, "Melbourne Looks to Toronto for Ways to Makes Streets Safe," *Vancouver Sun,* October 26, 1991b, p. C9.

DAUNCEY, G., "New Council Offers a Humane Victoria," *Victoria Times-Colonist,* December 6, 1990.

FARROW, M., "Campbell River's Heart Beats in African Town," *Vancouver Sun,* September 4, 1991, p.1.

FROMM, D., *Collaborative Communities: Cohousing, Central Living, and Other New Forms of Housing with Shared Facilities* (NY: Van Nostrand Reinhold, 1991).

Hamilton Spectator, "Hamilton Women's Group Plans to Take Safety Audit of City," reprinted in *Vancouver Sun,* September 18, 1991, p. A4.

INSTITUTE FOR RESEARCH ON PUBLIC POLICY, "Sustainable Development: The Urban Dimension: An OECD Urban Mandate for the 1990s," prepared for Canada Mortgage and Housing Corporation for consideration by the OECD Group on Urban Affairs, September 21, 1989.

LEVI, C., "Growing Fish Salad: An Experiment in Integrated Aquaculture," *Nor'Easter,* Spring 1991, pp. 14-17.

LOS ANGELES DAILY NEWS (LADN) with NEW YORK TIMES NEWS SERVICE, "L.A. City Council To Vote on Total Restaurant Smoking Ban," *Vancouver Sun,* October 16, 1990, p. A5.

LOWE, M.D., "Shaping Cities: The Environmental and Human Dimensions," Worldwatch Paper 105 (Washington, D.C.: Worldwatch Institute, 1991).

MATHUR, B., ed., *Perspectives on Urban Health* (Winnipeg: University of Winnipeg, Institute of Urban Studies, 1991).

MCCAMANT, K. AND C. DURRETT, *Cohousing: A Contemporary Approach to Housing Ourselves* (Berkeley: Habitat Press, 1988).

MINISTRY OF EDUCATION (Victoria, Australia), "Ministerial Policy: Environmental Education" (Melbourne: Ministry of Education, 1990), quoted in Victorian Environmental Education Council (VEEC), *Educating For Our Environment* (Melbourne: VEEC, 1991).

NEWMAN, P., "Successful Ageing, Transport and Urban Design," presented to Conference on Successful Ageing, Canberra, Australia, November, 1991.

NEW YORK TIMES NEWS SERVICE, "San Francisco to Get VDT Regulations," *Vancouver Sun*, December 27, 1990, p. A13.

ORR, D., quoted in Victorian Environmental Education Council (VEEC), *Educating For Our Environment* (Melbourne: VEEC, 1991).

PERLMAN, J.E., "The Mega-Cities Project," presented to the World Congress of Local Governments for a Sustainable Future, United Nations, New York, September 5, 1990.

STATE OFFICE OF DEVELOPMENT COOPERATION (SODC), *Bremen's Development Cooperation* (Bremen, Germany: Senator of Economy, Technology and Foreign Trade, State Office of Development Cooperation, 1990).

TAYLOR, C., "Taking Back the Night," *Vancouver Sun*, October 19, 1991, p. B5.

TOWNS AND DEVELOPMENT, "Getting to Know Towns and Development" (The Hague: Towns and Development: Local Initiatives for Global Development, n.d.).

URBAN ECOLOGIST, "Ecological Rebuilding in the United States," *The Urban Ecologist*, Fall 1991.

VICTORIAN ENVIRONMENTAL EDUCATION COUNCIL (VEEC), *Educating For Our Environment* (Melbourne: VEEC, 1991).

ZWEIG, R., "Development of an Integrated Aquaculture System at the Southeast Correctional Center in Bridgewater, Massachusetts" (Cambridge, MA: MIT Sea Grant Program, 1990).

12

Investment and Purchasing

> *"Public purchasing policy and the promotion and maintenance of standards are central to an effective environmental strategy. They complement the activities of trade and industry and affect the quality of life of all sectors of the community."*
>
> ACC 1990

Government investment and purchasing has a great influence in the local economy. For example, in 1989 total government purchases in the U.S. amounted to approximately $916 billion or about 20% of the gross national product. About 13% of these purchases were made by state and local governments. Municipal investment and purchasing is particularly important in terms of setting an example for private purchasers, creating new markets, and stimulating sustainable economic development.

Municipal purchasing policies are often critical to the success of other sustainable community programs. For example, despite winning a United Nations environmental award in 1989, Ontario's Blue Box recycling system was soon suffering as municipalities realized the program did not pay for itself (Reguly 1992). As many communities have found out the hard way, municipal expenditures on recycling programs are not useful or cost-effective if there is no local demand for businesses which make recycled or reusable products.

Corporate Environmental Responsibility
"By adopting these principles, we publicly affirm our belief that corporations and their shareholders have a direct responsibility for the environment. We believe that corporations must conduct their business as responsible stewards of the environment and seek profits only in a manner that leaves the Earth healthy and safe. We believe that corporations must not compromise on the ability of future generations to sustain their needs.
We recognize this to be a long-term commitment to update our practices continually in light of advances in technology and new understandings in health and environmental science. We intend to make consistent, measurable progress in implementing these principles and to apply them wherever we operate throughout the world."

(The Valdez Principles)

TOOLS

The Valdez Principles

The Coalition for Environmentally Responsible Economies (CERES) is a broad coalition of environmental organizations and socially responsible investment groups formed to promote environmental responsibility among businesses and local governments. In September 1989 CERES set forth the Valdez Principles as broad standards for evaluating corporate activities that directly or indirectly affect the biosphere. The Principles were adopted to help investors make informed decisions and in the hope of working with companies to create a voluntary mechanism of self-governance. The Valdez Principles call for elimination or minimization of pollution, sustainable use

> *"Governments are formed to preserve and protect the general good. Protecting the environment, safeguarding human health and preserving the national habitat should be an integral part of every government's environmental responsibilities. Local governments, in their own operations and in their regulation and monitoring of actions by others, should be model environmental citizens."*
> New York City's Environmental Charter 1990

of natural resources, reduction and safe disposal of waste, energy conservation, environmental risk reduction, marketing of safe products and services, damage compensation, hazard disclosure, selection of environmental directors and managers, and annual environmental audits.

Canadian corporate signatories include McDonald's Restaurants of Canada, Delta Hotels, Air Canada, VanCity Savings, and B.C. Tel. At least 40 local governments are considering environmental investment guidelines based on the Valdez Principles; at least five jurisdictions have already adopted guidelines.

CERES provides information and assistance in relation to the Valdez Principles, corporate shareholder campaigns, and community efforts to encourage local governments to adopt environmental investment policies (see Resources).

The Environmental Charter for New York City

Introduced by New York City Comptroller Elizabeth Holtzman in conjunction with Earth Day 1990, this is a generic document that can be adapted by other North American local governments. The Environmental Charter pledges local governments to develop programs to provide clean water (assure water quality, conserve water, and improve sewage systems); improve air quality (reduce vehicle pollution, incineration, and other emissions); expand recycling and minimize waste; foster sound energy

> **Health-Conscious Divestment**
> The City of Pittsburgh, Pennsylvania has divested itself of stock in tobacco companies.
> (see Associated Press 1991)

policy; plan for environmentally responsible growth; implement environmentally sound procurement policies; enforce laws and improve oversight capacity; encourage environmentally responsible business practices; maximize citizen education and involvement; and implement the goals of this charter (develop timetables, annual audits, periodic re-evaluation, environmental subcabinet of key government agencies, collaboration with colleges and universities, and public involvement in monitoring implementation and compliance). For access information see Resources.

INITIATIVES

Statement of Principle on Environmentally Sound Purchasing

In June 1989, the City of *Toronto* and Metropolitan Toronto Department of Purchasing and Supply hosted a symposium of Canadian purchasing officials on the purchase of reusable and recyclable and reclaimable materials. Toronto City Council's version of the symposium's statement of principles reads:

"That in order to increase the development and awareness of Environmentally Sound Products, all departments, in conjunction with Purchasing and Supply staff, review their contracts and tender specifications for goods and services, to ensure that wherever possible and economical, specifications are amended to provide for expanded use of products and services that contain the maximum level of

270

> ***Creating Markets for Recycled Materials***
> Many US local government procurement policies give
> a 5-10% cost preference to products made with post-
> consumer recycled materials, even though they may
> initially be more expensive. In the long run, it is in the
> interest of local governments to build up markets –
> and demand – for recycled materials.

post-consumer reusable or recyclable waste and/or
recyclable content, without significantly affecting the
intended use of the product or service, and that it is
recognized that cost analysis is required in order to ensure
that the products are made available at competitive prices."
(City of Toronto 1989)

Governments Incorporating Procurement Policies to Eliminate Refuse (GIPPER)

An *Ontario* intergovernmental committee called
Governments Incorporating Procurement Policies to
Eliminate Refuse (GIPPER) has been established to address
procurement's contribution to solving the waste crisis
problem. GIPPER is comprised of representatives from
both waste management and purchasing departments of
federal, provincial and municipal levels of government
and other concerned organizations. GIPPER intends to
incorporate environmental considerations into purchasing
procedures, with the goal of an overall, national, 50 per
cent reduction in waste generation by the year 2000. The
focus of the procurement policies will be to:
"a) Reduce the quantity of waste produced by
government bodies and associated agencies, boards,
commissions and affiliated contractors.
b) Provide markets necessary to promote and sustain
waste reduction, reuse, recycling and recovery of
materials initiatives.

c) Develop a process to facilitate co-operative or joint purchasing among the different levels of government so as to substantially influence and enhance item b) above." (GIPPER, n.d.)

Writing Environmental Practice Into Tender Documents

The *West Sussex* (U.K.) County Council's documents supplied to contractors invited to tender for the buildings cleaning contract includes these requirements in respect to equipment and materials:

"The contractor shall prepare, mix and use all cleaning materials and use all equipment in a safe manner and to the satisfaction of the authorised office, and shall keep the same when on the council's premises under proper control and safe keeping, and shall ensure that all cleaning materials are properly, accurately and clearly labelled on their containers. The contractor shall use his best endeavours to provide, for the purposes of this contract, materials whose manufacture, use and disposal have the least practicable harmful impact on the environment." (ACC 1990)

RESOURCES

GOVERNMENTS INCORPORATING PROCUREMENT POLICIES TO ELIMINATE REFUSE (GIPPER). For more information contact:
Lou Pagano, P. Eng.
Chairman of GIPPER
Dept. of Purchasing and Supply
City Hall
Toronto, Ontario M5H 2N2
Tel: 416/392-7311   Fax: 416/392-0801

THE COALITION FOR ENVIRONMENTALLY RESPONSIBLE ECONOMIES (CERES). For more information contact:

CERES
711 Atlantic Ave.
Boston, MA 02111
Tel: 617/451-0927

CONSERVATREE INFORMATION SERVICES, *The Government Procurement Kit.* Topics include creating markets for recycling and purchasing policies. Available from:
Conservatree Information Services
10 Lombard St., Suite 250
San Francisco, CA 94111
Tel: 415/453-1000

LOCAL GOVERNMENT COMMISSION, *Local Government Procurement and Market Development* (1989). A how-to guide for adopting a recycled product purchasing policy. Available from:
Local Government Commission
909 12th St., Suite 205
Sacramento, CA 95814
Tel: 916/448-1198

CITY OF NEW YORK, OFFICE OF THE COMPTROLLER, *The Environmental Charter for New York City* (1990). Available from:
The City of New York
Office of the Comptroller
1 Centre Street
New York, NY 10007-2341

References

ASSOCIATED PRESS, "California Is Urging Sale of Tobacco Stocks," *New York Times,* January 31, 1991, p. A13.

ASSOCIATION OF COUNTY COUNCILS (ACC), ASSOCIATION OF DISTRICT COUNCILS, AND ASSOCIATION OF METROPOLITAN AUTHORITIES, *Environmental Practice in Local Government* (London: Association of District Councils, 1990).

CITY OF NEW YORK, *The Environmental Charter for New York City* (New York: City of New York, Office of the

Comptroller, 1990).

CITY OF TORONTO COUNCIL, Report No. 33, Item 17, adopted September 21, 1989.

GOVERNMENTS INCORPORATING PROCUREMENT POLICIES TO ELIMINATE REFUSE (GIPPER) "Fact Sheet" (Toronto: GIPPER, n.d.).

LOCAL GOVERNMENT COMMISSION, *Local Government Procurement and Market Development* (Sacramento, CA: Local Government Commission, 1989).

REGULY, B., "Blue Boxes: Why They Don't Work," *Financial Times of Canada,* February 3, 1992, p. 1.

PART THREE

Planning and Administrative Tools

Part III is devoted to the successful implementation of the concepts and ideas in Parts I and II. As in Part II, these chapters include planning tools, practical initiatives, and associated resources which have helped municipal and local governments move toward sustainable communities. While not every tool will "fit" every community, many of them will fit quite well.

This section includes strategies and techniques for getting good ideas "off the shelf," involving the public, and overcoming bureaucratic inertia. It concludes with some lessons for designing effective sustainable community development policies.

13

Leadership by Example

While progress in environmental management appears to be the order of the day, a look at even recent history gives cause for concern. For example, in 1990 Toronto made headlines around the world by becoming the first city to commit itself to reducing its 1988 level of carbon dioxide emissions 20% by 2005. Included in its "call for action" was a goal of "significantly reducing the number of commuting autos" and a strategy to "promote significant reductions in the energy intensity of transportation in the city" by promoting public transit, bicycling and walking (see City of Toronto 1989). Yet *ten years earlier* Toronto City Council had passed an energy conservation by-law designed, among other things, to encourage development and redevelopment that would contribute to energy-efficient urban form, reduce the need for transportation, discourage automobile use and encourage public transit and bicycle transportation (see Lang and Armour 1982). That the same environmental legislation was passed twice in ten years is a strong indicator that the earlier measures were not implemented.

Another example of purported progress is the recent mushrooming of municipal and local government environmental departments, coordinators, task forces, staff committees, and citizen boards. At one level this certainly deserves applause. Yet a major survey of environmental management in nearly 3,000 North American local governments *in 1973* found that 20 percent had staff environment committees, 40 percent had

> **Knowing Your Constituency**
> "In a recent survey of German cities [...] people
> overwhelmingly favored greater emphasis on public
> transport even if that meant less support for
> automobiles. Varying by city size, the extent of popular
> response advocating greater investment in public
> transport ranged from 95 percent of people surveyed
> in Berlin, to 93 percent in Munich, 88 percent in
> Hamburg and Düsseldorf – and a low of 58 percent, in
> Troisdorf. Yet a separate poll of local politicians in
> the Munich area found that most were certain their
> constituents would favor the car over public
> transport."
>
> (Lowe 1991)

designated environmental coordinators, and 24 percent
had citizen environmental boards. Inadequate funding,
uncertainty and delay in program administration,
inadequate communication with senior levels of
government, and inadequate technical assistance were all
perceived in the mid-1970s as major impediments to
adequate local responses to environmental problem solving
(see Magazine 1977). Nearly 20 years later, this list still
sounds familiar.

How can we encourage sustainable policymaking and
ensure sustainable implementation? Local government is
an influential employer in most communities. The first
step toward sustainable administration is leadership by
example, particularly "greening" City Hall. We need to
put our own house in order, using tools such as
environmental audits, staff training, eco-counselling,
environmental impact assessment, and state-of-the-
environment reporting.

> *"We ask our citizens to change their behaviour, to leave their sacred cars at home, to pay a higher price for the future, and moreover, to vote for us. This is a real challenge for the leadership in our democracy. But in a sustainable city that thinks globally, the future of our planet has to be more important than the outcome of the next election."*
>
> Amsterdam Mayor E. Van Thijn 1991

> *Co-ordinated vs. Ad-hoc Development*
> **"The process of re-urbanization is obviously more difficult without a strong planning commitment to it [...] Some overall, co-ordinated vision for the city which takes account of re-urbanization's many other social, economic and equity impacts is clearly desirable. Certainly re-urbanization will have less satisfactory results in terms of the quality of developments and their impacts on established areas if the process is allowed to occur in a merely *ad hoc* way."**
>
> **(Kenworthy and Newman 1990)**

TOOLS

Local Government Styles of Response With Respect to Global Warming

Style	*Examples*
1. Flout the law	[...] Use illegally polluting vehicles.
2. Merely obey the law	Do no more, or less, than is required.
3. Set a good example within the administration	Intra-office recycling; use natural gas vehicles.

"Style

4. Advocate within jurisdiction	Encourage reduction, reuse, and recycling; promote transit and district heating.
5. Legislate within jurisdiction	Ban certain materials at landfill sites; local restrictions on automobile use.
6. Advocate outside jurisdiction	Push for tighter automobile pollution standards; promote inter-city rail.
7. Seek new legislative authority	To tax automobile ownership; to ban sale of items made with CFCs.
8. Legislate outside jurisdiction	Ban sale of items made with CFCs; ban use of many kinds of packaging."

(Gilbert 1991)

Environmental Auditing

"An environmental audit (EA) is based on an assessment of the environmental impacts of the authority's policies and practices. In some cases these will be known, or easily identifiable, whilst in others, it will be possible only to indicate the likely consequences. The policy review should encompass all activities of the authority, and all departments and arms of the service. It should not be restricted to 'official' or approved policy, because much local government practice has evolved through tradition, or results from informal decisions of staff.

Given the wide-ranging nature of such a review, and the differences which exist between authorities, only a general indication can be given here of the matters to be covered. However, many features will be common to most authorities. These might include:
    • the authority's existing environmental objectives and

policy statement(s) strategy/charter
* mechanisms and structures for co-ordinating environmental issues and inputs into all departments and service delivery
* purchasing policy
* use, conservation and recycling of resources and materials by/within the authority
* vehicle fleet management
* health and environment of the workplace and public areas managed by the authority
* estate management (land and buildings) and design
* consumer advice and protection
* environmental education
* transport policies and their implementation
* waste management policies and their implementation
* land use planning policies and their implementation
* environmental enhancement and conservation policies and their implementation
* energy consumption, energy policy and energy efficiency measures
* investment policy
* mechanisms for involving staff in the EA and securing their co-operation
* mechanisms for monitoring the effectiveness and implementation of the EA" (ACC 1990)

Staff Training

"If environmental initiatives are to be integrated effectively into mainstream services, particular effort is needed to ensure that the authority's own staff are properly involved. Before staff can be asked to develop and pursue initiatives, they must first understand and support the reasons for what they are being asked to achieve. This applies as much to junior field staff as to senior managers within service departments. A range of devices will be needed,

Local Authority (LA) Mechanisms for Conducting an Environmental Audit

	1) In-house team (existing staff)	2) In-house team (new specialist staff)
Cost	Cheapest	Most expensive but could be most cost-effective
Overall environmental expertise	May not be comprehensive	Excellent and LA controls what it gets
Knowledge of authority	Excellent	Limited at first but will grow
Knowledge of area	Excellent	Limited at first but will grow
Objectivity	Bound to be affected by LA culture	Good to excellent
Ease of management & control	Good	Good
Commitment to long-term implementation	Depends on other duties and priorities	Excellent
Continuous involvement in monitoring & review	Depends on other duties and priorities	Excellent

3) *External consultant*	4) *Combined in-house and consultants*
More expensive than 1)	More expensive than 1)
Excellent (if right consultant selected)	Excellent (if right consultant selected)
Likely to be nil or very limited	Good
Depends on firm's experience but could be nil or limited	Good
Excellent	Good
Not as easy as 1) or 2)	Not as easy as 1) or 2)
Non-existent	Mixed
Non-existent	Mixed

(ACC 1990)

such as seminars and staff newsletters, which have been used successfully in the past. Whatever the methods, key staff and elected members need to understand:

- *the environmental agenda:* staff must be familiar with global, regional and local environmental issues, and grasp their political and economic implications
- *the environmental lobby:* an appreciation of the demands and attitudes of local and national interests
- *the environmental impact of their own service:* the influence of the day-to-day services for which they are responsible
- *the environmental role of their own service:* how their department or section can contribute to solving environmental problems

Promoting such understanding does not necessarily require formal training. But it does require some thought as to how the authority can tap into available expertise (in the form of published material, its own staff, local environmental groups) and disseminate it (through in-house journals, environment newsletters, departmental briefing) to staff." (ACC 1990)

Eco-Counselling

More than 500 eco-counsellors are at work throughout Europe (*Germany, Switzerland, Austria, Italy, Spain, the UK, France, Luxembourg,* and *Belgium*). The concept of environmental counselling was originally developed in Germany (in 1985) as a means of providing detailed, impartial and practical environmental advice to individuals on an individual or small-group basis (e.g., schools, women's groups, businessmen, householders) on matters ranging from energy conservation to water pollution. The central idea is that the environmental adviser, largely by virtue of his or her personal contact with members of the community in which he or she works, can achieve small-scale but long-term behavioural change which in turn can lead to a large-scale improvement in the environment.

Eco-counsellor training programs and even masters degree programs in environmental counselling are now being offered in Europe. While courses on law and economy, etc. are offered, the central foci are environment and communications. Trainees gain expertise in technical, legal, administrative and economic fields, but most important is their experience in animating discussions, presenting issues clearly and simply, diplomacy, teamwork and cooperation with different partners.

While financing is necessary to cover training, salaries and materials, local authorities are increasingly accepting that these costs are low compared with a) the potential job-creation possibilities and improved market standing for those involved in the clean technology and environmentally oriented sectors, and b) the avoided economic and social costs of environmental damage. Estimates from Austria indicate that local eco-counsellors typically produce savings double to their costs through identification of waste reduction measures. Often local authorities are able to co-finance schemes with the assistance of government aid, local businesses or sponsorship. (see Eco-Conseil 1991; World Congress of Local Governments for a Sustainable Future 1990)

State of the Environment (SOE) Reporting

Some local governments are considering a community-based state of the environment (SOE) report for their region (see Resources). Inspired by national and international SOE reports, the idea of these efforts is to develop broad perceptions of ecosystems and our relationships with them, and to identify ecological approaches to planning and designing urban areas, on which residents and governments can

---

Eco-Conseillere Job Description

The job description for an Eco-Conseillere in the French town of Saint Orens (pop. 9,000) is typical of other municipal "ecology counselor" or "environmental advisor" positions in dozens of European communities. It calls for resolving disputes, acting as an environmental advisor to city council, working with the city employees in charge of green space and walking paths, signing off on city purchases to ensure they will not harm the environment, helping in general to preserve the quality of life by acting as an environmental advocate with both elected and appointed city officials, and working with local schools in helping to design environmental education and class projects.

(see *PIA* 14(8) August 1990)

---

ponder and act. As with all SOE reporting, the question of appropriate indicators presents a major challenge, especially at the local government level. Ideally, SOE indicators should be key measures that most represent the state of the environment and that collectively provide a comprehensive profile of environmental quality, natural resource assets, and agents of environmental change.

Environmental Impact Assessment

"Environmental impact assessment is a planning tool that integrates environmental considerations into project planning, development and implementation. In order to be effective, environmental assessment has to be a decision making tool. The application of an effective environmental assessment process ensures that potential environmental effects – physical and social – are identified and mitigative measures put in place to minimize or eliminate these impacts. Effective environmental assessment requires that the environmental implications of a proposal be

> ### Eco-Counselling Resolution
> "[...] 9. The Permanent Conference asks the regions and local authorities: [...]
>
> IV. to create, within their administration, a special department with a global approach to environmental questions to undertake the necessary coordination and also to inform and advise citizens, notably by the creation of posts for environmental advisers;
>
> V. to ensure that their administration has enough qualified environment personnel to be able to effectively to carry out the tasks in this area which will fall to the local authorities in the future;
>
> VI. to set up, within their administration, a means for the protection of the citizen (of a mediating nature) or a specific service within existing institutions, which every citizen can consult for environmental problems."
>
> (Council of Europe 1986)

considered prior to taking or making irrevocable decisions and as early in the planning process as possible. The assessment of a proposal should include the concerns of the public with regard to both physical and social environmental evaluation." (City of Ottawa 1990)

INITIATIVES

Municipal Environmental Offices/Positions
Municipal environmental offices/positions have been created in many jurisdictions. Some Canadian examples: *Vancouver* has created a Special Office for the Environment. *Burnaby*, B.C. has an "ecosystem" planner. *Calgary* has an environmental coordinator. *Toronto* has created an energy efficiency office. Some US examples: *Irvine*, California has hired an environmental program administrator. *Baltimore's* Regional Council of

Governments has a director of environmental programs. *Portland* has an Energy Office, *San Francisco* has a Bureau of Energy Conservation, and *San Jose* has an Office of Environmental Management.

Environment First Policy

The City of *Waterloo's* "Environment First Policy" evolved out of an Environmental Think Tank initiated by the Mayor with the full support of his Council and senior staff. It focuses on creeks and stormwater management, flood plain management, environmentally important areas, urban vegetation, and parks and open space development. In addition to individual strategies, the policy is intended to develop a broad-based, systematic approach to environmental enhancement at the local level. A position of Environmental Coordinator for the city was created as part of the policy (see City of Waterloo 1991).

Environmental Protection Office

The City of *Toronto* has an Environmental Protection Office which provides research and policy development services to City Council, other municipal departments, and external groups and agencies. The office has a professional staff of ten, ranging from information officers to researchers to an industrial hygienist (see Davies 1991).

Développement Viable

In *Montreal,* studies commissioned by the city have recommended the adoption of an approach directed to *développement viable,* based on the concept of the city as an "eco-socio-system." The city will attempt to incorporate sustainability dimensions into its development plan and implement a comprehensive framework for the evaluation of development and transportation plans against sustainability criteria (see Richardson 1990).

Assistant Mayor for the Environment

Bordeaux, France's environmental programs are run by the elected "green" assistant mayor for the environment. The assistant mayor chairs a number of public/private committees that promote, monitor and administer environmental initiatives (see *PIA* 14(11) November 1990).

Green Economic and Social Strategy

Sheffield, U.K.'s *Sheffield 2000* Development Strategy includes a "green growth network." Its activities include developing a dialogue between environmentalists and industry within the City and the region to promote joint working and to achieve agreed objectives; identifying and promoting emerging new environmental products and services; investing in environmental research and development; developing an integrated approach to urban policy planning within the City Council; implementing green strategies and promoting best practice within institutions, and developing a city-wide green economic and social strategy (see Sheffield City Council n.d.).

Overcoming NIMBY

New York City is pioneering a way of overcoming the NIMBY (Not In My Back Yard) syndrome by ensuring that LULUs (locally unwanted land uses) are distributed equitably among resisting neighbourhoods. The planning department will calculate a ratio, comparing each neighbourhood's jail beds, halfway houses, group home rooms, and other existing LULUs to the overall population. Neighbourhoods will not be expected to carry more than their fair share of facilities and affluent neighbourhoods that have previously lobbied successfully in the NIMBY mode will no longer be able to turn away every unwanted facility (see *PIA* 15(1) January 1991).

```
                    Acronym Glossary
   NIMBY        Not In My Back Yard
   LULU         Locally Unwanted Land Use
   NIMTO        Not In My Term of Office
   NIMBL        Not In My Bottom Line
   BYBYTM       Better Your Back Yard Than Mine
   NIABY        Not In Anyone's Back Yard
                    (e.g., toxic waste)
   YIMFY        Yes In My Front Yard
                    (e.g., bicycle paths)
```

RESOURCES

ASSOCIATION OF COUNTY COUNCILS, ASSOCIATION OF DISTRICT
COUNCILS, AND ASSOCIATION OF METROPOLITAN AUTHORITIES,
Environmental Practice in Local Government
(London: Association of District Councils, 1990). The
three U.K. national local authority Associations teamed
up to produce this impressive notebook-style publication
in an attempt to raise environmental awareness throughout
local government. The first edition concentrates on
examples of best available practice within U.K. local
authorities; while few of these are in themselves relevant
to North American municipal and local governments, this
book would be a good model for a similar effort on this
continent. Available from:
    Wendy Aylett
    Association of District Councils
    26 Chapter Street
    London, U.K. SW1P 4ND
    Fax: 071 233 6551

THE LOCAL GOVERNMENT COMMISSION is a California
organization providing technical assistance to local

governments. The Commission is developing energy efficiency guidelines for cities in the areas of land use, transportation, solid waste recycling, and energy conservation in buildings. One very valuable Commission publication is "Model Ordinances for Environmental Protection," available from:

Local Government Commission
909 12th St., Suite 205
Sacramento, CA 95814
Tel: 916/448-1198

THE INTERNATIONAL CITY MANAGEMENT ASSOCIATION (ICMA) is the professional and educational association for appointed administrators and assistant administrators serving cities, villages, boroughs, townships, counties, and councils of governments. ICMA's membership also includes directors of state associations of governments, other local government employees, members of the academic community, and concerned citizens who share the goal of improving local government. In terms of environmental management, ICMA offers assistance in solid waste management, ground water protection, and wastewater treatment. ICMA also publishes *Cities International,* a quarterly newsletter on municipal development and management training programs in developing countries. For more information, contact:

International City Management Association
777 N. Capitol Street, N.E.
Washington, D.C. 20002-4201
Tel: 202/289-4262

PUBLIC TECHNOLOGY, INC. (PTI) is the technical arm of the International City Management Association and the National League of Cities, and a non-profit organization that helps local governments throughout North America cut costs and improve services through practical use of technology and management systems. With funding from the US Environmental Protection Agency, PTI organized an Urban Consortium Environmental Task Force to conduct applied research to address local environmental problems, develop innovations and transfer results. For more information, contact:

Public Technology, Inc.
1301 Pennsylvania Avenue, N.W.
Washington, D.C. 20004
TEl: 202/626-2400

THE FEDERATION OF CANADIAN MUNICIPALITIES (FCM). publishes *Forum*, a bi-monthly publication. In 1991 *Forum* introduced a new column promoting municipal environmental initiatives. Available from:

Federation of Canadian Municipalities
24 Clarence Street
Ottawa, Ontario K1N 5P3
Tel: 613/237-5221   Fax: 613/237-2965

THE INTERGOVERNMENTAL COMMITTEE ON URBAN AND REGIONAL RESEARCH (ICURR) is an information exchange service and research program. In 1991 ICURR co-sponsored a management symposium on "Implementing Sustainable Development in Municipalities" with the Association of Municipal Clerks and Treasurers of Ontario. ICURR documents and publishes information on sustainable urban development in Canada. For more information, contact:

Intergovernmental Committee on Urban and Regional
    Research
150 Eglinton Avenue East, Suite 301
Toronto, Ontario M4P 1E8
Tel: 416/973-5644   Fax: 416/973-1375

ENVIRONMENT CANADA distributes a newsletter on *state of the environment reporting.* Available from:

SOE Newsletter
State of the Environment Reporting
Corporate Policy Group

Environment Canada
Ottawa, Ontario K1A 0H3
Tel: 819/953-1448
TORONTO's **state of the environment (SOE) report** is
an example of one community's experience with this tool.
Toronto: State of the Environment (May 1988) is available
from:
Department of Public Health
City of Toronto
City Hall
Toronto, Ontario M5H 2N2

References

ASSOCIATION OF COUNTY COUNCILS (ACC), "Association of
District Councils, and Association of Metropolitan Authorities,
Environmental Practice in Local Government" (London:
Association of District Councils, 1990).

CITY OF OTTAWA, "Urban Environmental Conservation
Strategy: Framework Document" (Ottawa: City of Ottawa,
Department of Engineering and Public Works, 1990),
discussion paper.

CITY OF TORONTO, *The Changing Atmosphere: A Call To
Action* (Toronto: City of Toronto, 1989).

CITY OF WATERLOO, *Environment First 1990 Review Report*
(Waterloo: City of Waterloo, Report CAO 91-15, 1991).

COUNCIL OF EUROPE, Resolution 171 on "The Region, the
Environment and Participation," produced by the Permanent
Conference of Local and Regional Authorities in Europe
(Strasbourg: Council of Europe, 1986).

DAVIES, K., "The Role of Environmental Considerations in
Municipal Decision-Making in Canada and Some Preliminary
Comments on Municipalities and the Proposed Canadian
Environmental Assessment Act (Bill C-13)," unpublished
paper prepared for The Federal Environmental Assessment
Review Office, September 1991.

ECO-CONSEIL, "Introducing Environmental Counselling for
Local Authorities in France: A Successful Experiment"
(Strasbourg: Institut Pour Le Conseil En Environment,
1991).

GILBERT, R., "Cities and Global Warming" (Toronto: Canadian Urban Institute, 1991).

KENWORTHY, J.R., AND P.W.G. NEWMAN, "Cities and Transport Energy: Lessons From a Global Survey," *Ekistics* 57(344/345):258-268, 1990.

LANG, R. AND A. ARMOUR, *Planning Land to Conserve Energy: 40 Case Studies From Canada and the United States* (Ottawa: Lands Directorate, Environment Canada, 1982).

LOWE, M.D., "Shaping Cities: The Environmental and Human Dimensions," Worldwatch Paper 105 (Washington, D.C.: Worldwatch Institute, 1991).

MAGAZINE, A.H., *Environmental Management in Local Government: A Study of Local Response to Federal Mandate* (New York: Praeger Publishers, 1977).

Public Innovation Abroad (PIA), various issues

RICHARDSON, N., "Regional Overview Paper: Canada" (Toronto: University of Toronto Centre for Urban And Community Studies; draft prepared for the Colloquium on Human Settlements and Sustainable Development, June 21-23, 1990).

SHEFFIELD CITY COUNCIL, *Sheffield 2000: The Development Strategy* (Sheffield, UK: Sheffield City Council, n.d.).

VAN THIJN, E., Mayor of Amsterdam, remarks to World Cities and Their Environment Congress of Municipal Leaders (Toronto: August 25-28, 1991).

WORLD CONGRESS OF LOCAL GOVERNMENTS FOR A SUSTAINABLE FUTURE, *Congress Report* (Cambridge, MA: International Council for Local Environmental Initiatives, 1990).

14

Environmental Administration

As noted in the previous chapter, the road to sustainable development is paved with failed efforts to incorporate the environment into everyday municipal decision-making. The first step toward sustainable administration is leadership by example.

Unfortunately, energy-efficient light bulbs and reusable china in the City Hall cafeteria will not in themselves achieve sustainable development or slow global climate change. These kind of well-intentioned initiatives are but small steps toward creating sustainable communities.

The second step toward sustainable administration is conceptual and organizational. One of the greatest obstacles to sustainability is the reductionist administrative mindset that subdivides problems and prevents the left hand of government from understanding what the right hand is doing. For example, despite considerable trumpeting of the Canadian government's *Green Plan*, an analysis of the 1991 federal budget and spending estimates concluded that Ottawa spent billions of dollars in 1991 on programs and policies that *create* pollution and *encourage* environmental degradation (see RFI 1991). Such bureaucratic schizophrenia is perpetrated at all levels of government as well as throughout academia.

Sustainable communities cannot be achieved through the kind of fragmented and bureaucratized administration that characterizes senior government. At the community level the issues of, for example, transportation, land use, economic development, public health, environmental protection, and housing affordability cannot be successfully managed as separate problems by separate agencies using separate strategies.

Conventional wisdom considers the environment as an administrative problem, to be solved by better management – understood as cutting the environment into bite-size pieces. This approach seems increasingly unable to deal effectively, sensitively, and comprehensively with environmental complexities.

Rather than the environment as an administrative problem, it would appear that administration is itself an environmental problem. The alternative to conventional municipal administration is an emerging form of what has been called "environmental administration." It can be characterized as non-compartmentalized, open, decentralized, anti-technocratic, and flexible (see Paehlke and Torgerson 1990). Community "Round Tables" on the environment and the economy may prove to be a good example of environmental administration.

It will take a great effort over a long time to turn the system of local government into a paragon of environmental administration, though try we must. In these transition decades, however, an effective and popular way to implement sustainable community development is urgently required.

Tools for Environmental Administration are organized in three sections: principles, process, and strategies. Examples of current fledgling attempts to develop sustainable forms of administration are described under Initiatives.

TOOLS

Principles

Principles for Sustainable Development and Urban Management

"• Local governments/authorities must assume the responsibility and marshall the resources to address the environmental problems facing their communities.
• Present and future generations have a right to a healthy and productive environment.
• Sustainable development approaches must give priority to the alleviation of poverty.
• Development strategies and projects should be judged from their long-term environmental impacts not just from their short-term gains.
• Polluters should pay for the costs of remediation, but it is even more important to prevent pollution and the waste of resources in the first place.
• Human communities must understand and respect the ecosystem processes of which they are an integral part.
• Those potentially affected by the environmental risks of development projects should have the opportunities to participate with full information in decisions about them." (Toronto Declaration on World Cities and Their Environment 1991)

Principles for Innovative Policy Making

The Organization for Economic Cooperation and Development's (OECD) Group of Urban Environmental Experts believes this set of principles could form the basis for ambitious, far-sighted urban environmental policy making.

"1. There is a need to redefine and intensify co-operation between different levels of government. Each governmental level – local, regional, national – is

responsible for taking the initiatives to protect the environment.

2. *Co-operation between the public and private sectors must grow. The private sector should be involved in designing solutions to environmental problems.* The financial participation of the private sector is indispensable if urban environmental projects, above all those involving major infrastructure planning on the local level, are to be successful.

3. *Minimum environmental standards must be established – and enforced.* In some cases, enforcing existing standards may produce better results than creating new ones. Proper enforcement cannot take place without the involvement of local authorities. Wherever possible, local authorities should endeavor to go beyond minimum requirements proposed at a higher governmental level.

4. *The local community must take part in devising and implementing environmental policies.* Local initiatives stimulate greater awareness of local problems and potential. Innovative local approaches should be widely disseminated.

5. *Prices must incorporate environmental and social costs.* Sustainable development requires that environmental capital not be dissipated. Until environmental impact is internalised in accounting procedures, decisions by investors and consumers will not be based on realistic information. Certain kinds of information on environmental and social effects may be available most readily at the local level. Local taxes and fees may be the most appropriate way to internalise some of these costs.

6. *Synergies that can contribute to environmental protection must be identified.* In a synergistic relationship, mutually enhancing activities are more productive when

they are co-ordinated than when they are carried out separately. Classic examples are production processes in which excess heat is used as part of a district heating system or in combined heat and power provision.

7. *Short-term decisions must be taken within the framework of long-term strategies.* Political as well as private sector decision making often tends to be based on short-term considerations, while a great deal of urban planning is necessarily long-term. Short-term economic growth which exploits non-renewable resources is increasingly seen as producing only illusory income, and a permanent loss of wealth." (OECD 1991)

Operating Principles

"In thinking about how to achieve environmental objectives, it is important to establish 'operating principles.' For example, a local government might decide that, in pursuing its objectives, it will:

- consult widely and welcome comment about its current performance and potential contribution
- seek to promote freedom of information on all matters relating to the local environment
- work in partnership to pool resources and expertise
- seek to promote an awareness and understanding of environmental issues throughout the local community
- recognise that prevention is better than cure and seek to ensure that its own action and that of others reflects this principle
- employ a careful approach in its own practices, and encourage others to do the same, by assuming that an activity is environmentally damaging unless proven otherwise, and recognising that where the environmental consequences of an action have not been properly established, it should seek other methods which are known to be environmentally safe

> ***Difficult Decisions and Public Participation***
> **Planners and policy analysts are rightly concerned
> about the dislocations, economic costs, and potential
> inconveniences associated with sustainability
> measures and their distribution across society. Polls
> do suggest that the public is willing to make some
> sacrifice to achieve ecological stability. However,
> both the gain and the pain of adjustment should be
> shared fairly by community members. Participation
> in the decision process by affected groups
> "can help make the attendant redistribution of costs
> and benefits fairer and more widely understood.
> Democratic mobilization is essential to the
> achievement of such policies in the face of the
> opposition [by vested interests they] inevitably
> engender." (Paehlke and Torgerson 1990)**

- recognise that long-lasting or irreversible changes are more significant than those which are short-lived or easily reversed
- seek to prevent pollution wherever possible, but when it does occur, accept that the polluter should pay and ensure that its own committees take account of this principle in decisions about council services
- ensure equal access and opportunities for all sections of the community, including disadvantaged groups, to a safe and pleasant environment" (ACC 1990)

Process
Good Practice
"Good practice is marked by the implementation in particular of three principles:
- The principle of partnership. The recognition that no one organisation or profession has the capacity on its

own significantly to advance environmental protection: hence the need for partnership with other professions and organisations
* The principle of proactivity. Prevention is not only better than cure, it is a vital ingredient when it comes to environmental protection issues
* The principle of participation with the community. Sound environmental protection will only be secured if the community is encouraged to participate in formulating and implementing policy." (ACC 1990)

Getting Public Involvement and Commitment
"To gain and maintain involvement and commitment:
* The authority must put its own house in order. It will need to acknowledge its own shortcomings (in its purchasing practice and so on) and show a commitment to overcoming them
* The authority must demonstrate a willingness to listen and to learn. In this field more than most, local authorities are slowly acquiring expertise. The best way of doing this is to canvass the views and draw on the expertise of others
* It is important to match words and deeds. The local authority may not succeed in achieving all of its environmental targets, but it must make a serious attempt at doing so
* The commitment needs to be visible. Using newssheets, departmental briefings, open meetings, the local media and other means, the authority must inform both its own staff and external audiences of its efforts
* Policies must be understood. Complex environmental issues must be translated into objectives and measures that can be easily grasped by staff, other organisations, and the general public" (ACC 1990)

Facilitating Community Participation

"Community participation helps ensure that decisions are sound and all parties will support them. It is facilitated by:

- conducting consultations where the people are;
- working with traditional leaders, and the full range of community groups and organizations;
- ensuring that the scope of consultation is appropriate to the decision being made;
- limiting the number of management and consultative bodies to which communities have to relate;
- giving communities and other interested parties adequate, readily intelligible information and enough time to consider it, contribute to proposals themselves and respond to invitations to consult;
- ensuring that consultations are in a culturally acceptable form. For example, indigenous people with a tradition of decision making by communal discussion should not be expected to respond with a written submission from one representative. If indigenous consultation mechanisms exist, they should be used;
- ensuring that the timing of consultations is right. Consultation must not take place so early that no useful information is available, or so late that all people can do is react or object to detailed proposals."
(IUCN 1991)

Community Involvement

"Communities should initiate and be involved in all stages of environmental action, from setting objectives and designing activities to doing the work and evaluating the results. Participation should be as broad as possible, involving all segments of the community, and emphasizing that individual actions can make a difference. The participatory approach aims for fair consideration of all viewpoints in reaching reasoned and informed decisions. It takes all factors into account, including people's feelings and values. It draws on all relevant knowledge and skills, and uses 'expert' assistance with care and sensitivity.

Evaluation should be continual; objectives should be re-examined and (if necessary) redefined. Plans should be subject to modification in light of experience. Information should be exchanged among the participants and, if possible, with others engaged in similar activities. Assessment, monitoring and evaluation are essential, preferably using participatory methods. Monitoring helps to inform people of progress, since they sometimes forget how far they have come. Independent evaluation is useful so that people can develop a body of experience from which everyone may learn." (IUCN 1991)

Strategies

Preparing Local Strategies

"Preparation of local strategies enables communities to express their views on conservation and development issues, defining their needs and aspirations, and formulating a plan for the development of their area to meet their social and economic needs sustainably.

Local strategies enable the communities involved to define and achieve the kind of development that is most appropriate for them. If approved by the responsible government, each such strategy could form the basis of land-use policies and a land-use plan for the area. Local strategies could usefully be undertaken as part of a national or subnational strategy, but if neither of these is available there is no reason why local strategies should not be done independently.

The geographical scope of a local strategy should be defined by the community (or communities) undertaking it." (IUCN 1991)

Means of Implementation

"In general, municipalities have a number of means of

implementing sustainable development in their communities:

Regulations	emission standards, environmental quality standards, subdivision codes, building codes, health codes, zoning by-laws, development charges, land use plans, covenants, restrictions on the operation of vehicles or industries during certain hours, etc.
Incentives and Disincentives	preferential taxation, transfer of development rights, easements, bonus and penalty provisions, pricing policies (e.g., for solid waste disposal), effluent fees, low-interest loans, etc.
Public Investment	in highways, sewers, schools, open space, public housing, community centers, direct land purchases, etc.
Education	demonstration projects, public meetings, mall displays, etc." (Reeve 1988)

Implementation Strategies

An implementation strategy for municipal sustainable development will require the following:

1. Undertaking an awareness/education program for city staff, businesses, institutions and the general public in order to develop an understanding of the concept of sustainable development and the need for its implementation.
2. Reviewing the official plan and strategic plan of the municipality in the context of sustainable development, and implementing the appropriate zoning and environmental site plan techniques.
3. Undertaking energy and environmental audits of the

municipality's operations, making them less material and energy intensive.

4. Investigating the social and environmental cost of municipal programs/services and development, bringing the true cost of resources onto the balance sheets.

5. Developing appropriate incentive/inducement programs to secure the cooperation of developers, builders, businesses and householders using by-laws, levies, permit fees, user fees, fines and bonusing.

6. Lobbying senior levels of government for the legislation and regulations necessary to meet the municipality's sustainable development objectives." (Ryan 1991)

Strategies for Sustainability

"Successful strategies have four components in common:
- consultation and consensus building;
- information assembly and analysis;
- policy formulation;
- action planning and implementation.

Demonstration projects may also be undertaken so that participants can see concrete results from the strategy while it is being developed [...]

A local strategy by a single municipality can be developed within a year. Strategies involving several communities are likely to require more time, because of the need to reach agreement among them all.

The results of a strategy are the agreed policies and the actions taken to put the policies into practice. A key step in the development of a strategy is the preparation of a strategy document. This provides a summary description and analysis of the people, economy, environment, and institutions of the area; and sets out the agreed policies and action plan.

The basic organization of a strategy consists of a steering committee and a secretariat. The steering committee should be representative of the main participants in the strategy. It is responsible for overall direction of the strategy, and ensuring the full participation of all interest groups.

The secretariat undertakes the day-to-day management of the strategy's development. It is responsible for organizing consultation and consensus building, assembly and analysis of information, and drafting the strategy document. The secretariat also produces a newsletter or equivalent to keep everyone informed of the strategy's progress." (IUCN 1991)

Revising Official Community Plans (OCPs)
"Where official community plans already exist, but do not appropriately address sustainable development concerns, municipalities could revise the contents of their current official plans to provide:
- a full description of the municipality's natural systems and processes;
- a full description of the flow of energy and materials through the urban ecosystem (especially toxic wastes and their disposal sites);
- explicit policy statements on conservation and related goals;
- environmental, social, and economic policies to realize these goals;
- a listing of environmentally sensitive areas to be protected and explanations for this listing; and
- ways to encourage landowners to exercise stewardship."
(Reeve 1988)

Rethinking Property Taxes
"Several economists [...] have called for differentiated treatment of land and buildings in property taxation. Whereas a higher tax on buildings encourages holding land unused or allowing buildings to deteriorate, a higher tax on land often encourages efficient use of the property

> ### A Dual Property Tax System
> Local governments typically assess vacant properties at far less than than their market value, effectively rewarding property owners for keeping their land idle [...]Cities can go a step further to tax vacant land more heavily than developed parcels. To avoid spurts of sprawled growth, however, it is critically important to combine these tax strategies with clearly defined growth frontiers – such as greenbelts and urban growth boundaries–that contain development within the existing urban area [...] Fifteen U.S. cities levy a higher charge on land than on buildings to spur the regneration of their blighted land. When Pittsburgh introduced a sharply graded dual tax system in 1978, the number of vacant lot sales, new building permits, and new dwellings quickly increased. At the same time, demolitions declined."
>
> (Lowe 1992)

[...] Several cities, including Pittsburgh, have put [this approach] into effect. The results have been impressive. None of these cities has abolished the tax on buildings. Chiefly they have simply raised the taxes on land and lowered those on buildings. In Pittsburgh, city taxes on land were raised to 12.55% while leaving the tax on buildings at 2.475%. Since county and school taxes were not adjusted, the actual relation of the two rates was about three to one. This was sufficient to precipitate a major building program in the city. It also brought additional funds into the city treasury [...]

Land should be taxed at a higher rate than improvements [...] Just what difference in rate is required to encourage improvements cannot yet be stated, but the experience of Pittsburgh and other Pennsylvania cities suggests that even a two-to-one ratio gets results [...] even a reduced version of this tax would meet all local needs by capturing much of the gain from rising land values. To put this land tax into local hands, is, therefore, to free localities from depending on state and federal financial help and the accompanying control [...]" (Daly and Cobb 1989)

"The Environmental Charter for Local Government
Declaration of Commitment
This authority will seek to promote the conservation and sustainable use of natural resources and to minimise environmental pollution in all of its own activities, and through its influence over others. This authority will review all of its policies, programmes and services and undertakes to act wherever necessary to meet the standards set out in this charter.

Policy development
1. *Develop an energy policy* based on energy conservation and clean technology, and establish a cross-departmental Energy Management Unit.
2. *Develop a recycling policy* including provision of public collection or deposit facilities, a recycling officer, an in-house recycling scheme, a commitment to using recycled materials and payment of or lobbying for rebates for recyclable material taken out of the waste stream.
3. *Develop a strategy for monitoring and minimising pollution* in the local environment including pollution caused by its own activities. It will make use of all available measures, including publicity and enforcement.
4. *Develop transport and planning policies* to minimise the use of cars, and encourage public transport, cycling and walking. Also to encourage fuel efficiency, the use of unleaded fuel and the fitting of catalytic converters to minimise pollution from vehicle emissions.

5. *Develop an environmental protection and enhancement strategy* including measures to protect and enhance public open spaces, wildlife habitats and streets. Full consideration will be given to the particular needs of disadvantaged groups. The authority will adopt environmentally sustainable methods of land management (which do not threaten wildlife interest) for parks, open spaces, and verges, and promote organic and sustainable methods in agriculture and countryside management.

6. *Develop a health strategy* which recognises the links between the environment and public health and includes implementation of an amended health and safety policy which has full regard to environmental hazards.

Implementation mechanisms

7. Reform the internal mechanisms of the council such that an adequately resourced cross-departmental body such as an *Environmental Protection & Monitoring Committee* exists to develop and monitor environmental strategies and policies.

8. Commission a regular *Environmental Audit* covering the state of the local environment, and the impacts of all existing policies and practices on the local and wider environment.

9. Encourage and enable public participation in all council activities through *freedom of information,* consultation and publicity. Provide environmental *information and education services* for the public and businesses.

10. Make environmental requirements part of its *purchasing and procurement policy,* including its building specifications and in selection of investments.

11. Revise the relevant statutory and non-statutory *development plan(s)* to take into account the environmental policies outlined by this charter.

12. Through its *planning functions,* promote sustainable development, in particular through the explicit use of environmental criteria in development control and the provision of information on relevant environmental issues to all developers.
13. Implement the policies of this charter in *grant aid conditions* and in *contract tender specifications.*
14. Require committees and departments to consider the environmental implications of their policies and activities as a routine part of *policy development and performance review.* The authority will require all reports prepared by or for it to include a statement of the expected environmental impacts.
15. Support and promote measures through local authorities' associations and other bodies for changes in *national legislation* to improve authorities' powers to implement these policies." (Friends of the Earth, U.K., 1989)

INITIATIVES

Environmental Commitments and Legislation
As described in previous chapters, several cities have made commitments to reach environmental targets, such as a 10% increase in energy efficiency by 2000 (*Portland,* OR and *San Jose,* CA), reducing waste 50% between 1988 and 1998 (*Seattle*), and reducing emissions of carbon dioxide 20% by 2005 (*Toronto* and *Vancouver*).

Community Round Tables on the Environment and the Economy
Round Tables on the Environment and the Economy have been established in several Canadian communities to bring diverse perspectives together to identify common ground and work collectively toward the goal of sustainable

"We in local government are closest to our communities. We are closest to the people who must participate in a very direct and active way if the transition to sustainability is to have any hope of success. We are uniquely situated to assist in the evolution of new social values and practices. We can encourage co-operation between the sectors of the community with a stake in the environment and in development and sustainability. We can act as a catalyst for local action beyond the boundaries of our own jurisdiction [...] Although the Peterborough [Ontario] Committee on Sustainable Development is not a formal part of the municipal government structure, it has strong links with the city: the municipality provides financial support and a meeting room. Council has, by resolution, accepted the Committee as its advisory body on such matters. I and another member of Council sit on the committee, along with several City staff members [...] We are beginning to identify an agenda for action by local government and other sectors of the local community. In this regard, we established a Policy and Planning Subcommittee that developed proposals for 'greening' our Official Plan."
Peterborough Mayor Sylvia Sutherland 1991

development. Local sustainable development Round Tables have been set up in *Peterborough, Burlington, Kitchener, Guelph, Muskoka, Skeena,* and the Capital Regional District of *Victoria,* to name just a few. In the Province of *Manitoba*, the Department of Rural Development offers consulting and financial assistance to Community Round Tables. Each one prepares a "Community Vision Statement," which is "a social, economic and environmental game plan" for community development, using citizen input. The document establishes goals, priorities and an action strategy. Special effort is made to coordinate the Community Vision Statement with other local programs such as capital works, land use plans, business strategies, environmental protection, and Healthy Communities (see Foulds 1990; NRTEE n.d.; BCRTEE n.d.).

311

Environmental Enforcement
The Dutch municipality of *Weert* (pop. 40,000) has an intensive system of environmental enforcement based on an active licensing policy. The police department is authorized to enforce environmental laws, and the Weert police have taken the initiative to organize a course on environmental affairs.

Another Dutch municipality, *Apeldoorn* (pop. 147,000), has an environmental investigation team to monitor source separation. If the team comes across an offence, their first action is to provide information and try to persuade people. Only later do they use their authority to fine offenders (see ANM 1990).

Richmond, California has an environmental police officer. The *Los Angeles* police department has a hazardous waste squad (see PBS 1990).

Council Mission Statement on Sustainable Urban Development
"City Council accepts that change is an on-going phenomenon in cities which must be managed within the parameters imposed by the overriding aim of preserving a lasting habitat for humanity and wildlife. It also recognizes that economic prosperity can provide us with the capability to support wise resource management, to meet social needs and to improve environmental quality. Therefore, City Council supports an approach to managing urban development which balances the right of the individual and the needs of society with the need to conserve our natural resource base and enhance the natural environment, thereby promoting the health of *Ottawa's* inhabitants and communities" (City of Ottawa 1991).

Sustainable City Strategy
San Jose, California's City Council adopted its Sustainable

City Strategy in September 1989. This policy aims to "promote a sustainable future by conserving 10% of the projected energy use in all sectors in the year 2000 so as to enhance the liveability, economic strength and well-being of the City's residents and businesses and reduce environmental problems, particularly emissions that contribute to global warming." (City of San Jose 1991)

The Sustainable City Strategy is designed to effect change through education and persuasion, technical and design assistance, financial incentives, municipal operations, and policy and regulation. During Year One (1990-91) essential programs included residential information and education, public school education, and lighting and appliance point of sale programs; technical assistance, solar access, and the city's Innovative Design & Energy Analysis Service (IDEAS); municipal facilities energy management, street maintenance and surface improvements, and traffic signal management programs; housing energy efficiency rehabilitation, urban forestry, transportation demand management, growth management and land-use planning programs.

Government-Community Partnerships
The Municipality of *Metropolitan Toronto* and the *City of Toronto* are the host community for the International Council for Local Environmental Initiatives (ICLEI). For the first three years, the local governments are providing ICLEI with rent-free office space, seconded research and support staff, and approximately $500,000 in financial support (see Municipality of Metropolitan Toronto 1990).

Boston has granted the power of eminent domain to a community group in Roxbury. The Dudley Street Neighborhood Initiative, an advocacy and planning association of residents, social service agencies, businesses, and churches, plans to buy 200 properties and build 500 units of mixed-income housing. The city has committed $1.5 million in low-interest loans to help finance the purchases (see Peirce and Steinbach 1990).

RESOURCES

THE INTERNATIONAL COMMISSION FOR LOCAL ENVIRONMENTAL INITIATIVES (ICLEI) is a newly established (September 1990) international agency dedicated to helping local governments address environmental issues. It was founded by more than 200 municipal officials (representing 42 countries) at the World Congress of Local Governments for a Sustainable Future at the United Nations in New York. ICLEI is governed by and for local governments and local government associations. Its mission is to help local governments work to prevent environmental problems before they happen, respond to problems when they arise, and enhance both the natural and built environments at the local level. ICLEI is working with municipal leaders around the world to develop a strategy document, *Local Agenda 21,* as a follow-up to the UNCED in June 1992 in Rio de Janeiro. The *Urban CO$_2$ Project* is another ICLEI initiative, designed to identify means to reduce greenhouse gases from urban areas of the industrial world. ICLEI recently opened its North American headquarters in Toronto. For more information, contact:

The International Council for Local Environmental
   Initiatives
New City Hall, East Tower, 8th floor
Toronto, Ontario M5H 2N2
Tel: 416/392-1462   Fax: 416/392-1478

ORGANIZATION FOR ECONOMIC CO-OPERATION AND DEVELOPMENT (OECD), *Environmental Policies for Cities in the 1990s* (Paris, OECD, 1990). This report examines various existing urban environmental improvement policies, proposes ways and means to improve policy coordination with regard to urban environmental impacts, and describes policy instruments available to national, regional and local governments. It also assesses local initiatives in three areas of concern: urban rehabilitation, urban transport and urban energy management, and proposes policy guidelines for improvement in these areas. The report emphasizes the need to develop long-term strategies, adopt cross-sectoral approaches, facilitate cooperation and coordination, enable polluters to absorb environmental and social costs through fiscal and pricing mechanisms, set and enforce minimum environmental standards, increase the use of renewable resources, and encourage and build upon local initiatives. Several descriptions of urban environmental policies and programs in OECD countries are included.

FRIENDS OF THE EARTH (U.K.), *The Environmental Charter for Local Government* (London: FOE, 1989). This package includes the 15-point Charter (reprinted in this chapter), a guide to local government in the U.K. (including a glossary of council jargon), and a book of 193 practical recommendations. In addition to many of the topics covered in the present volume, the *Charter* recommendations cover everything from employment policies (drop any requirement for transport planners to be Members of the Institute of Civil Engineers) to travel allowances (which should not discriminate against the non-car user). Available from:
Friends of the Earth
26-28 Underwood Street
London, U.K. N1 7JQ
Tel: 01 490 1555   Fax: 01 490 0881

TIM ELKIN, DUNCAN MCLAREN, AND MAYER HILLMAN, *Reviving the City: Towards Sustainable Urban Development* (London: FOE, 1991) is also available from

FOE/UK. Unfortunately, this volume will be of little interest to most readers outside of the UK.

LOCAL SOLUTIONS TO GLOBAL POLLUTION (LSGP) is a clearinghouse which provides technical assistance in developing pollution prevention programs on the community level and in the workplace. Their materials and information are directed toward local government officials, grassroots groups, citizens, businesses, and employees. LSGP is an outgrowth of an informal clearinghouse established by Berkeley City Councilmember Nancy Skinner in response to requests for information on polystyrene foam/plastics legislation and other innovative environmental programs. LSGP's emphasis is on source reduction and pollution prevention. A variety of information packets containing fact sheets, ordinances, background articles, etc. are available from:

Local Solutions to Global Pollution
2121 Bonar Street, Studio A
Berkeley, CA 94702
Tel: 415/540-8843 Fax: 415/540-4898

THE PLANNERS NETWORK (PN) is an association of professionals, activists, academics, and students involved in physical, social, economic, and environmental planning in urban and rural areas who believe that planning should be used to assure adequate food, clothing, shelter, medical care, jobs, safe working conditions, and a healthy environment. PN publishes a bi-monthly newsletter. Available from:

Planners Network
1601 Connecticut Ave., N.W.
Washington, D.C. 20009
Tel: 202/234-9382 Fax: 202/387-7915

References

ASSOCIATION OF COUNTY COUNCILS (ACC), ASSOCIATION OF DISTRICT COUNCILS, AND ASSOCIATION OF METROPOLITAN AUTHORITIES, *Environmental Practice in Local Government* (London: Association of District Councils, 1990).

ASSOCIATION OF NETHERLANDS MUNICIPALITIES (ANM), *Municipal Environmental Policy in the Netherlands: Setting Out For Sustainable Development* (The Hague: Association of Netherlands Municipalities, 1990).

BRITISH COLUMBIA ROUND TABLE ON THE ENVIRONMENT AND THE ECONOMY (BCRTEE), *Sustainable Communities: Getting Started* (Victoria: BCRTEE, n.d.).

CITY OF OTTAWA, *Official Plan, Volume I: The Primary Plan* (Ottawa: City of Ottawa, February 1991), final draft.

CITY OF SAN JOSE, *Sustainable City Strategy 1991-1992* (City of San Jose, California: Office of Environmental Management, March 1991).

DALY, H.E. AND J.B. COBB, JR., *For the Common Good: Redirecting the Economy Toward Community, the Environment, and a Sustainable Future* (Boston: Beacon Press, 1989).

ELKIN, T., D. MCLAREN, AND M. HILLMAN, *Reviving the City: Towards Sustainable Urban Development* (London: Friends of the Earth, 1991).

FOULDS, D.W., "Environmental and Economic Sustainability Go Hand in Hand," *Municipal World,* July, 1990, p. 5.

FRIENDS OF THE EARTH (U.K.), *The Environmental Charter for Local Government* (London: FOE, 1989).

INTERNATIONAL UNION FOR CONSERVATION OF NATURE (IUCN), THE UNITED NATIONS ENVIRONMENT PROGRAMME (UNEP), AND THE WORLD WIDE FUND FOR NATURE (WWF), *Caring for the Earth: A Strategy for Sustainable Living* (Gland, Switzerland: IUCN/UNEP/WWF, 1991).

LOWE, M.D., "City Limits," *Worldwatch* 5(1), Jan/Feb, 1992. pp. 18-25.

MUNICIPALITY OF METROPOLITAN TORONTO, Council Meeting Minutes, December 5, 1990. Appendix A: Report No. 34 of the Management Committee.

NATIONAL ROUND TABLE ON THE ENVIRONMENT AND THE ECONOMY (NRTEE), *Sustainable Development and the Municipality* (Ottawa: NRTEE, n.d.).

ORGANIZATION FOR ECONOMIC COOPERATION AND DEVELOPMENT (OECD), *New Environmental Policies for Cities* (Paris: OECD, 1991).

PAEHLKE, R. AND D. TORGERSON, eds., *Managing Leviathan: Environmental Politics and the Administrative State* (Peterborough: Broad View Press, 1990).

PEIRCE, N.R., AND C.F. STEINBACH, *Enterprising Communities: Community-Based Development in America, 1990* (Washington, D.C.: Council for Community-Based Development, 1990).

PUBLIC BROADCASTING SYSTEM, *The Race to Save the Planet* (Boston: WGBH, 1990).

REEVE, N., "Sustainable Development in Municipalities: Making It Work," position paper of the Forum for Planning Action (Vancouver: FPA, 1988).

RESOURCES FUTURES INTERNATIONAL (RFI), "Ottawa Creates Pollution," analysis commissioned by Southam News, in *Vancouver Sun*, April 23, 1991.

RYAN, J. (Burlington, Ontario Alderman), "Existing in Harmony with the Environment," *Municipal World* 101(3): 3-5, March 1991.

SUTHERLAND, S. (Peterborough Mayor), remarks to the Association of Municipal Clerks and Treasurers of Ontario (AMCTO) and Intergovernmental Committee on Urban and Regional Research (ICURR) Management Symposium, "Implementing Sustainable Development in Municipalities," Hockley Valley, Ontario, May 9, 1991.

TORONTO DECLARATION ON WORLD CITIES AND THEIR ENVIRONMENT (Toronto: World Cities and Their Environment Congress of Municipal Leaders, August 28, 1991).

15

Beyond Municipal and Local Government

> *"The effectiveness of urban planning can be fully achieved only if governments remove the conflicting incentives posed by other national policies [...] [For example,] raising national gasoline taxes to a level that more accurately reflects the true costs of driving [...] would give an enormous boost to more efficient urban land use and raise revenues for investment in a broader range of transport options."*
>
> Lowe 1992

The previous chapters in this section identified the first two steps toward sustainable administration. The first is leadership by example. The second is to recognize that conventional municipal administration is itself an environmental problem and that we need a new form of "environmental administration" which is non-compartmentalized, open, decentralized, anti-technocratic, and flexible. For our communities to become sustainable communities, however, we also need to take a third step.

The third step toward sustainable administration is improving the context for sustainable community planning and governance. This requires looking beyond the local level toward regional, provincial/state, and federal policies and programs. These programs should use means such as sustainability goals and targets, planning grants, technical assistance, and timelines. They should encourage, enable, and empower those communities which have already started to plan local initiatives for a sustainable future, and require the rest to begin.

*"Premises of the National Growth Management
Leadership Project [see "Resources"]*

1. To achieve both a healthy economy and a healthy
environment, land development must be planned for
and 'managed' *in balance with* land conservation goals.
Public policies that emphasize economy over
environment (i.e., 'anything goes' development) or
environment over economy (i.e., 'no-growth') are *both*
counterproductive to community and regional well-
being.

2. To balance development and conservation goals,
effective growth management policies should clearly
determine where and when development *will* go and
where it will *not*. Sensible land use planning can lend
greater certainty and stability to the economic
development process, while enhancing initiatives by
governments and private land trusts to buy land of
special conservation or recreational value.

3. Regional or state-wide growth management goals
and policies are needed to provide a *comprehensive*
and systematic means of addressing concerns such as
traffic congestion, housing costs, and pollution.

4. Integration of local planning ordinances and
regulations with state and regional goals and policies
is essential to ensure that planning is both consistent
and comprehensive.

5. Federal policy also exerts a major influence on
the ability of state, regional, and local governments to
manage growth and should be structured to support
sound growth management at all levels of government.

6. Growth management benefits many diverse
constituencies, providing opportunities to build
consensus about the future of a community or region
among homebuilders, economic development
interests, environmentalists, neighborhood
associations and minority communities."

(NGMLP, n.d.)

Priority actions
"Sustainable urban development is only possible when local governments are given adequate powers, and develop effective capabilities. They need to manage change in the context of an ecological approach so that cities can support more productive, stable and innovative economies while maintaining a high-quality environment, proper services for all sectors of the community, and sustainable resource use. These conditions are most likely to be met if all interest groups participate, and if government is active, decentralized, representative, and supportive of citizen efforts."

(IUCN 1991)

TOOLS

Regional Cooperation
"Compact growth of cities also hinges on regional cooperation, an important tool for handling conflicts between the interests of individual localities and those of the broader region. For instance, many municipalities compete for high tax-yielding development and misuse their zoning powers to shut out land uses that yield little tax revenue or require public spending for social services. Such 'fiscal' zoning leads communities to exclude low-income housing, which leaves neighboring jurisdictions with the burden of providing affordable homes. Fiscal zoning can also accelerate the economic drain from central cities, as suburbs seek to replenish public coffers by establishing massive commercial zones to attract taxpaying businesses. Cooperation among competing localities is difficult to achieve without specific laws at the state or provincial level." (Lowe 1992)

Mayors' Commitments

Recognizing the significance of local efforts to solve global environmental problems, and frustrated by lack of leadership from senior levels of government, some 130 mayors from 75 countries gathered in Toronto on August 25-28, 1991 to sign *The Toronto Declaration on World Cities and Their Environment*. The declaration noted that cities provide enormous, untapped opportunities to solve environmental challenges; that local governments must and can pioneer new approaches to sustainable development and urban management; and that local governments must assume the responsibility and marshall the resources to address the environmental problems facing their communities. Among other things, the mayors pledged that their local governments will:

- be models of environmental responsibility;
- establish detailed plans for sustainable management and development;
- provide incentives and restructure fines, taxes, and fees to discourage pollution;
- establish the means and capacity to enforce compliance with environmental laws and agreements;
- urge other levels of government and international agencies to provide resources and support for the financing, management and policy-making authority necessary to achieve sustainable development and to alleviate poverty in their communities;
- work together on a regional basis to address common environmental challenges;
- establish programs whereby the cities of the developed world will devote resources, if feasible under law, to environmental projects in the developing world;
- call on national governments to seize the current opportunity for redirecting military expenditures into environmental and social programmes. (see Toronto

Declaration on World Cities and Their Environment 1991)

Goal-Oriented Planning

Sustainable community planning works best in the context of a supportive regional, provincial or state planning framework. The key is goal-oriented planning – that is, planning for sustainable community development. Governance systems in some regions have been relatively successful in planning and managing for a healthy environment. Some of the characteristics of those systems are:

- A regional or provincial/state framework which requires all municipalities to create plans for achieving a set of regional or provincial/state planning goals.
- Coordination of all plans and programs adopted by local governments and provincial/state and federal agencies.
- Provincial/state agency programs that affect land use and resource management are reviewed to see that they are consistent with the planning goals.
- Affected agencies have opportunities to comment on or object to local comprehensive plans as they are being drawn up.
- Once a local plan has been acknowledged, the agencies are obligated to carry out their programs in accordance with it.
- After its acknowledgement, a local comprehensive plan becomes the controlling document for land use and resource management in the area it encompasses.

Some examples of supportive planning contexts in *France, Norway, Finland, Holland* and *Oregon* are described under Initiatives. The Oregon program is an example of goal-oriented planning that provides a North American model for sustainable development planning.

INITIATIVES

National Programs

In *France,* the Environment Ministry is supporting a nationwide program of municipal plans for the environment. The program engages city administrations in a multi-year action program to improve the urban environment. Specifics include air, water and noise pollution control, waste reduction and recycling, urban green space, civic art and architecture and related measures to better the quality of urban life (see *PIA* 15(4), April 1991).

In *Norway,* the MIK Program is a direct application of the imperative in the Brundtland Commission report to "think globally – act locally." MIK stands for "Miljovern i Kommuner," equivalent to "environmental work in municipalities." It was initiated during 1988 in 90 of Norway's 443 municipalities and is probably the largest local environmental program ever undertaken in one country. Interest in the programme has been overwhelming.

The objective of this program is to test administrative and organization models which can lead to a strengthening of the environmental efforts in the municipalities. Each Norwegian municipality requests participation in the program. The local public then chooses an environmental consultant who fosters interdepartmental collaboration. To increase public participation, the consultant must also promote the building of community social networks. The end result is to be the production of a communal "environmental and natural resource" program for each municipality. The work is thus designed to invite input from the community and create learning networks with other communities.

The Ministry of Environment has recommended that

the municipalities establish an independent environmental committee. This model enables the municipal authorities to create a political body which can concentrate on environmental issues, will have the necessary legal measures and authority and, at the same time, can have an overall view of environmental projects in the municipality.

The experiment involves political as well as administrative reorganization. The delegation of authority to the trial municipalities is an important element in the MIK program. They will get increasing formal authority to take care of local environmental tasks and their own priorities will be central. Later this will be extended to all municipalities in the country. This approach to implement environmental policy at the local level also reflects Norway's national strategy for development towards a sustainable future (see Bjork and McLaren 1990; OECD 1990).

In *Finland*, municipalities have statutory tasks in the field of environmental protection. In each municipality there is a statutory Board of Environmental Protection in charge of the general administration and planning as well as of permit and supervision issues in this sector. Officials with responsibility for environmental protection have been engaged by municipalities during the last ten years and presently there is at least one specialist, often biologist, geologist or geographer, in environmental protection in about 300 of Finland's 461 municipalities.

The Association of Finnish Cities, the Finnish Municipal Association, the Ministry of Environment and a selection of municipalities have launched two projects on municipal contributions to a sustainable future. The project on the consideration of sustainability in municipal activities has so far determined three major capabilities of a municipality to work for a sustainable society (see Jalkanen 1990):

- A municipality should be an arena for politicians and especially for citizens to have open discussion about and to make democratic decisions on the long term objectives for the sustainable future. These objectives must guide all municipal activities and direct the private sector as well.
- A concept of sustainability should be one of the major aspects along with economical and operational ones in the strategic planning and implementation of municipal activities.
- A municipality should introduce the environmental impact assessment (EIA) as an essential part of its activities.

A second project, running from 1989 through 1991, focuses on introducing the EIA into the routine activities of Finnish municipalities to:

- systematically ensure that the essential information of environmental impacts of municipal activities is available for the political decision makers;
- detect the cumulative impacts of various activities taking place within municipal boundaries; and
- provide specialists involved in permit and supervision issues with appropriate environmental information at early stages of decision-making.

In 1989 *The Netherlands* Government presented the National Environmental Policy Plan (NMP), a major step towards an integrated environmental policy. NMP+ in 1990 was a further reaching version. The plan is based on the principle of sustainable development, as defined by WCED. Major elements in this approach are: closing substance cycles from raw material to waste as much as possible; reducing the use of fossil fuels combined with an increased use of renewable energy; and promoting product and production process quality. Typical of this policy is the tendency to take measures at the source, while removing the causes of pollution. The municipal environmental tasks consist partly of implementing national and provincial policy aims, but there is also room for municipalities to develop their own local policy (see ANM 1990).

Provincial/State Programs

Provincial or state legislation can require each town's land use to be compatible with specified regional interests, but leave the actual planning process up to the local community. In the US, such legislation has given new force to urban planning in eight states: *Florida, Georgia, Maine, Massachusetts, New Jersey, Oregon, Rhode Island,* and *Vermont*. All cities and counties in these states are required to plan their own development according to stipulated goals, such as energy conservation, protection of open space, and provision of affordable housing. These statewide planning requirements not only enhance regional cooperation, but they also give cities the backing they need to apply a comprehensive, long-term vision to their land use planning (see Lowe 1992; Wexler 1992).

Oregon's statewide planning program was launched with the enactment of legislation in 1973 which calls for all of Oregon's cities and counties to adopt comprehensive plans that meet state standards known as the Statewide Planning Goals. These goals (e.g., to provide for widespread citizen involvement; to preserve and maintain agricultural lands; to conserve energy) are general standards for land use planning. Planning remains the responsibility of city and county governments, but it must be done in accordance with these statewide standards (Rohse 1987). Oregon's program, which is directed by the Land Conservation and Development Commission (LCDC) and administered by the Department of Land Conservation and Development (DLCD), was named the "Outstanding Land Use Program

> *"If anybody's opposed to land-use planning, I just tell 'em,
> 'How would you like it if I moved my hog operation in next
> door to you?' That turns them into land-use planners pretty
> quickly."*
>
> Stafford Hansell,
> hog farmer and
> former Oregon land-use planning commissioner,
> in Fulton 1991

in the Nation" in 1982 by the American Planning
Association. The national Fund for Renewable Energy
and the Environment also rated Oregon's planning program
as the best in the country in 1988 (see Secretary of State
1989).

In conjunction with Goal 12 (Transportation) of the state
land use planning program, in 1991 LCDC and DLCD
issued the Oregon Transportation Planning Rule to address
urban sprawl, traffic congestion, and air pollution through
an integrated approach to land-use and transportation
planning. The rule requires several innovative policies,
including:

- Every city and county must plan for increased use of
  alternative transportation modes. Land-use plans
  and local ordinances must make specific provisions for
  transit and for bicycle and foot travel.
- The state's four largest urban areas must plan to
  reduce per capita vehicle miles travelled (VMT) by 10
  percent over the next 20 years and by 30 percent over
  30 years.
- The Portland metropolitan region must reconsider
  land-use designations, densities, and design standards
  (i.e., more compact development) as a means of reducing
  travel demand and meeting transportation needs.

The new rules will be phased in over a five year period
(see APA 1992; NGMLP 1991).

Regional Cooperation

Legislation has successfully foiled fiscal zoning in the state of Minnesota since 1971. All of the municipalities in the *Minneapolis-St. Paul* region are required to pool a portion of their commercial and industrial tax base – thus reducing the competition between them for commercial and industrial development. Forty percent of the increases in business tax proceeds are pooled and then distributed throughout the metropolitan region according to each community's population and overall tax base.

"This tax-base sharing system has not only reduced the usual incentives to court the most lucrative land uses throughout the region, but has also narrowed the gap between the per-capita tax-base of the richest and poorest communities from a ratio of roughly 13:1 to a more equitable 4:1." (Lowe 1991)

Municipal Foreign Policy

Many Canadian and US municipalities have taken municipal foreign policy initiatives such as establishing sister-city programs. *Los Angeles, Pittsburgh and Baltimore* each passed "Jobs with Peace" ordinances requiring their staffs to prepare and publish annual reports on the local economic impacts of military spending. *New York City* has lobbyists in Washington, D.C. and at the United Nations. *Seattle* and *Dallas* have funded Offices of International Affairs to oversee trade, sister cities, and tourism. Over the last decade more than 100 cities have refused to invest or enter contracts with firms doing business in South Africa (see Global Communities 1992).

RESOURCES

THE INTERNATIONAL COUNCIL FOR LOCAL ENVIRONMENTAL INITIATIVES **(ICLEI)** was created to improve the capacity and authority of local governments to plan and manage their communities for sustainability. For more information, contact:

The International Council for Local Environmental Initiatives
New City Hall, East Tower, 8th floor
Toronto, Ontario M5H 2N2
Tel: 416/392-1462   Fax: 416/392-1478

THE NATIONAL ROUND TABLE ON THE ENVIRONMENT AND THE ECONOMY reports directly to the Prime Minister of Canada with the objective of supporting the emergence of sustainable development in Canada. Provincial Round Tables also exist throughout Canada. For more information, contact:

National Round Table on the Environment and the Economy
1 Nicholas Street, Suite 520
Ottawa, Ontario K1N 7B7
Tel: 613/992-7189   Fax: 613/992-7385

THE NATIONAL GROWTH MANAGEMENT LEADERSHIP PROJECT **(NGMLP)** is a coalition of state and regional conservation and planning organizations in 18 states. Founded in 1988, the NGMLP advocates regional and statewide land use planning as a policy tool to address land conservation, housing, transportation and other key growth management concerns. In 1992, the NGMLP opened an Office of Federal Policy in Washington, D.C. to monitor opportunities for strengthening federal programs and policies related to growth management efforts at the state and regional level. NGMLP's study on "Managing Growth to Promote Affordable Housing" found that modest increases in housing densities and a wider range of housing types can positively influence the affordability of housing on a regional basis. LUTRAQ, a national research project on the land use, transportation, air quality connection, is expected to produce valuable new computer models of transit-oriented (vs. auto-dependent sprawl) land use development patterns when it is completed in 1992. The NGMLP also publishes a newsletter, *Developments.* For more information on the NGMLP contact:

NGMLP Main Office
1000 Friends of Oregon
534 SW 3rd Ave.,
Suite 300
Portland, OR 97204
Tel: 503/223-4396
Fax: 503/223-0073

NGMLP Office of Federal Policy
915 15th St. NW #600
Washington, D.C. 20005
Tel: 202/628-1270
Fax: 202/628-1311

For information on the State of *Oregon's* land-use planning program, contact:

Land Conservation and Development Commission and Department
1175 Court Street, N.E.
Salem, OR 97310
Tel: 503/373-0050

THE CENTER FOR POLICY ALTERNATIVES is a non-profit center on progressive policy for state and local government. Since 1975, the Center has provided public policy models, direct technical assistance and a broad publications program for the public and public officials. The Centre's Environmentally Sustainable Development Program produces *Policy Alternatives on Environment,* a quarterly state report containing original articles and summaries of state actions in sustainable development. For more information, contact:

Center for Policy Alternatives
1875 Connecticut Ave., NW, Suite 710

Washington, DC 20009

Tel: 202/387-6030   Fax: 202/986-2539

THE INSTITUTE FOR POLICY STUDIES publishes *Global Communities*, a newsletter of reports on issues such as economic conversion, nuclear free zones, municipal environmental initiatives, and municipal foreign policy. Available from:

Global Communities
Institute for Policy Studies
1601 Connecticut Ave, NW
Washington, D.C. 20009
Tel: 202/234-9382   Fax: 202/387-7915

References

AMERICAN PLANNING ASSOCIATION (APA), "From the Capitals," *Planning* 58(2):5, February 1992.

ASSOCIATION OF NETHERLANDS MUNICIPALITIES (ANM), *Municipal Environmental Policy in the Netherlands: Setting Out For Sustainable Development* (The Hague: Association of Netherlands Municipalities, 1990).

BJORK, S., AND N. MCLAREN, "Environment and Health: The Norwegian Response," in Urban Ecology, *Report of the First International Ecological City Conference* (Berkeley, CA: Urban Ecology, 1990).

FULTON, W., "The Second Revolution in Land-Use Planning," in DeGrove, J.M., ed., *Balance and Growth: A Planning Guide for Local Government* (Washington, D.C.: International City Management Association, 1991).

GLOBAL COMMUNITIES "Municipal Foreign Policy: News and Commentary" *Global Communities* Winter 1992, pp. 6-7.

INTERNATIONAL UNION FOR CONSERVATION OF NATURE (IUCN), THE UNITED NATIONS ENVIRONMENT PROGRAMME (UNEP), AND THE WORLD WIDE FUND FOR NATURE (WWF), *Caring for the Earth: A Strategy for Sustainable Living* (Gland, Switzerland: IUCN/UNEP/WWF, 1991).

JALKANEN, P., "The Role of Finnish Municipalities on the Way Towards the Sustainable Future" (Helsinki, Finland: Environmental Department, The Finnish Municipal

Association, 1990), unpublished paper.

LOWE, M.D., "Shaping Cities: The Environmental and Human Dimensions," Worldwatch Paper 105 (Washington, D.C.: Worldwatch Institute, 1991).

LOWE, M.D., 1992. "City Limits," *Worldwatch* 5(1), Jan/Feb, pp. 18-25.

NATIONAL GROWTH MANAGEMENT LEADERSHIP PROJECT (NGMLP), *Developments* 2(1):5, Summer 1991.

NATIONAL GROWTH MANAGEMENT LEADERSHIP PROJECT (NGMLP), "Fact Sheet" (Portland: NGMLP, n.d.).

ORGANIZATION FOR ECONOMIC COOPERATION AND DEVELOPMENT (OECD), *Environmental Policies for Cities in the 1990s* (Paris: OECD, 1990).

Public Innovation Abroad (PIA), various issues

ROHSE, M., *Land Use Planning in Oregon* (Corvallis, Oregon: Oregon State University, 1987).

SECRETARY OF STATE, *Oregon Blue Book 1989-90* (Salem, Oregon: Secretary of State, 1989).

TORONTO DECLARATION ON WORLD CITIES AND THEIR ENVIRONMENT (Toronto: World Cities and Their Environment Congress of Municipal Leaders, August 28, 1991).

WEXLER, P., *Cool Tools: State and Local Policy Options to Confront a Changing Climate* (College Park, MD: Center for Global Change, University of Maryland, 1992).

Toward Sustainable Communities

16

Lessons for Policymaking

While the initiatives described in this book are encouraging, it appears that most local governments around the world experience external institutional constraints on the development and implementation of local sustainability policies. Recognizing the significance of local efforts to solve global environmental problems, and frustrated by lack of leadership from senior levels of government, some 130 mayors from 75 countries gathered in Toronto on August 25-28, 1991 to sign "The Toronto Declaration on World Cities and Their Environment."

The declaration points out that nearly half of the world's people will live in urban areas by the turn of the century, and that the way these urban areas are developed will largely determine our success or failure in overcoming environmental challenges and achieving sustainable development. It notes that cities provide enormous, untapped opportunities to solve environmental challenges; that local governments must and can pioneer new approaches to sustainable development and urban management; and that local governments must assume the responsibility and marshall the resources to address the environmental problems facing their communities.

Local governments are coming to recognize their responsibility to develop sustainable communities. Taken together, the initiatives described in this book begin to delineate a strategy for encouraging a globally conscious culture of sustainability in our cities. They also indicate some practical suggestions for both local and senior government officials on how to design effective sustainable community development policies. The key features of any sustainable development policy framework should recognize that:

- *Sustainable development requires sustainable communities:* Global sustainable development requires local authority and capacity for sustainable urban management and development. Despite the concentration of population in urban areas, most city and local governments do not have the regulatory and financial authority required to effectively contribute to sustainable urban development. Other levels of government must provide resources and support for the financing, management and policy-making authority necessary for local governments to achieve sustainable development in their communities.

- *Rules can and must be changed:* Many urban policymakers are stuck in the paralysing belief that our market society and our bureaucratic nation-state system cannot be changed in any basic sense. To play by those rules means that both the environment and the less fortunate members of society always lose until eventually everything is lost.

- *Sustainability can mean "less" as well as "more":* So long as sustainable development is conceived merely as "environmental protection" it will be understood as an "added" cost to be "traded" against. Once sustainable development is conceived as *doing development differently,* such trade-offs become less critical: the new focus is instead on finding ways to *stop* much of what we are already doing and use the resources thus freed for socially and ecologically sustainable activities.

- *Where the market works, use it:* As one utility executive recently explained his sudden interest in energy

---

Allocating Resources to Local Governments

"In order to make wise land use decisions, cities need more generous national funding for infrastructure, education, and social services. Experience in the industrial countries has demonstrated that placing the burden of all these costs on property taxes can lead local governments to act irresponsibly – for example, allowing ecologically destructive development of valuable open space, or excluding low-taxpaying land uses such as affordable housing. Deteriorating municipal services, along with failing roads, bridges, and sewerage systems in major urban areas worldwide, testify to the need for giving more financial resources to cities."

(Lowe 1991)

"The enduring legacy of the environmental movement is that it has taught us the distinction between price and cost. Price is what the individual pays. Cost is what the community pays. The marketplace works efficiently only when guided by accurate price signals."

Morris 1990

---

conservation, "the rat has to smell the cheese." Create incentives for ecologically sound practices. Well-designed ecological incentive programs are also cost-effective, since larger expenditures for clean-up and restoration are avoided.

• *Where the market fails, don't be afraid to mandate changes:* The prevailing economic orthodoxy is that we must have a political and economic environment that welcomes foreign-owned companies and supports business through a reduction in regulations to become

337

globally competitive, even if it requires a form of economic "shock treatment" (Bramham 1991). Yet the evidence may suggest otherwise. For example, in 1989 Los Angeles adopted a far-reaching mandatory environmental plan which, among other elements, phases out the use of petroleum-based transport fuels over the next 20 years. No less a source than *The Economist* attributes California's economic success as the capital of a US $130 billion a year environmental services industry to strict environmental laws – the toughest in the world (see *The Economist* 1991). This would not have been possible if Los Angeles had opted instead to impose a modest gasoline tax to encourage energy efficiency (see Morris 1990).

• *Polluters should pay for the costs of remediation, but it is even more important to prevent pollution and the waste of resources in the first place:* This principle is particularly significant in the debate over "green" taxes. Governments can reflect new priorities without increasing the total tax burden by shifting taxes away from income and toward environmentally damaging activities. If governments substituted taxes on pollution, waste and resource depletion for a large portion of current levies, both the environment and the economy would benefit. For example, The Worldwatch Institute estimates that a set of potential U.S. green taxes (particularly on carbon content of fuels and on generation of hazardous wastes) could substitute for reducing income taxes by nearly 30 percent (see Postel 1991).

• *Social equity is not only desirable but essential:* Inequities undermine sustainable development, making it essential to consider the distributive effects of actions intended to advance sustainable development. Growth management ordinances in many western U.S. cities, for example, enacted to safeguard the environment and protect the quality of community life, have caused local housing supplies to tighten, driving up prices and causing serious affordability problems for low- and moderate-income households. As these households leap-frog across preserved open space to less expensive communities in the region, additional commuting, traffic congestion, and air pollution threaten the very quality of life at which the control measures were aimed in the first place (see van Vliet 1990).

• *Public participation is itself a sustainable development strategy:* To a considerable extent, the environmental crisis is a creativity crisis. By soliciting the bare minimum of public "input," rather than actively seeking community participation from agenda-setting through to implementation, local and senior decision-makers have failed to tap the well of human ingenuity. They have failed to recognize that *only* from this well can the myriad challenges necessary to redevelop our communities for sustainability be successfully met. Effective and acceptable local solutions require local decisions, which in turn require the extensive knowledge and participation of the people most effected by those decisions, in their workplaces and in their communities.

Sustainable development requires that we develop our communities to be sustainable in global ecological terms. This strategy can be effective not only in preventing a host of environmental and related social disasters, but also in creating healthy, sustainable communities which will be more pleasant and satisfying for their residents than the communities we live in today.

Sustainable communities will emphasize the efficient use of urban space, reduce consumption of material and energy resources, and encourage long-term social and ecological health. They will be cleaner, healthier, and less expensive; they will have greater accessibility and cohesion; and they will be more self-reliant in energy, food and economic security than our communities now are. Ecologically sustainable communities will not, therefore, merely "sustain" the quality of urban life – they will *improve* it.

References

BRAMHAM, D., "Scholar Urges Vast Change in Attitude: But Transition Will Cost Jobs" [report of lecture by Harvard University economist Michael Porter], *Vancouver Sun,* November 21, 1991, p. E2.

THE ECONOMIST, "Going Green in Smog Valley," reprinted in *Vancouver Sun,* November 20, 1991, p. D9.

LOWE, M.D., "Shaping Cities: The Environmental and Human Dimensions," Worldwatch Paper 105 (Washington, D.C.: Worldwatch Institute, 1991).

MORRIS, D., *An Environmental Policy for the 1990s: Fashioning the Molecular Basis for a Green Economy* (Washington, DC: Institute for Local Self-Reliance, 1990).

POSTEL, S., "Accounting for Nature," *Worldwatch* 4(2): 28-33, March/April 1991.

VAN VLIET, W., "Human Settlements in the U.S.: Questions of Even and Sustainable Development" (Toronto: University of Toronto Centre for Urban and Community Studies; draft prepared for the Colloquium on Human Settlements and Sustainable Development, June 21-23, 1990).